Euro trains - www.e
Rail Europe - 08705 848848
8am - 9pm Mon-Friday

First-Time Europe

www.dfds.co.uk (Boats to/from Denmark)
08705 333000 written and researched by

Louis CasaBianca

with illustrations by

Jerry Swaffield

Easyjet - 0871 2442366

ROUGH GUIDES

www.roughguides.com

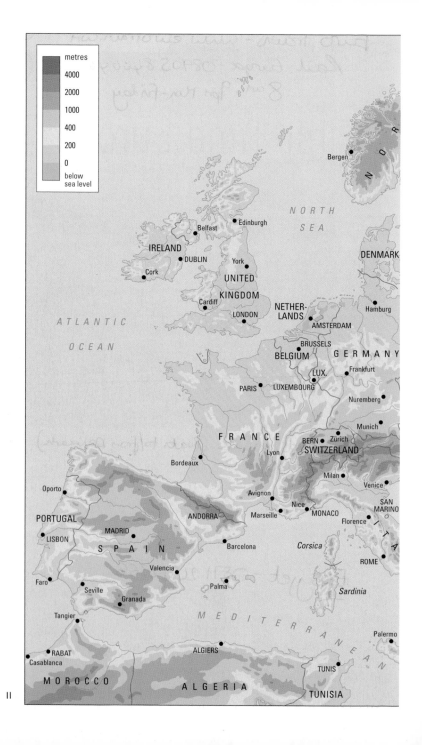

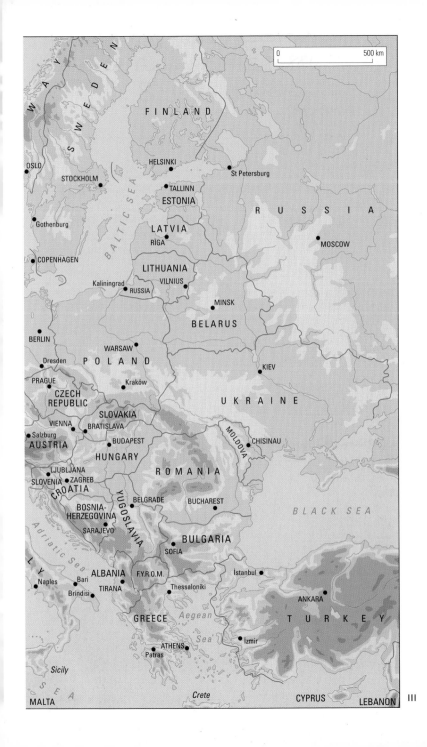

Introduction to

First-Time
Europe

I know you're at least thinking about going to Europe, or you wouldn't be reading this book. Every year thousands of people just like you head to Europe for the first time, and I'd guess all of them want the best trip they can get for the money. This book is intended to help someone taking one of those trips see Europe as cheaply and as enjoyably as possible. The first time I traveled to Europe I just picked up and went, and had to learn the hard way. That trip was a wonderful experience, but it would have been much easier, and certainly less expensive, if someone who had been there before had given me his or her advice. Now, several years and much European travel later, this book contains the advice I give to friends before their first trip.

The very first and most important piece of advice I can give you is one word: GO! If you have the time, and can find the money somewhere, anywhere, just GO! You will not regret it, I promise you. When you walk into St Peter's in Rome and look down a central aisle longer than two football fields, over the spot where Charlemagne was crowned twelve cen-

War cemeteries and memorials

Twice in the last century, much of Western Europe was a battlefield. During the First and Second World Wars, millions of young men were sent to fight in Europe, and tens of thousands of them remain there today, in hundreds of British, Commonwealth, and American cemeteries. There are few experiences in Europe which are more affecting than visiting one of these places – peaceful, immaculately tended, and indescribably sad.

British and Commonwealth cemeteries are concentrated near Bayeux, and in eastern France and Flanders, especially around the Somme and Ypres. Whenever possible, survivors of those killed were given a chance to add a personal message on the headstone of their son or husband. American cemeteries are typically much larger and more formal, with row after row of white crosses interspersed with Stars of David. American cemeteries are typically open from morning until sunset, while Commonwealth cemeteries are open 24 hours a day.

Along with the actual cemeteries there are larger war memorials throughout Europe. The memorial arch at the Menin Gate in Ypres bears the names of 55,000 British men (part of an inconceivable total of 85,000) who died near Ypres and who have no known grave, their bodies swallowed up in the mud of the Western Front. Every night at 8pm, rain or shine, the road through the gate is closed and members of the Ypres Fire Brigade play "The Last Post" on silver bugles. For Americans, the cemetery at Colleville-sur Mer, directly over Omaha Beach, seems to resonate most deeply. Many of the 9387 men interred at Colleville died on that beach, within a few minutes of their landing on French soil. Finally, no Canadian should visit France without visiting the Vimy Ridge Memorial. No Canadian needs to be told why.

turies ago, and then give a glance to the right and see Michelangelo's *Pietá*, you will not regret going. When you sit on a beach in the Greek Islands and watch the sun set into the Aegean Sea, and listen to the others on that beach laughing and chatting in six languages as the ouzo and wine get passed around, you will not regret the time and money it took to get there. When you wake up in Paris and have a choice between going to the Eiffel Tower, or the Louvre, or Versailles, or Notre Dame, or the Cathedral at Chartres, or a dozen other wonders only a walk or a train ride away, your trip will seem very cheap indeed. That's not to say that you shouldn't try to go as inexpensively as possible; in fact, this book is written in large part to help you do just that. But later in life, when you look back and ask yourself whether it was worth it to go when you did, I promise you the answer will be "Yes." If you have the time and the money, do it. If you have the time, but think you don't have the money, keep reading, and maybe I can show you that Europe for a few weeks, or for a summer, can be a lot cheaper than you think.

This book is about the nuts and bolts of travel, especially with regard to planning, saving money, and getting the most out of a trip

And, if the whole process of going seems like too much of a bother, too much planning

Russia

For those feeling adventurous and looking for something out of the ordinary, there's one place I'd especially recommend as a side trip: Russia. Don't believe the hype about Russia being some kind of lawless nightmare of mafia shootouts and out-of-control crime (it isn't), though grinding poverty is widespread. Despite this, the Russian people will, with the slightest excuse, share their food, cigarettes, time, and lives with you. Combine that with jaw-dropping museums and architecture, and an atmosphere, especially in winter, that simply drips romance, and Russia is a trip worth taking.

Getting a visa to Russia is a major bureaucratic pain in the neck. Basically, to get into the country a Russian citizen needs to sponsor your stay. In practice, there are a few hostels and hotels who will "sponsor" you when you make a reservation. After your hostel or hotel gets back to you, usually by fax, you will need to visit a Russian embassy with your sponsor's invitation, your passport, a wad of cash, and some passport photos in hand. Expect a long time standing in line, and bring a pen. The best jumping-off points for Moscow are Warsaw and Tallin, and the best for St Petersburg is Helsinki. The contacts below are a good start on the visa/accommodation hunt. Bon voyage.

Host Family Association
ⓔalexei@hofak.hop.stu.neva.ru.
Arranges home stays in Moscow and St Petersburg as well as the Baltic capitals.

Moscow Guest House
ⓦtghmoscow.hypermart.net/map.htm.

St Petersburg International Hostel PO Box 8, FIN-53501, Lappeenranta, Finland (snail mail to Russia via Finland), ☎+7 (812) 329-8018, ⓕ+7 (812) 329-8019, ⓔryh@ryh.ru.

and time, remember the following: by spending a summer in Europe you will visit countries that are both much older and very different from your own, and gain a new perspective on your own country as a result. You will meet people who happily live lives very different from your own. And you will see some of the greatest creations of the human mind and spirit: legendary wonders of art and architecture that form a large part of the collective heritage of the human race. That's why you're going to

Europe, not to hunt for the cheapest hostel or the best rate of exchange. Remember this during all the dry talk about money and packs and all that practical stuff.

Why go cheaply?

As recently as fifteen or twenty years ago, seeing Europe by staying in hostels or small hotels and using a Eurail train pass was pretty much a student option. No longer. Savvy travelers have recognized the rewards of such a trip in comparison with a much more expensive tour. Because of this, although I am speaking mainly to college students, recent graduates, and teachers who are planning budget trips for several weeks, the advice in this book should be useful for independent travelers of all ages. Indeed, if you are an "older traveler" finally getting to go to Europe for the first time, or someone who's going back after having served there in World War II, I would like to add a special farewell. To those who are

now realizing that European trip they have dreamed of for years or decades, congratulations. I hope it's the best trip of your life.

Travelers with larger budgets who want to avoid bland hotels and crowded tours may also find the information contained here very useful as a worthwhile introduction and reference.

This is not a guidebook. There are plenty of excellent guides available to every conceivable region of Europe. This book is about the nuts and bolts of travel, especially with regard to planning, saving money, and getting the most out of a trip. I can't guarantee that everything in this book is right for every traveler; after all, my advice reflects primarily my own experiences. But I can promise that I will help the first-time traveler avoid some very common mistakes and frustrations, save time and money, and skip the sometimes painful learning process I went through. This is the book I needed and couldn't find before I left on my first trip. I hope you find it helpful on yours.

Note: All prices listed in this book are in US dollars unless otherwise noted.

reasons to come to Europe

It's not possible to see the whole of Europe on a short trip – and I don't suggest you try. But to give you a taster of where you might go and what you might see or experience, here's my personal selection of the best that Europe has to offer.

01 **Art** How to put this politely... every major art museum in Europe contains more great works than any museum outside of the continent. Yeah, that pretty much says it.

02 Your compatriots You don't know how much of an American/Australian/Briton/Canadian/New Zealander/South African/etc you are until you've left your home and met some of your countrymen on the road.

03 The Alps Why climb in the Alps? Because they're there. And because they're spectacularly beautiful and full of friendly, astonishingly fit climbers and hikers from all over the world.

04 The French Riviera Yes, the Riviera does have plenty of giant yachts and walnut-brown, gold-bedecked women, but the best things about the south of France – the sun, the flowers, the blue sky and the even-more-blue water – are free, even to scruffy backpackers.

05 Pamplona For pure excitement, there's no festival like it. To participate, instead of just watch, all you need is the guts to climb the fence and face the bulls.

06 **Oktoberfest** This festival actually begins in September, and ends on the last full weekend in October. Somehow or other, those at the festival manage to down roughly four hundred thousand liters of beer every day, for sixteen days.

07 **The trains** With a Eurail pass in hand, Europe's trillion-dollar train system becomes your property, and you can use it like it was a borrowed mule.

08 **Paris** I've lost count of the number of times I've visited Paris, but the last time I visited, I found myself rushing through breakfast to get out and see the city.

09 **Rome** When London and Paris were both clusters of wooden huts, Rome was already the capital of an empire. There are fifty churches in Rome, any one of which would be the wonder of any country besides Italy. Since they're in Rome, they're taken for granted.

11 (Some) hostels Almost always cheap, usually fun, and occasionally filled with people who are a joy to eat, drink, talk, argue, and travel with.

10 Castles There are castles all over Europe, and most of them look exactly as you might expect – turrets, towers and massive walls of stone. I have to admit, there is something very satisfying about standing on a castle wall and ordering your friends to be dragged off to the dungeon.

12 The Dalmatian Coast Hundreds of islands, thousands of beaches, and almost all of the tourists are Europeans.

14 Slovenia Slovenia is a small, beautiful, peaceful, friendly country that is, today, what Western Europe was like in the 1950s. Visit now before it's gone.

13 Roman ruins The Romans built their roads and bridges to last forever, and, as of this writing, they seem to have succeeded. Scattered throughout Europe, but especially in Spain and southern France, Roman bridges, aqueducts, and theaters are in use every day.

15 Tuscany and Umbria These two provinces contain the classic Italian land-scapes, with ancient stone villages set among mountains, vineyards, and olive groves.

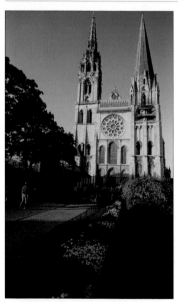

16 Cathedrals You simply can't find anything like them anywhere else on earth, and nothing like them will ever be built again.

17 Europeans A dozen trips, thirty countries, a hundred distinct regions, thousands of encounters, and I can recall hundreds of people who were friendly and helpful, and maybe ten who weren't.

18 **Music/opera/dance** Even the smallest town can surprise you with remark-ably good cultural performances, while in some cities – Vienna, Berlin, and Prague, for example, great music is inseparable from the city's identity.

19 **The Greek Islands** If you can get away from the tourist hordes, the Greek Islands are pure magic. Blazing sun, clear water, and tiny villages of white-washed stone.

20 **London** The United Nations has nothing on London. Greater London isn't a city so much as worldwide human society in miniature. Expensive, crowded, and endlessly fascinating.

Contents

Colour section

The guide

Basics

Index + small print

List of maps

First-Time Europe

Guide

1

Planning your trip

Calvin Coolidge (the 30th President of the United States) once said that if you look up the road and see ten troubles coming toward you, nine of them are going to run off the road before they get to you. That's the attitude to have in planning and getting ready for a trip to Europe. Remember, tens of thousands of people just like you went to Europe last year and had a great time. So will you. Plan, but don't overplan. Prepare, but don't stress out over every detail. To be honest, if you were to throw away this book, pack a tote bag, and hit the airport tomorrow, you could probably go and have a great time. With some planning and advice, though, you could have a much better time for about half the price. You're way ahead of the game by buying this book, so relax. I've made all the mistakes already, and you get to hear about them now instead of repeating them.

Your passport – first things first

This is an absolute essential – you won't be allowed on the plane without one. If you don't have a passport, send away for one as soon as possible. *Don't put this off.* Seriously, if you don't have a passport and especially if you don't have your birth certificate handy, the best thing you can do is put down this book right now and start the process immediately. If you already have a passport, note that some countries require a passport to be valid for a certain amount of time *after* you enter that country. If your passport is going to expire within six months of the beginning of your trip it's probably worth renewing it.

American passports

To get an American passport, you will need (1) your birth certificate or other proof of citizenship; (2) proof of identity (like a driver's license) with a signature; (3) an application form, available at any large post office, courthouse or passport office; and (4) two passport-sized photos as described on the form. The pictures, form, and so forth, can be mailed from any large post office (the postal clerk will check your ID) or taken directly to a passport office. (Passport offices, listed in the phone book under "Federal Government, Department of State," are located only in major cities.) If you don't have a copy of your birth certificate, send away for it *immediately* – the process can take a while, and until you have your birth certificate or other proof in hand, you can't apply for a passport. Other forms of proof, such as certificates of baptism, are described in detail on the form. Passports are good for ten years (five if you're under 16) and cost $45 ($25 for under-16s). Figure that into your budget. As you might expect, there is a flood of applications every spring. During the height of the summer, well after the peak application period, there can still be as much as a five-week processing wait. Other times of the year it may take

six weeks, or five days, or three weeks. The moral of this story is pretty obvious: get yours now.

If you are panicking as you read this because you have a thousand dollars' worth of non-refundable airline tickets for next week and no passport, take heart. For some extra money (a $35 surcharge), you can get a passport expedited. You can apply for an expedited passport from a passport agency or a large post office. Expedited passports will be processed within three business days of receipt by a passport agency – use express mail to get it there as fast as possible and pay the extra fee for the passport office to express mail it back to you; if this deadline cannot be met by the agency, the additional fee will be refunded. Specific information on expedited passports can be obtained when you pick up your application; or try the Passport Services website at ⓦwww.travel.state.gov/passport_services.html.

If your situation is truly desperate, there are services on the Web that can get your passport to you in about 24 hours – albeit for a hefty fee. One example is Passport Express (ⓦwww.passportexpress.com), who will ship your new or renewed passport for a fee of $150 ($100 if you can wait a week) plus government fees. The service, and others like it, essentially acts as your proxy at the passport office by showing up and doing all the paperwork for you. If you live in a city with a passport office, you can drop in just as quickly and do it yourself.

Canadian passports

Applications can be obtained from passport offices, which are located in major cities, or from any large post office. (I've been told that going directly to passport offices is best, if you can do it.) Applications can also be downloaded from the Web. Full details on the requirements are provided with each application form, but you'll need two current photos, and have the application form and one photo signed by an eligible guarantor. You must also provide original evidence of Canadian citizenship, any previous Canadian passport, certificate of identity or refugee travel document issued to you in the last five years, and the appropriate fee (Can$85 for an adult, Can$35 for a child aged 3–15, and Can$20 for a child under 3). Passports should be ready in ten days if the application is delivered by hand, or twenty if it's mailed. For more information, call

☎1-800/567-6868 or check online at ⓦwww.dfaitmaeci.gc.ca/ passport.

British passports

The United Kingdom Passport Service (UKPS) charges £30 for a new passport (£16 for a child), and requires the usual application form, photographs, proof of identity and proof of Britishness. Expedited services are available. Along with various passport offices and about 2400 post offices and travel agents, the UKPS has moved a great deal of their operation to the Web, and they have a pretty good site with tons of information at ⓦwww.ukpa.gov.uk – or you can call them on ☎0870/521 0410.

Australian passports

Aussies can apply for passports at over 1700 post offices throughout the country. After filling out the somewhat complicated form, you will need to appear for an interview, which may require an appointment. Aussie passports cost a fair bit: Aus$144 for a regular passport, Aus$72 for seniors. You should have your passport in hand in about three weeks. For those in a hurry, and within three weeks of departure, a priority service is available. For $60 extra, the fee guarantees the processing of an application by a passport office within two full working days (48 hours), provided the applicant has met all the other requirements. Call toll-free ☎131 232 for more information, or go to ⓦwww.passports .gov.au.

New Zealand passports

Along with a consenting witness – who will need to sign the backs of photographs and be available to answer questions from the government over the phone – Kiwis will need the following to get a passport: proof of citizenship, proof of identity, two identical photos, application fees, and application forms (which can be obtained from a travel agent or downloaded). Fees are NZ$80 for an adult passport, and NZ$40 for those under 16. Passports should come back to applicants within about two weeks, unless you opt for the quicker "Urgent Service" (NZ$160/120) or "Callout Service"

(NZ$330/290). Call freephone ☎0800/225 050 or go to Ⓦwww
.passports.govt.nz for more info.

Visas

A visa is a special notation, stamped or glued into your passport,
that allows you to enter and exit a country. Something like: "Bearer
is hereby granted leave to travel in Elbonia from June 1, 2001 –
August 31, 2001, for the purpose of tourism."

Visas are an unfortunate holdover from the days when European
borders meant something. Today, visas are little more than bureaucratic inconveniences, and some can be surprisingly expensive,
especially for Canadians. Fortunately, very few Western European
countries still require them, and fewer Eastern European countries
do each passing year. See Basics #1 for more on visas – especially
if you are from Canada, Australia, or New Zealand.

Planning

Now that your passport application is in the mail, the next thing to
do in any serious planning is to get an overview. This part is easy
and fun. Just find a large map of Europe and let your imagination
loose. Paris? The Norwegian fjords? Liters of beer in Munich? The
nightlife in Amsterdam? Jazz clubs in Prague, and the Charles
Bridge? Pubbing and clubbing in London? The ruins of Pompeii?
The midnight sun in Sweden? One country for a month, or the
highlights of five different nations? Get an atlas or a large map that
covers all of Europe, and some coffee-table books from the library,
and wander at will. One of the true joys of travel is seeing for yourself a place that, in photographs, looks too exotic and beautiful to
be real. To get some of those enticing pictures, look for books
called *Insight Guides* at the library. These books have great photographs but are not very useful for traveling. Also, *National
Geographic*, at one time or another, has published a story on just
about every place in Europe. Most libraries also have video collections that include documentaries and/or tourist office productions
about Europe.

National tourist offices

This is another one of the fun parts. Just call or write the national tourist offices listed in Basics #3 and in a few days your mailbox is miraculously full of brochures. Their heavy, glossy pages are covered with pictures of beautiful sights and happy, smiling people. Even a toxic waste dump would look like heaven in one of these.

This type of information is good for getting a first glimpse of a country, and especially for revealing places, sights, or monuments you may never have heard of. When you call tourist offices, let them know your intended budget and your specific areas of interest. Ask for maps, since good maps can be expensive, and tourist office maps are sometimes of surprisingly high quality. Maps of entire countries or regions are needed to plan effectively. If you have any special interest, such as long-distance walking, bicycling and so on, ask for information on that, too. Most tourist offices have an incredible amount of information, and most of it is free for the asking. Before leaving on your trip, copy whatever information you need out of these glossy brochures and then leave them at home – they're too heavy and awkward to carry with you.

Tourist offices on the Web

Most European countries are scaling back on expensive tourist offices abroad, and putting more and more content on the Web. Below are the official websites for a number of European tourist authorities. If your destination of choice is not listed below, try Ⓦwww.visiteurope.com, which has links to semi-official sites for every country in Europe.

Austria	Ⓦwww.austria-tourism.at/us
Belgium	Ⓦwww.visitbelgium.com
Britain	Ⓦwww.britishtouristauthority.com
Denmark	Ⓦwww.visitdenmark.com
Estonia	Ⓦwww.visitestonia.com
Finland	Ⓦwww.mek.fi
France	Ⓦwww.francetourism.com
Germany	Ⓦwww.germany-tourism.com
Hungary	Ⓦwww.hungarytourism.com
Ireland	Ⓦwww.goireland.com
Italy	Ⓦwww.enit.it

Latvia	ⓦ www.latvia-usa.org/golatvia
Luxembourg	ⓦ www.visitluxembourg.com
The Netherlands	ⓦ www.holland.com/
Norway	ⓦ www.visitnorway.com
Poland	ⓦ www.polandtour.org
Portugal	ⓦ www.portugal.org
Scotland	ⓦ www.visitscotland.com
Spain	ⓦ www.okspain.org
Switzerland	ⓦ www.switzerlandtourism.com
Sweden	ⓦ www.gosweden.org
Wales	ⓦ www.visitwales.com

Other travelers

There is nothing like up-to-date first-hand information. If you know somebody who has been to Europe recently, give them the third degree. Don't take everything they say as gospel truth (or for that matter, everything *I* say); after all, you are a different person going at a different time. But if they rave about a quiet little village you've never heard of, consider a visit. If they mention a specific hotel that was the site of a mouse convention, or the home of herds of corn-fed cockroaches, write that name down and avoid it.

In addition, the Internet is a great place for sharing travel tips and information. You'll find a number of travel-related message boards all over the Web where you can post your specific questions and get good first-hand advice back. It's best to be as specific as possible on these boards; avoid "Anyone been to Paris lately?" types of questions and remember to take the advice with a grain (or boulder) of salt. A list of travel-talk websites is in Basics #9.

Deciding on an itinerary

The next step is a bit harder – deciding what you want to see, and how best to arrange your trip to see it all. The most common entry and exit points to and from Europe are London, Amsterdam, Paris, Frankfurt, and Milan, and it is generally cheapest to fly in and out of those cities (see Chapter 4, "Getting There" for more on this). Once you have a rough list of what's important to you, and a rough itinerary, you can start thinking about when and how to get there. When you're doing your planning, don't plan too rigidly. When

you get to Europe you will hear of places, meet people, and find out about events that may cause you to change your plans. Leave some days open so you can do this along the way.

A word of advice about *how much* to plan to see. A typical list of the "must-see" cities might include London, Paris, Rome, Florence, Venice, Prague, Amsterdam, Munich, Berlin, Madrid, and Vienna. But notice that if you were to spend a week in each place – and allow, say, twelve days for moving around – you'd have to spend from June 1 through August 28 in Europe to visit them all. You would also miss Greece, Ireland, Scandinavia, Scotland, and Switzerland completely, be wretchedly sick of traveling by the second month, and arrive home totally exhausted.

The point is this: you can't see all of Europe in one summer, and it's not even fun to try. Remember, you only get one chance to see a place for the first time, when everything is fresh and new. The first time you see Paris, give it the five days or so that it deserves. Going there for a day will simply be unsatisfying and will inevitably diminish the experience the second time you go. I'm not one of those snobs who claims you have to spend weeks in a place to really say that you've been there. I am saying, however, that if you try to do and see too much your trip will become a blur of trains, hostels, museums, paintings, and churches that all run together after a while.

Plan realistically. Figure out what is really important to you, go see those cities or things at a reasonable pace, and don't get caught up in the "I've got to complete my list" syndrome. If this is going to be your only trip for a long time, it's understandable that you want to see as much as possible. But when you're in Europe, if you ever feel you *have* to go sightseeing, rather than you *get* to go sightseeing, you're pushing too hard. Take a break at this point. Planning to visit a beach resort, or just making a long stay in one spot about halfway through your trip, is a good idea if you think you might need a bit of a rest.

When to go

For most of us, summer is the travel season, whether we like it or not. Certainly the vast majority of students and teachers will be traveling between May 15 and September 15. The good and bad aspects of travel during the summer are obvious: the weather is nice, but the crowds are not. So for the first time (and not the last), I will repeat one of the Three Great Truths of European travel: GO EARLY. The best time to travel is in early May. Spring is in the air, European students are still in school, the summer hordes have not arrived, and it's as good as it's going to get. What this means to students and teachers is that it will be worth your while to leave as soon as possible after school is out. While you shouldn't go directly from your Organic Chemistry final to the airport, don't wait around just to catch a concert on June 10 when you could have gone on May 30.

One word of warning: many European schools take their students on "educational" trips during May. Some of the "education" provided on these trips seem to include screaming football matches in hostel hallways until 1am. If you are hosteling in May, always ask if you will be sharing your hostel with a school group, or you may go to sleep to the not-so-sweet sounds of children at play.

Travel quality peaks around June 1, before the tourists really start to arrive from abroad, declines steadily throughout June and July as more and more Europeans hit the trail, and then drops off a cliff in August, as millions of French, Greek, and Italian tourists go on a vacation frenzy. Almost all French and Italians take their holidays during August. This means that not only are beaches and major attractions crowded, but also many shops and restaurants are closed, and others may have shorter hours. Bear in mind, too, that actually traveling at the beginning or end of August is very unpleasant, with massive traffic jams and overcrowded trains and ferries.

Weather is another factor to consider. A traveler who spends a summer in Europe can expect some very hot days and nights in southern Europe (Spain, Italy, Greece) and warm days with cool nights in most other places. Rain is possible anywhere at any time, especially in Britain, Ireland, and Scandinavia, so it is advisable to bring a light rain jacket or small umbrella. Outside of the south, layered clothing is a good idea because days can include chilly mornings, hot afternoons, and cool evenings. More detailed weather information, on specific countries, is best obtained from a national tourist office. Europe is a big place, and it is hard to generalize about continent-wide weather conditions.

Off-season travel

I have spent quite a bit of time in Europe in the winter months, including a Christmas in Venice. Despite the cold, there are some definite advantages to visiting off season. Aside from the obvious reasons to go in the winter, such as skiing or snowboarding, the lack of crowds is the best reason to visit from October through March. Venice, for example, is a totally different city in the winter, and actually feels quiet and peaceful. (Those who have only seen Venice in summer, when rampaging hordes of tourists overrun the city like army ants, may find this hard to believe.) Also, most towns and cities have some sort of Christmas/New Year's festival. Museums in all cities are typically empty, especially on rainy days, and hotel rooms are generally cheaper, although the most touristy hotels and resorts will probably be closed or deserted, especially from about December 10 through New Year's.

If you are considering a trip to Europe in the winter, take a look at a globe. Notice that London is about the same latitude as Montreal and is well north of Maine. The southern parts of Sweden, Norway, and Finland are at the same latitudes as parts of Alaska. Bottom line: it can be bitterly cold anywhere in Europe over the winter, even in places that are roasting hot in the summer. (The coldest I have ever been in my life was in Naples in January.) The cold can be compounded by drafty hotels and the European habit of only heating a few rooms at a time. (More than once I have woken up in a European hotel, let out a breath, and watched a little cloud of condensation form.) Bring some seriously warm clothes, polypro underwear, gloves, a hat, and a lightweight sleeping bag to put on top of all-too-thin blankets in all-too-cold hotel rooms.

Classes and reading

If you're thinking about a trip to Europe some time well in the future, say in six months or a year, one of the best things you can do now to prepare is to take a course in Art History, European History, or Architecture. A survey course in Art History, in particular, will vastly increase the relevance and interest of all of those paintings and statues. Most of the truly unique attractions of Europe, particularly in Italy and France, involve art and/or architecture in one form or another. Knowing even the basics about the major artists of the various periods will vastly increase your enjoyment of their works. If you don't have the time or opportunity to take a course, any decent library will have several metric tons of those big glossy books on art and artists. My personal favorites are the *Time-Life History of Art* series – about thirty books, each concentrating on one particular artist and his world. They are designed for the general population, have beautiful illustrations, and are well written. Unfortunately, they've been out of print for a while, so look for them in libraries. Look also for the Thames & Hudson art books: well-illustrated paperbacks, each of which covers a particular artistic or architectural style or era. Of course, any major bookstore will have loads of new, glossy picture books on every conceivable artist. In any book, if you see a painting or piece of sculpture you like, note where it is (the location is usually written right next to the picture), then go see it when you get there. When you do, be prepared for a surprise, since what is beautiful on a page in a book is very often spectacular in real life, particularly sculptures. Along with books on artists, also look for books which concentrate on the contents of a specific museum – these can often be more practical for someone traveling to only a few cities.

No matter how much time you spend reading about art and architecture, I don't think you'll regret it. I've certainly never heard anyone say that they have. On the other hand, I've lost count of the number of times I've heard someone say, "I wish I knew more about this stuff, so it was more to me than just a bunch of paintings."

Languages

One of the most humbling experiences an American (or Australian or Kiwi) can have in Europe is to meet a teenager who speaks three or four languages. For true humiliation, spend a few minutes at the Amsterdam Visitors Bureau and watch the 20-year-old behind the desk switch from Dutch to German to Spanish to English to French and back to Dutch again without batting an eyelash. It's almost as bad in Scandinavia, where my pitiful efforts in Danish or Swedish are usually met with "How's it going – anything I can do for you, just let me know, okay?" I know – and have used – all the excuses: the United States and Canada are huge countries, we don't have as many languages as close to us as Europeans do, and so on. Those statements are indeed true, but not much help when you're trying to function and get around in a different culture. The ability to speak a language, even a little, will add tremendously to the enjoyment of visiting a country, and will work wonders when dealing with the local residents. Even a phrasebook or dictionary, especially if you are going to be spending a long time in one country, can be very useful.

By speaking the local language you're making an obvious effort to reach out, while simultaneously showing respect for the local culture, and that will be noted and appreciated. (Canadians will find their French very useful in this regard, especially if they make it known that they are from Canada.) Also, while it may be true that "everybody speaks English" in the big cities, that will not be the case out in the sticks. Even a single semester or quarter of a language, or an adult school class, is well worth taking. I know how much the moderate amount of Spanish I can speak has meant to me. I once gave my seat on a bus to an older woman in Spain, who refused to take it out of pride. When I managed to say "It's only because you look like my girlfriend," her laughter was worth all of those miserable verbs conjugated over the years. I don't know who said it, but this quote is both beautiful and appropriate:

Saber otra lengua es tener otra alma.
To know another language is to possess another soul.

Planning how to get around

Once you've got a rough idea of where you want to go and what you want to see, the next step is deciding how to get around to all those great places and things.

Planning this step is kind of a chicken-or-the-egg situation, in that you won't know what's the best way to get around until you've tried it, but you have to plan (and buy train passes if necessary) before you head for Europe. This next section will discuss the options available that require planning before you leave. Other options that don't require as much planning, such as hitching and ride-share, are covered in Chapter 6, "Getting around."

Trains

For most people budgeting their way around Europe, there is a simple answer to the transport question: buy a train pass in some form, or just some train tickets, and hit the tracks. There are good reasons for this: European trains are generally fast, convenient, reliable, and they seem to go everywhere. During the summer, they are full of travelers from dozens of countries, and you can meet some very fun people. They're a great way to travel.

If you only want to see two or three cities, then you should probably buy individual train tickets between those cities, rather than a pass. If you want to go to more than four or five cities, especially if they are in different countries, then consider a train pass. The most popular kind of pass, at least for visitors from outside Europe, is the "Eurail" pass, which comes in a number of forms and covers from three to seventeen countries. These allow either unlimited travel over a period of time, or travel on a certain number of days within a given time period (say, five days within a month). You'll find more information than you thought possible on train passes and their various validities and restrictions in Basics #2 – there's too much to put in here. Take some time with it, even though the material is a bit dry. Remember also that any good rail agent can quote you individual point-to-point ticket prices, to help you decide whether or not you need a rail pass at all.

Citizens or subjects of EU countries are ineligible for Eurail passes, but get an even better deal with InterRail passes, also discussed in Basics #2.

Finally, even if the train is your transportation choice, don't skip the rest of the information in this chapter. You may find a situation where some other way of getting around will work for a side trip, or when your pass runs out.

WARNING: *Eurail and other train passes should be purchased before leaving for Europe.* There are a few major cities (London, for example) where *some* types of passes may be available if you can prove that you have been in Europe for less than six months, but they cost several hundred dollars more than if purchased outside of Europe. It is far easier to buy a pass before you leave. If you are already in Europe, as a student, for example, you can have a pass bought for you and sent out with a moderate amount of difficulty. Contact any pass vendor (listed in Basics #2) for specific information.

Airplanes

One of the best things to happen to European travel in years has been the recent explosion of low-cost no-frills airlines operating out of Britain. For decades, most air travel in Europe was controlled by national airlines who, because they were virtual monopolies, could effectively charge what they liked, and the customer could either take it or leave it.

Well, those days are over. Along with competition from the low-cost carriers, the plunge in air travel after the September 11 attacks was too much for the weakest national carriers. Sabena, Belgium's national airline, actually went bankrupt, and Swissair quit flying entirely (though a new national airline, Swiss, was set up a few months later). Other carriers are fighting to survive against the smaller, more responsive no-frills airlines; British Airways has even dramatically slashed its European fares in a bid to recapture some of the market from its rivals.

New no-frills airlines are starting up all the time, but some of the longest established are listed in Basics #4 on p.229. Some pointers on these airlines:

- The vast majority of their flights are from smaller airports, such as London Stansted, or from smaller cities, such as Bologna, Lyon or Faro. Check out exactly where you're flying to, as some airports served by the no-frills carriers are a long way out of town: you might think you're flying to "Bologna", but in fact end up landing in Forli, 60km from Bologna. The extra money (and hassle) spent on transport from Forli to Bologna may or may not be worth the saving you make on the flight.

- The no-frills airlines are much easier to deal with on the Web than on the phone – in fact, their goal is to sell 100 percent of their tickets online if possible. As a result, all of these airlines have excellent websites.

- While almost all low-cost airlines advertise ridiculously low fares, such as £10 from London to Spain, these are usually available only on the Web, only at odd times, and only in limited supply. Don't believe that you can always get a £10 flight from London to, say, Italy, any time you want. You can't.

- Even though you make a reservation on the Web and don't get a ticket, you still need to bring either printed itinerary or a confirmation number at the airport. If your airline needs a printed itinerary, you should have a printer handy when making the reservation.

- For really cheap tickets, avoid flying on Fridays, Sundays, and holidays, and outside the peak summer holiday months. You'll get the best prices if you book well in advance, though it's also worth keeping an eye on the airlines' websites for news of their special offers, which is where you get the truly great deals.

No-frill bargains aside, you will find that planes are still a bit more expensive than trains. Airplanes are very useful, however, for special cases, such as flying to remote locations that would otherwise involve lengthy and complicated travel. For example, a plane trip from London to the Greek Islands compares very favorably with the same trip by train – it costs about the same, but takes four hours as opposed to the better part of two days. This is a slightly special case, where flights are regular and cheap, and the destination is hard to get to by train and boat. If you are planning a long round trip to a specific destination, take the time to calculate how much it will cost you in incidental fees (port taxes, departure taxes, etc), time and travel days, and/or train pass days. If time is short or the routing is long and complex, it just might be worth your while to fly. See Chapter 6, "Getting around," for more on this.

Even before the Internet boom, the center of cheap European flights was London, and some truly amazing deals can still be found among the multitude of discount travel agencies located there. If you're thinking about going to Greece or Turkey, on to Israel or to Egypt, or even just Spain or Portugal while on your European trip, consider flying into and out of London. There are a number of ways to track down these cheap non-Internet flights. *Time Out*, a London magazine, always has a lot of ads for cheap flights, as does the *Evening Standard*, a London newspaper. However, perhaps the best (certainly the cheapest) sources for cheap flights are the freebie magazines, most of them aimed at Australian and New Zealand travelers. They are available from self-service bins and budget accommodations all over the city, and contain ads from discount travel agencies for flights all over Europe and the world. Of these, *TNT*, specifically geared to the budget traveler, is the best. In the States or Canada, copies may be available at large bookstores or at Tower Records. Failing that, the *TNT* address is: 14–15 Child's Place, Earls Court, London SW5 9RX, England (☎020/7373-3377). Send away for a copy well in advance of your trip, and see if some of the available flights fit your plans and your budget. These will change by the time you get there, but at least you will get an idea.

Also, remember that many of the best deals are last-second, stand-by, or some other wrinkle on normal air travel. If you are in London prior to flying home, you may find an incredible deal and be able to spend the last week of your trip in Israel rather than in London. It's worth calling around to the discount agencies on arrival in London (see p.229) to check this out.

Boats and ferries

If you are planning on taking a boat to Europe, have your butler return this book for a refund, as you don't need my advice on saving money.

While in Europe, however, there are numerous ferries, lake steamers, and riverboats for those in the mood to set sail, many of which are cheaper with a Eurail pass. These discounts are listed on the back of the free map that comes with that Eurail pass. If you're visiting the Greek Islands, you'll undoubtedly travel by ferry at some point, and you probably will if you're traveling from London to the rest of the continent (although there's also the option of the Channel Tunnel). One "cruise" line that might interest budget travelers is the Norwegian Coastal Steamer Route, or "Hurtigruten."

These boats leave Bergen and arrive six days later in Kirkenes, well above the Arctic Circle, having cruised through some absolutely spectacular scenery on the way. Fares are very reasonable, especially for Norway, since these are working boats and not meant specifically for tourists. Off-season fares (from September 1 to April 30) are extremely reasonable, and anyone in Europe at this time should consider this trip. The Norwegian Tourist Board can give full details – see Basics #3 for their address.

Buses

Unlike the United States, where riding Greyhound is like a sentence in a mobile prison, buses in Europe are generally clean, safe, reliable, and fast. In some countries – Greece and Portugal for example – express buses are faster than trains for some trips. This is also the case in Ireland, and, to a lesser extent, in England. If you plan on spending most of your time in these countries, then a train pass may not pay for itself. This is definitely so if you won't be traveling much.

If you are planning on visiting only major cities in a large number of countries, and are on a very tight budget, you might want to look into Busabout, a long-distance bus company based in

London. The buses travel a set route around Europe, hitting about seventy cities in a series of loops and spurs. Buses stop for the night at hostels that are affiliated with the company. Busabout is a viable alternative to a train pass, but a couple of warnings are in order here. The first is that a long-distance ride on a bus is much more uncomfortable than on a train. The second is that a standard Busabout pass does not cover Greece, Ireland, Hungary, or Scandinavia, as a Eurail pass would. A two-month unlimited-travel Busabout pass for those under 26 is $669 – cheaper than a train pass, though of course only good on the Busabout system. If you're interested in checking them out, Busabout has a fine website with an excellent description of their service at Ⓦwww.busabout.com. You can also get hold of them at Busabout, 258 Vauxhall Bridge Road, London SW1V 1BS, England (Ⓣ020/7950 1661, Ⓕ020/7950 1662, Ⓔinfo@busabout.co.uk).

Another bus option worth considering is the "slow coach" operation. These are also designed for ultra-budget types, and consist of a number of buses that follow a preset route around a particular country, dropping off and picking up travelers anywhere along the route. Basically, you buy a ticket for a certain amount of time, then jump on and off buses as desired. Be advised that these operations focus on the cheapest possible accommodations when they stop for the night. Check the London magazines mentioned on p.21 or at tourist offices in major European cities for these types of operators, or look for posters in hostels and budget accommodations.

Finally, if you are planning only a few trips between cities, say three weeks in London, followed by three weeks in Paris, followed by three weeks back in London, making those trips by bus is going to be your cheapest option. You certainly don't need a rail pass for such a trip.

Driving

A car is best for getting to out-of-the-way towns the train doesn't go to and for seeing the truly rural parts of a country. Towns and villages without train stations, at least those some distance from big cities and the highways, are bound to be quieter, more traditional, and see far fewer foreign tourists than rail towns do. I have traveled in some very out-of-the-way places, in both Europe and the Middle East, and the people were generally more friendly (or curious) and certainly less jaded. The downside is that traveling by car can insulate you from your surroundings: you don't meet people in the same way you do getting around by train, and you can end up feeling as if you're traveling in a bit of a vacuum.

If cars and the countryside go together like bacon and eggs, cars and cities go together like Twinkies and Tabasco. If you are interested mainly in rural areas and camping, think about a car. If you are going exclusively to major cities, the problems with parking, theft, and driving in traffic may not make it worth it. The expenses of renting a car can be horrific, especially if only paid by one person: generally $200–500 a week, depending on the country, for a car that moped riders will laugh at (easyCar – ⓦ www.easycar .com – is a cheaper alternative, if booked far enough in advance). Add to this the cost of gas (roughly the cost of champagne in most European countries), a hefty tax, a collision damage waiver fee, parking fees, road tolls, etc. All this makes renting only an affordable option for groups of two or more. Also, remember that every company has a minimum age for renters – either 21, 23, or 25.

One handy tip for those who do want to rent: it is always cheaper to arrange a rental vehicle before leaving instead of arranging it on the spot in Europe. It may also be cheaper to arrange a fly-drive package with a tour operator or travel agent. They will have much more buying clout than you as an individual, and even with their fees added on may be able to offer you substantial savings.

One friend, who is the king of the do-it-yourselfers, advocates buying a car, especially for motorhead types. If you are a good judge of cars, can make simple repairs, and can bargain hard, you may be able to buy a car, use it, and sell it a few months later for almost as much as you paid for it. Don't bet the return ticket on this, and remember that you may end up driving around Paris looking for a shop that sells Armor-All so you can spiff the old sled up before you sell it. However, that's part of the experience, and even if you don't get quite as much as you paid for it, you will probably end up saving money over the rental option. You might, however, want to leave this for a second or later trip.

The indispensable guide to driving, buying, leasing, and renting a car in Europe is *Moto Europa*, by Eric Bredesen. Eric and I have never met, but we've spoken over the phone off and on for the last seven years. I've used his book, and I trust his advice implicitly. Eric has posted the entire contents of *Moto Europa* on the Web for free at ⊛www.ideamerge.com/motoeuropa/index.html. Those who want hard copies of the book can order directly from the website – if you are considering a driving trip through Europe it will be $15 well spent.

Bicycles

If you haven't done a bike tour or two at home, I would strongly recommend against doing your first on your first trip to Europe. If you're going to pay the kind of money it takes to get across the ocean, you should make absolutely sure that you like pushing a bike around for six or eight hours a day.

Bike touring is one instance where an organized group trip, at least for first-timers, might make sense. Certainly the support that a company can provide, such as vans and repair facilities, can let the rider concentrate on biking rather than logistics. The classified section of any bicycling magazine (such as *Bicycling*) will have a number of ads for European trip outfitters, and the Web of course has dozens of tour operators. One warning, though: as with all types of tours, seemingly similar operations can have dramatically different levels of competence and professionalism. The best information you can possibly get on a company is a first-hand report from a rider who has recently taken a tour. A notice posted in a bike shop requesting first-hand accounts of European trips will probably get you more good advice than you can use.

Another option you might want to consider is a train/bike trip. Bikes are welcome on trains throughout Europe for a varying but usually small charge. By combining the two modes of transport, you will be able to cover much more ground than by bike alone. Remember that the train system in Europe goes nearly everywhere; if you get sick of riding or of headwinds, the nearest train station will often be only a few kilometers away. On your return you can astound your friends with the number of countries you covered. Some tips for the prospective biker:

- Normally, you can bring your bike on an airplane as one of your two pieces of checked luggage for no charge (Virgin Atlantic, United, and others have this policy, but call to confirm for your airline and flight). Call your airline of choice for further details on packing, but expect them to insist that the bike is packed in some sort of protective, durable packaging. Don't count on the airlines for that – get a box from a bike shop. You will probably need to check in an extra half-an-hour early.

- If you intend to rent a bike in Europe for a long ride, you might want to bring along a seat or a soft seat cover that you find comfortable. Rent-a-bike seats tend to be made from cast iron, or at least feel like it. Bringing your own helmet is also a good idea. I would never trust the safety of my skull to a rental helmet, or to no helmet at all. Bring one you have used before.

- Hopefully your bike weighs less than seventy pounds. If it does, you can pack other things in the box with it, both to avoid having to carry them with you and to cushion the bike. Pad your faithful steed well, as fixing a damaged bike is a rotten way to start a trip.

- If you are a super-serious biker, remember that a trip to Europe is not a race, calling for an ultra-light, stripped-down speed machine. Hard as it may be, put a bell or a horn on your handlebars, as well as a big, un-aerodynamic (but safe), mirror. Lights can also be a lifesaver when you don't make your destination by nightfall. Along with tools, spare parts, and a good solid lock, bring extra sunscreen and lip balm.

- I strongly recommend getting around major cities by public transport instead of by bicycle. Remember that local drivers and local cyclists know what to expect from each other. The instinctive reactions that serve you so well at home may be just the wrong things to do in Europe.

Despite much searching, I have yet to find a decent book about bike touring in Europe. The two I have found, *Cycling Europe: Budget Bike Touring in the Old World*, by Nadine Slavinski (Bicycle Books), and *Europe by Bike*, by Karen and Terry Whitehill (Mountaineers Press), are similar. They both have very short planning and basic information sections, and then present a number of routes and itineraries. Perhaps you can find something better in Europe.

If you are considering renting a bike while in Europe for a day or weekend, rather than as a primary means of getting around, see the section on bikes in Chapter 6, "Getting Around."

Walking

If you are a dedicated walker, you are in for a treat. There are tens of thousands of miles of recognized trails in Europe, especially in the main mountain ranges of the Alps and Pyrenees, and in Britain and Ireland. In the United States and Canada, long-distance walking usually means hiking through the wilderness and camping. In Europe, on the other hand, it can simply mean walking on a trail from cabin to cabin, or hostel to hostel, without the need for tent, groundsheet, sleeping pad, stove, and so on. In England you can easily hike from pub to pub over some truly beautiful farmland and end up gaining weight after walking eight hours a day. I'm sorry to say I've managed to do just that.

If you plan to do a walking trip, the first step is to write or call the tourist information offices listed in Basics #3 and request specific information on walking and hiking trails. Don't be surprised if you get more information than you can handle, particularly from Switzerland. Good maps are absolutely essential if you plan this sort of trip. It may not be as tricky as hiking in Alaska, but getting lost on the moors of England or in the mountains of France, Switzerland, or Italy, can be dangerous, especially considering the weather. After you arrive, excellent maps, some designed specifically for the walker, are available in most countries in Western Europe. If the local tourist office can't supply you with them, they can send you to someone who can. Invest in some even if you only plan a short hike.

WARNING: If you are planning on hiking in the woods of Eastern or Central Europe, see the health warning on tick encephalitis in Chapter 9, "In sickness and in health."

2

Budgeting

udgeting is a touchy subject. Some people are going
to have more money and/or different standards than
others, some people are going to get lucky and find a
great deal, while others may not. Also, everyone has
an optimum point where they feel the trade-off
between saving money and spending money is going to result in the
best trip. On one hand, you really do want to save money, but on
the other, you have spent quite a bit just to get to Europe, may not
be back for years, and want to get as much out of the trip as possible. If you have a fixed amount of money, and I mean really fixed,
the task is easier – you have to stick to that budget no matter what.
For everyone else, that "rock-solid" budget may prove alarmingly
expandable.

The brutal truth is that most of Europe is expensive. I took a
seven-week trip to Europe specifically to prepare for writing the
fourth edition of this book, and saved every receipt, logged every
expense, and tried to note every pound, mark, krone, or franc I
spent. It was an eye-opener. The minor expenses – tram tickets,
tube tickets, museums, phone calls, ice cream, newspapers, and so
on – really do add up. Don't be surprised if you go over even the
most carefully planned budget. Aussies and Kiwis should add about
US$400 to the budgets that follow to account for the higher air-
fares, while Brits can pretty much deduct the airfares altogether.

A realistic budget

The following is a budget for a typical two-month trip to Europe, for someone moving around quite a bit and seeing the sights. As you can see, it comes to about $4730/5180 (depending on age – see below), which is a realistic number to start with, with some of the inevitable budget bloat included. Note that the daily total, without transportation, is about $55. You could certainly do it cheaper than this if you tried, but when I say realistic, I mean that this is a good framework to start planning from. I don't want to give too low a figure, and even this budget will take some discipline. Increase all of these budgets by about $15 for every day you plan to spend in Denmark, Norway, Sweden, Finland, and Iceland. The budgets below are split for those under and over the age of 25. Those below that age are eligible for student fares and for cheaper rail passes.

Expenses

Airline tickets	$450/650	Getting around in cities	$400
15-day Flexi Eurailpass	$650/900	(50 days at $8 each)	
Accommodation	$1500	Documents	$100
(60 nights at $25 each)		(passport, student card, hostel card)	
Food/alcohol	$1080	Incidentals	$200
(60 days at $18 each)			
Museum and attraction admissions	$350	**Grand totals**	**$4730/$5180**

Middle- to low-range budgets

Going cheaper than the above is certainly possible. Airline tickets should be somewhat cheaper off-season, or a great deal or sale could cut their price. Don't plan on this, though; prices could just as easily go up. Camping would help the most and could cut that $1500 accommodation chunk by half. It would do this, however, at an increased cost in city transportation, and greatly increased time spent toting packs around. A cheaper train pass or a bus pass could help squeeze a bit, as could cheaper food and fewer incidentals – buying food at stores and cooking it for yourself can save major dollars. If you like pasta, or rather if you like cooking pasta, you can eat cheaply pretty much everywhere. Traveling as a couple, you can save some money over single travelers, and you will have more privacy while you save.

Unless you want to hitchhike, sleep in train stations, and eat bread three meals a day, I would count on spending an absolute minimum of about $3600/4000 (depending on age – see below) for two months. This is a daily total of about $35 per day, without transportation. Note that this last budget cannot be cut substantially anywhere.

Expenses

Airline tickets	$450/650	Getting around in cities	$500
10-day Flexi Eurailpass	$470/650	(50 days at $10 each)	
Accommodation	$750	Documents	$100
(50 nights at $10 each,		(passport, student card, hostel card)	
10 nights at $25)		Incidentals	$100
Food/alcohol (60 days at $15 each)	$900		
Museum and attraction admissions	$350	**Grand totals**	**$3620/$4000**

Rock-bottom budgets

If you are reading this and it seems that Europe is beyond your reach, take heart. A two-month trip with train pass is not mandatory. Below I have set out a one-month ultra-budget trip. This trip will require some major creativity on your part, especially in arranging transportation to where you want to go. And at seven dollars a day for city transportation, you will be walking a lot. You shouldn't hitchhike unless you are very comfortable with the idea, but you may be able to appeal to other hostelers who have a vehicle. Keep your ears wide open. I sincerely doubt if you could do better than this – certainly don't count on it.

Expenses

Airline tickets	$450/650	Getting around in cities	$210
Accommodation	$450	(30 days at $7 each)	
(10 nights at $25 each,		Documents	$100
20 nights at $10)		(passport, student card, hostel card)	
Food (30 days at $10 each)	$300	Incidentals	$100
Museum and attraction admissions	$200		
		Grand totals	**$1810/$2010**

If you think you can do it cheaper...

I'm sure there's some go-cheap commando out there who claims to have been traveling since 1995 on less than the $1810/$2010 I mention above. If you have done that, or know how to live on less than, say, $30 a day while seeing something of Europe, I'd love to hear from you. I cannot in good conscience advise a lower budget for the first-timer, unless you have extensive cheap travel experience in the States or your home country; or you have contacts in Europe who would be willing to put you up when you arrive penniless at their door. Do not try the "I can get there – I'll worry about getting back later" approach. And don't even think about the idea of "I can always appeal to my embassy – they won't abandon a fellow citizen so far from home." They will. Your nation's embassies overseas will barely notice if you drop dead in their doorways. Providing irresponsible travelers with money to get home is not their top priority, and believe me, they have heard every sob story known to man.

Don't overeconomize!

Those are the numbers. They may not be exact, but they do represent a realistic estimate of what a trip to Europe will cost. Remember that some of the expenses listed, such as food, would also have to be paid for if you stayed home. If you consider that you may not be paying rent while you travel, nor driving your car if you have one, the cost picture may look a lot better. Subletting or moving out of your apartment can obviously save a great deal of money and can mean the difference between going and staying for many people, especially students. I recommend subletting, but this is difficult in most university towns, so try to arrange it as early as possible.

At the risk of driving you into debt, here's my philosophy on spending on a European trip. If this is going to be the trip of a lifetime, spend a bit more and have the kind of trip you want. Students, trust me, $300 buys a lot more happiness at 20 than at 30, even if you could afford to take the whole summer off to go travel at that age. Since many students are graduating with a pretty hefty debt anyway, a few hundred bucks on top of that pile is not going to seem like much, especially when viewed from the distance of a couple of years. For both students and non-students, if you have the money, there are few better places to spend it than in Florence, Dublin, Barcelona, or Prague.

For those of you with no limit to your budget at all, you will find plenty of places in Europe that will be happy to take as much money as you can spend, and provide you with exquisite surroundings and impeccable service in exchange. A large resort is a large resort anywhere in the world; where Europe truly shines in upscale travel is in small, old, family-run hotels and inns that offer a level of personal service and hospitality that can't be found anywhere else. If you're going on a trip that includes these kinds of places, all I can say is: take me with you!

Working abroad

Here's a hot tip: there is one country where working to earn money for a European trip is better than any other. There are no language problems, no problems with taxes or laws, and the wages are relatively high. On top of that, prospective European travelers are welcomed wholeheartedly by the locals. This wondrous country, for Americans, is called the United States of America. Another profound truth learned at great pain. The best place for Americans to work to pay for a European trip is right at home. Why go to Europe and get some miserable low-paying job that barely covers food and rent when you could sacrifice some free time in the States and then travel without the need to work? Oh, yeah: "But I'll be in Europe while I work." True, but you will be working, possibly illegally, probably very hard, and probably for low wages, and all the while your vacation will be ticking by. Why not sacrifice some time at home and earn the money here, with housing, transportation, and all the other life issues already settled? Just my opinion. If you have a great job lined up in Europe, that's different. If the money earned is secondary to the purpose of being immersed more deeply in the culture, by all means, go for that job. But to earn money efficiently, there's no place like home.

For Canadians, Kiwis, Aussies, and those from other Commonwealth countries, the picture is slightly different. Britain has a policy of grudgingly allowing descendants of its former colonists back to the motherland to work, though with many restrictions. Commonwealth citizens with one or more grandparents born in Britain may not need a work permit at all, though they must apply for entry. Commonwealth citizens between ages 17 and 26 can apply to be "working holiday-makers" and stay for up to two years, though working no more than half the time of their stay. Be aware that these policies may have changed since this book went to press, so call the embassy of your country of interest for more information.

As far as working in the rest of the European Union, every country has different rules, and none are exactly screaming for hordes of travelers to come and take high-paying jobs. (France, for example, seems to have a ten percent unemployment rate as a national policy.) Brits have full EU privileges, of course, and Commonwealth citizens mentioned above may be able to use their British entry as a Trojan Horse to work in other nations. Also, if you have a parent or grandparent who emigrated from a European country, contact its embassy to see if you have any privileges. Germany, Ireland, and Greece, in particular, are supposed to welcome home prodigal descendants. Regardless of your status, if you wish to work in a particular country, contact that country's embassy months before leaving to get all details and necessary forms, well in advance. Even then, expect a few snags before it's over. Good luck.

WARNING: Any readers planning on working in Britain without permission, or entering Europe via Britain with the intention of working in another country, should see the section on British immigration officials at the end of Chapter 11, "Crime, safety, and sleaze."

Shorter trips

If you are working, rather than a student, teacher, or person of independent wealth, spending a whole summer wandering around Europe is probably not possible. For someone who has only two or three weeks to travel, the priorities change. Planning ahead to make the most of your limited time is essential, and a trip can and should be planned out day by day. Not very spontaneous, I know, but two weeks just doesn't allow for that. On the other hand, two weeks is plenty of time to see some truly wonderful places in Europe, and is a heck of a lot better than not going at all. Also, the short-term traveler has one huge advantage over the summer traveler: the ability to go before June or after August. If you have a choice, by all means avoid the summer crowds and heat and go in spring or early fall. Between October and April, however, you should expect some fairly cold weather, even in southern Europe. Some thoughts about a two- or three-week trip:

- Decide whether you want to explore one or two cities, or see the most famous bits of three cities. Anything more than three cities or (two regions) is going to be too much.
- Traveling by night train is recommended, especially if you are able to get a decent night's sleep in a somewhat noisy environment. More on this in the section on trains in Chapter 6, "Getting around."
- Carefully check the operating days and hours for any museums or attractions you especially want to see, and plan accordingly. These should be listed in your guidebook. Many museums in Europe are closed on Mondays, so you might want to plan on traveling then. There are exceptions to this rule; the Louvre, for example, is closed on Tuesdays, but open late on Mondays and Wednesdays. National tourist offices should also be able to tell you in advance if any major attractions are likely to be closed or under renovation. Be careful – a lot of renovation is going on these days.
- A full Eurail pass will not be necessary, and any train pass may prove too expensive unless you are really moving around. Do not buy a pass unless you are sure you will need it. Most travel agencies that sell Eurail passes also quote prices for individual train tickets. Compare the price of separate train or bus tickets with the cheapest possible pass (see Basics #2) that will cover your trip.
- Look very hard for an airfare that allows you to leave from the last city you plan to see, rather than one that requires you to fly out of the city you flew into. It is well worth paying a hundred dollars or more for this option, although it may not be necessary to pay anything extra at all.
- When all of the planning and expense is considered, a three-week trip is much more than a fifty percent improvement over a two-week trip. If you can borrow a week from next year's vacation

time, consider it. Also, if you can afford it, see if you can get another week off unpaid.

You really can see quite a bit in two weeks. If I were going for that length of time – and bear in mind that I like art, architecture, and that kind of stuff – I would probably advise something like this:

Day 1:   Fly to London.
Days 2–5:   London, and perhaps Cambridge or Oxford.
Days 6–9:   Channel Tunnel train to Paris. Paris, Chartres, and Versailles. Night train to Rome.
Days 10–13: Rome, with a day-trip to Florence.
Day 14:   Fly home out of Rome.
Day 15:   Fight jet lag, and drive your friends insane with jealousy by casually referring to "Firenze" and "Roma."

If you have three weeks, I would recommend adding one day in or around London, two days in Paris, two days in Florence and one day in Venice.

Veteran travelers may sneer at such a "short" trip, but who cares? In those two weeks you can see, roughly in order, Westminster Abbey, Big Ben, the Houses of Parliament, Trafalgar Square, the Tower of London and the Crown Jewels, Piccadilly Circus, Buckingham Palace, the British Museum and National Gallery, Cambridge University, the Eiffel Tower, Notre Dame, Versailles, the *Mona Lisa*, the Louvre, the Cathedral at Chartres, the Sistine Chapel, Vatican City, the Spanish Steps, the Trevi Fountain, the Colosseum, the Uffizi Gallery and Michelangelo's *David*. Or you could blow off this itinerary entirely and spend two weeks whooping it up in Paris, Provence, Milan, or Mallorca. Or, like one person I know, you could spend two weeks in Belgium and the Netherlands, ignore everything on the above itinerary, and still feel as if there was much more to see in those two small countries.

So you're hitting the tourist highlights and not spending a month hanging out in Parisian cafés drinking cheap wine and eating snails. So what? You've been to Europe once, and if you like it, you can always go back and see more, with all the experience gained on your first trip. And until that next trip you've still got Vienna, Munich, Berlin, and a dozen other incredible places to look forward to. Sounds all right to me.

Longer trips

One of my readers (Cathy from Montreal) wrote me a letter a few months ago, and said that I should have included a few words for those who are going to Europe for a long while, say for a semester or a year abroad. She was quite right and you may thank her for the following advice:

- For those who are going abroad to live, rather than travel continuously, "travel light" should be modified to something along the lines of "travel smart." Since you will have a base to store your things, you can bring a bit more stuff, but as always, bring what you need, and need what you bring.
- The normal airline limit of two seventy-pound bags plus carry-on should be enough to last you for quite some time, although if you are bringing books you may need another bag (at a cost of roughly one to two dollars a pound).
- I assume part of the reason you're going abroad is to get a better understanding of the country you're visiting. Don't try to re-create home by bringing it with you. (For example, don't bother with ten extra bottles of shampoo – Europeans wash their hair too and you're sure to find a new brand you'll like.) On the other hand, products like Walkmans, running shoes, cameras, and other consumer goods will cost much more in Europe (not to mention they use different outlets and voltage, discussed on p.69). They will be available of course, but at a stiff price. Bring these with you along with LOTS of film.
- Most European schools that cater to foreign visitors, especially those that specialize in languages, are not exactly hard-nosed about attendance. Most students seem to specialize in "learning by experience," and much of that "experience" seems to involve cafés, beaches, road-trips, and bars. Bring a daypack to use on those four-day weekend "educational trips."
- Don't buy a train pass or bus pass until you know how much traveling you'll be able to do. If you decide you need one, you can have someone buy you one in your home country and mail it to you.
- Take some time and find the cheapest possible way to call home (more about this in Chapter 10, "Communications"). Don't use "phone home" services which connect you with an English-speaking operator, such as AT&T USA Direct, on a long-term basis – it's way too expensive. You will probably find email is the cheapest way to stay in touch as often as you like, varied by the occasional phone call.

- If you are a student, you may have surprising rights in your country of choice, such as financial assistance with school costs, books, and so on – France, for example, will help buy your textbooks. You may have to do some checking, but it could be well worth your while.

Saving money

While in Europe you will obviously want to spend wisely, and not blow money unnecessarily. The most flexible budget items are museums and attractions, and food and drink, and the amount spent on either is entirely a matter of personal preference. My thoughts on these follow; as always, take them for what they're worth in your situation and on your trip.

Museums

Don't try to go cheap here. By all means, skip a museum because you're sick of them and don't want to see another painting for the rest of your life, but don't skip a major museum just to save money. For example, there is a copy of Michelangelo's *David* in the main square of Florence. Since there is usually a line, and always a charge (about $8 without a discount), to see the real thing, some people are satisfied to see the copy. They are making a huge mistake. I agree that $8 is a lot of money to pay to see one statue, but when you get home you will regret not seeing the real, honest-to-God *David* for about the price of a movie. (You should regret it, by the way. The copy is *nothing* like the real thing.) If you are going to a large number of museums, however, this can cost some serious money: five or six dollars here and there can add up. Some hints:

- Going to Europe without an International Student Identification Card (ISIC) or a youth or teacher card if you are eligible, or not using one if you have one, is simply throwing money away. See Chapter 3, "What to take," for more on these.
- Many cities sell "Tourist Cards" or "City Passports," good for admission to large numbers of museums or attractions. As a bonus, a few also offer head-of-the-line privileges. That's worth a lot on a hot summer day, believe you me. Check and see if a particular card allows unlimited entries for a certain time period, or only one per card. Then check and see how the cost stacks up against the cost of what you really want to see. If it's close, buy one, and you may end up going to more exhibits than planned, with some pleasant surprises. The existence of these cards is usually detailed in your guidebooks. Always check for them before arrival, or at the tourist office when you get there.
- Many museums have a reduced- or free-admissions day some time during the week or month. If this day is during the week, it can be worth waiting for. If it's on a Sunday, expect major crowds. If you want to visit a museum briefly, or for a second time, remember that some – the Louvre in Paris, for example – have reduced admission prices in the afternoon. Remember, many European museums are closed on Mondays.
- Whether or not to pay to see *David* is, at least in my opinion, an easy decision. Other museums housing less impressive or famous exhibits are not quite so easy. Again it's a judgment call, balancing money, interest, time, and tiredness, for you to make. Be wary of some smaller private museums, though. Many are little more than thinly disguised gift shops. The real finds are usually the obscure public museums, where you may be one of the only visitors. I have seldom regretted paying for a museum and have often found really marvelous things in small, out-of-the-way exhibits. Be warned, though: I deeply regretted not spending seven bucks to get into the Liberace Museum in Las Vegas, and actually visited the museum on my next Vegas trip, so I may have a different standard than you . . .

Food and drink

Food and drink, especially if you drink alcohol, are probably the all-time European budget-busting champions, with food taking overall honors by a nose. Whenever possible, buy food in stores, head for the nearest park, and chow down. This can lead to a somewhat dull diet of bread, yogurt, cheese, and fruit (the four basic European traveler's foods), but you won't spend much money and you will eat fairly well. Most Europeans (the English and Scandinavians are notable exceptions) have a different idea of what breakfast means than do most of their visitors – typically some form of bread and coffee – so be sure to ask what you are going to get before buying that hostel breakfast. In Scandinavia, hostel breakfasts are typically fairly elaborate affairs of yoghurt, muesli, fish, and so on, and are usually very good deals. Whenever you have a chance to all-you-can-eat in Scandinavia, you should – and eat until you are bloated like a beached whale. Food is very expensive in those countries. In England, the cholesterol assault known as the full English breakfast (eggs, sausage, bacon, toast, beans, cereal, grilled tomatoes, mushrooms, and tea) can keep you going until dinner if you adopt the same tactic of scarfing until you can barely walk.

The McDonald's factor

You *will* go to and eat at a *McDonald's* when you are in Europe. If you're an American, yes, I know that you wouldn't be caught dead in one while in the States, and, yes, if you took a date to one in your hometown, you would face a hurricane of ridicule and abuse. Yes, I know that you are going to Europe to experience authentic foreign culture, not transplanted American fast food. However, you will go to and eat at a *McDonald's* while you are in Europe. Why? The bathrooms will be the initial lure. Semi-clean, free, convenient bathrooms with guaranteed toilet paper can be few and far between in some cities (Paris springs to mind instantly). When you have once crossed the threshold, half the battle is over, and you are all but lost. The familiarity starts to work: "Hey, this is just like back home. . ." "Smells pretty good, and I can get something familiar, in a hurry, and it's not too expensive. . ." "Well, maybe just this once. . ." And the next thing you know you're chowing down a double bacon McCheeseburger, large fries please, and a medium Coke. Resistance is futile. Though you have been warned, it will help you not. The Golden Arches will triumph in the end.

Eating out can be one of the really charming aspects of European travel. Remember, though, "authentic" and "local" do not always mean "expensive." Good, cheap restaurants can be few and far between, especially in cities, but they do exist: the best sources of information on such places are your hostel or pension staff, your fellow travelers, and your guidebook, usually in that order. The usual list of thoughts and experiences:

- Restaurants that appear in guidebooks should be treated with caution, as they may be overrun with tourists.
- Likewise, any restaurant that caters excessively to tourists should be avoided, just as you would avoid the same type of place at home. Menus in English are usually a bad sign.
- Some of the things that come free in Canada, the States, or other countries, such as bread, butter, and so on, sometimes cost extra in Europe. If something magically appears on your table that you did not order, you should inquire about its price.
- You can often eat at bars as well, but you should know that in continental Europe prices for the same item in a bar or café can increase dramatically when you sit at a table, instead of standing at a table or at the counter, if any. This is less true the farther north you go, culminating with the traditional English pub or Dutch "brown café," where you can sit anywhere you like.

Alcohol

Alcohol, while often expensive, is certainly a big part of going out in Europe. I think it was Woody Allen that was thrown out of a restaurant in France for not ordering wine with a meal. German and British beers, French and Italian wines, Spanish sherries and Portuguese ports, Scotch and Irish whiskies, anisette, grappa, ouzo – the list goes on. Some of it great, some of it interesting, some of it (Italian Cynar, Scandinavian aquavit) just plain vile. And depending on the country, it can be either dirt cheap or incredibly expensive. In Scandinavia, the price is so high that it has made alcohol consumption something of a regional mania. In other places, especially Eastern Europe (beer) and France and Italy (wine), alcohol may be cheaper than soft drinks, especially if you buy it from a supermarket.

When in Europe, it's worth spending a bit more and trying a better version of the local product as opposed to brands sold internationally – or even in other parts of the country. Whatever it is may take some getting used to, but that's part of the experience. On the downside, be aware that drunk tourists are a criminal's dream – if you're going out to get hammered, go in a group. Note also that the legal limits for blood alcohol while driving in most, if not all, European countries are very low. More than one beer will put you over the limit in Sweden. The penalties for drunk driving are savage, too; if I remember right, a 0.08 blood alcohol content (three or four beers) results in a mandatory two- or three-week jail sentence in Norway. The designated driver was an established institution among European teens twenty or thirty years ago. If you and your friends are driving to a night out, use one.

What to take

The best advice I can give on this subject, and the second of the Three Great Travel Commandments, is the following: Travel Light. I know you've heard it before, but I doubt you believe it. Consider this: every first-time traveler I have asked has said that they wished they hadn't brought so much with them. Every one. Please, please, please, believe me. I have met Australians who have been traveling for six months with a daypack. I once made a two-week side trip from London to Cadiz, Spain, via Madrid, Paris, and Granada, also with a daypack. The freedom was incredible. I truly believe that the most important thing you can do to ensure an enjoyable trip is to bring only what's genuinely necessary with you. Clothes are the worst culprit – bringing too many will make you feel that you spent two months doing nothing but carrying a giant mass of dirty laundry around Europe. I can think of one idiot who brought so many clothes on his first trip that he had to pay an excess baggage fee. (I've learned my lesson since then.) You will be happiest if you bring no more than what you can carry on to the airplane: a large, well-made daypack or a small travel pack. If you can carry all that you've brought around a museum, you've done just about right on the weight.

I can practically hear the snorts of disbelief and derision as you read this: "Yeah right, pal, like I can really live two months out of a daypack." Well, no, actually you can live out of a daypack indefinitely. You honestly can. Someone once said: "Figure out exactly what you need for your trip, then bring twice the money and half the clothes." Words of wisdom. Some of the benefits of packing light:

- You don't have to check your bag when flying, and therefore never lose control of your things. While others may have their bags sent to Zambia, you are sitting pretty. This is no joke. Having your bags lost is a miserable experience. Never check anything you will need during the first day or two in a new country.
- You can spend more time, if you so choose, looking for accommodation, and don't have to fight that common, desperate desire to accept any place to stay just so you can take off your damn pack. Believe me, you'll appreciate this greatly when you're on the road.
- You aren't chained to a bag. After a week of travel with too much stuff, that's how it feels, and it gets worse. For example: You have a 1pm train. You would like to spend the morning in a museum or a park. With tons of stuff you either have to leave your things at your hotel or hostel, if possible, and return there before catching the train, or leave your things in a locker or at the left-luggage office in the train station, and then go back out. When you're light and mobile, you just put on your pack, go where you want to go, and only go to the station to catch your train.
- The mental strain is less. You'll understand it better once you're in Europe, but a big bag is just a major headache to worry about, almost like a traveling companion you hate. There is a definite feeling of release after you find a place to leave your stuff, roughly equivalent to being let out of school. If you have a really big bag, the feeling is like being let out of a cage.

Carry-on baggage

Airlines' maximum carry-on size varies, despite what some authors claim. Typically, length plus width plus height must be less than 45 inches, with some airlines allowing 55 inches. Weights allowed vary from a pathetic thirteen pounds on British Airways to a back-straining forty pounds on American. Call your airline for details. It used to be that you were rarely challenged on your carry-on baggage unless it was suitcase size; however, be warned that all airlines have been cracking down on carry-on baggage regulations lately. If you must take all that luggage with you, try putting it in two small carry-on bags – most airlines won't make a federal case of it. No matter what, after you've decided on two or three airlines, call and check on their policy.

Essentials

As I'm sure you're sick of hearing already, packing light is A Very Good Thing. On the other hand, there are many items that are essential and should be brought with you, and some others that are very handy but might not be immediately obvious. There is a checklist of stuff to take in Basics #11, but I'm also going to go through my recommendations of what to bring and what not to bring item by item. If you're buying things specifically for your trip, remember that quality is definitely cheapest in the long run. In particular, the six things you do not want to skimp on are your main pack, daypack, camera, shoes, guidebook, and map(s). Each of these is vital to your trip, and saving money by buying a cheap version of any of them is asking for trouble.

The best book on selecting packs, shoes, and a number of other relevant items is *Backpacking One Step at a Time* by Harvey Manning (Vintage Books). Although this book is written primarily for campers, the sections on packs, boots, and equipment are more than worth the price. Manning has probably forgotten more about those three subjects than I ever knew.

Luggage

I almost called this section "backpacks" because the idea of suitcases seems so outlandish. Backpacks are hard enough to carry around. Suitcases, gym bags, duffle bags, anything designed to be carried by hand, including bags with one shoulder strap, have no place on any trip that involves using public transportation and walking. Any budget traveler will be doing both of these quite a bit. Luggage with wheels is made for airports, and will not last if used extensively on sidewalks or streets. (I have a slide of a woman pulling a suitcase with wheels across a cobblestone piazza in Italy.) Even if you will be using your own or a rental car, backpacks of one sort or another are the way to go. If you don't like the idea of backpacks, then buy a travel pack and use it as a suitcase; that way you will have the ability to switch carrying modes if you find that carrying your things by hand is too difficult. Leaving the suitcases home goes double for older travelers. Break the habits of a lifetime and invest in a travel pack. Trust me, you'll be glad you did.

No matter what you choose, buy something solid that will last a lifetime, especially since buying something new in Europe will bankrupt you. Also, attach a large, solid name tag with your name, a dollar or two, and the phone number of someone at home inside your bag. That way, if your bag is lost and found, the finder can call, at your cost, and let someone know where it is. After getting to Europe, another tag, with phone number, on the outside is a good idea, especially if you lock your bag. Also, sewing a clip on the inside of your bag and clipping away any keys you might need on your return keeps them safe and out of the way.

Travel packs ✓

A travel pack is basically soft luggage, with a very simple internal frame, shoulder straps, a waist belt, and a flap that can be used to cover the straps and belt and convert the whole thing into a suitcase. These packs are probably the best choice for most travelers, especially those not intending to do much hiking with their packs on. They certainly are extremely popular, although they are marginal at best for long walks, and anything over a mile or two with one is going to be unpleasant, especially if the pack is fully loaded. For short walks, however, they are fine, and light years better than duffle bags or suitcases. A major plus of travel packs is that they usually have a zipper around the perimeter of the bag that allows the whole pack to be split open, thus avoiding lots of digging and groping around. Since travel packs are designed for travel rather than hiking, they can almost always be locked up – a very handy feature. Cost: $150–250.

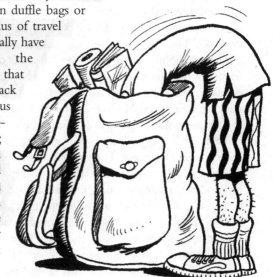

Backpacks

Backpacks fall into two main categories: those with external frames and those with internal frames. Although external frames are often looked upon as obsolete or "low-class," they are still the best choice if you are going to be walking long distances with your pack on roads or trails. If you are planning on walking in Switzerland or trekking in Scotland, if walking is in any way the focus of your trip, this is the way to go. The disadvantages of an external frame are its rigidity, making it difficult to fit into lockers, the tendency for the frame, straps, and buckles to be damaged when checked on airplanes, and the typical lack of any way to lock the darn thing. If you are going to travel with an external frame, box it up before putting it on the plane to Europe. If you don't, the baggage system may destroy it, and you can watch the pieces come spilling out onto the carousel (along with chunks of your camera, shreds of your clothes, dirty underwear, and so on). For the return, if you can't find a box, tighten the straps up and then mummify it with a roll of plastic packing tape. A decent external frame pack will cost $120–250.

A good internal frame pack carries a load almost as well as an external frame and is somewhat less liable to damage. However, you should still tighten straps, and box or tape it if possible before entrusting it to an airline. Internal frames usually reflect a more modern design than external frames and have become the packs of choice for most hikers. This is not entirely a reflection of utility, however. The latest word on carrying a large load is that external frames are slightly better if you are on streets or trails, while internal frames, which more closely hug the body, are better for scrambling on rocks and across rough country. If that's the primary purpose of your trip, you probably have a backpack already. Completely locking an internal frame is usually not possible. Cost: $150–300.

An *essential* backpack tip is that nothing beats experience. Before buying a new backpack, borrow one of the same type from a friend, get their thoughts on it, load it up with clothes and books, and take it for a walk around the neighborhood. I guess if you truly want to be realistic, walk from house to house, up and down stairs in blazing sun, to simulate a search for accommodation in Rome. Also, most backpacking shops, especially the small ones, will have experienced employees who can give the shopper tons of advice. Once you settle on the type you want you can start shopping around (see Basics #7 for a list of suppliers). Don't wait until the last minute to buy your pack – order or buy it at least a month before you go. When you get it, as before, load it up with stuff and take it for a good long walk at least once. If you can't get comfortable with it, or you find some problem and have to return it, that's the time to find out, not the day you intend to leave. By the way, if you take about ten of those walks, you will not only know your backpack better, but will also have a much better idea of how much your pack really weighs (taking that leather trench coat to Europe may not seem worth it after all), you will have spent lots of time out in the healthy fresh air and sunshine, and your feet will not rise in savage protest when you start your march across Europe. I have to admit that I haven't always prepared like this. You can read about the gruesome consequences later.

WARNING: No matter what kind of pack you get, try to avoid those that only load from the top. A zipper which allows you to open the whole thing up is *essential* as far as I'm concerned. Having spent a month digging blindly through a bag, then, in frustration, pouring everything out to get to the one thing I wanted, which was always at the bottom, I will never go to Europe with a top-loader again.

Packing your backpack

How you pack and wear a backpack is almost as important to your comfort as how much goes in it. Ideally, you want the smallest possible pack that conforms to your body shape as much as possible. This will keep the weight on the waist belt and off your shoulders and will greatly increase the ease of carrying your pack. Almost all modern packs have external straps to tighten the whole thing up after packing. If you've got them, use them, and get your pack as tight and compact as you can.

When carrying a load, at least fifty percent of the work should be done by the waist belt. Your belt should be as tight as is comfortable, and you should be able to slide a finger or a hand through the front of your shoulder straps when standing straight up. The whole aim of good packing is to get as much weight as possible bearing vertically on your hips and legs, and as little as possible pulling back and down on your relatively weaker shoulders. If your pack does not have a waist belt, don't take it to Europe unless it's the size of a daypack. Trust me on this one.

Finally, it's a good idea to take a large waterproof bag to cover your backpack in case of rain. If you expect rain on your trip, get a solid one made of plastic, vinyl, or waterproof cloth. If you are pretty sure of good weather, two large plastic bags will serve.

Daypacks

A good daypack should be your constant companion, containing your camera, film, notebook, guidebook, maps, and all those bits and pieces you need every day. If you follow my advice, you'll get a big one and live out of it. If not, then go for a medium-sized, high-quality lockable version. Spend some time finding one that you like, since you will be using it a lot. As with your main pack, I recommend getting one with a zipper that goes around the perimeter of the pack, so you don't have to pour out all of the contents to find a small item. By the way, fanny packs are no substitute for a daypack; they are too small, and are much more vulnerable to theft.

Some travel packs have daypacks that zip onto the larger pack. While this seems like a neat idea, it puts your most important and valuable things hanging out there in the breeze, out of your sight and out of your feeling, and practically in the hands of razor-wielding thieves. A terrible idea. It is far better to leave enough space to fit your daypack inside your main pack, where it will be out of sight, and leave you only one piece to worry about. If this is too heavy, or you don't have space, wear your daypack in front of you, as you will see most experienced travelers doing. This will also help balance the weight of your main pack when you walk.

Locks

Most travel packs can and should be locked with a small padlock. It's best not to buy the tiny locks you see advertised in travel equipment catalogs; you can get the same thing for about one-fifth the price at a hardware store. Either way, these locks won't stop someone who's determined, but they will discourage the casual or opportunistic thief.

Clothes and accessories

I've said it before and I may as well say it again here – try to keep your clothes to an absolute minimum. This is where most people lose the battle against excess weight.

Remember also that all of your clothes are going to get some hard use. One school of thought says that because of this, you should bring old stuff; another says that because of this, new things would be better. I prefer to bring new things; after a few weeks on the road I look scroungy enough without old or worn clothes adding to the effect. Also, remember that you can always buy clothes on the road if you need them.

For both men and women, the list should look something like the following:

- One pair of long pants, preferably not faded blue jeans if you intend to do some stepping out. Also, long pants or skirts are required in some churches, most notably St Peter's in Rome. New black Levis have served me well but are a bit hot in the summer. I usually buy something lighter when the weather gets hot and shorts are inappropriate. One belt as well.
- One nice short-sleeved shirt with a collar.
- Three T-shirts all in good shape, and none of them white. Bring one "nice" T-shirt, and two that are as light as possible without being flimsy. Use the first type for everything up to and including going out, and the second for those days when all you need is something to keep you from being topless. Again, don't bring white! (Thanks and a tip of the hat to Chris in Denver.)
- One long-sleeved Oxford-type shirt, definitely not white, or a similar shirt for women. Women might also want to include one more long-sleeved top for use in countries where bare female skin is frowned upon in public.
- One hooded sweatshirt or a fleece jacket. A nice-looking dark sweater can also serve many of the same functions, and can also be worn on a more dressy occasion. Sweatshirts with college names look touristy, but can be good for trading with European students.
- Two pairs of shorts, again non-white.
- Five sets of underwear. Add a set of long underwear if you are going somewhere cold.
- Five pairs of socks. If you're going to a cold area, make two pairs of these wool.
- One pair of no-kidding, fully functional walking shoes. See p.50 for more on this.
- A pair of solid walking sandals (rather than a pair of cheap thongs), for slimy showers, the beach, or kicking back.
- Your rain gear. Again, see p.50 for more.
- A hat with a brim. If you're going into the mountains or to a cold area, a wool watch cap also.
- A bandanna or two. The red kind, usually seen around the necks of golden retrievers, has 1001 uses. Women should also include some form of head covering to wear in churches and in some of the smaller Mediterranean villages.
- A bathing suit, preferably one that can be used as extra underwear or shorts.

- A skirt for women, preferably long, loose, light, and opaque. Not too long, though, as you will probably be climbing stairs in it.
- A coat in some form, loose enough to layer over other things. If this can also serve as your raincoat (see below), so much the better.

Shoes

A blister the size of a pencil eraser can make you absolutely miserable on vacation. Larger ones can make you wish you'd stayed home. Wearing a pair of cheap, too-old, too-new, or poorly fitting shoes to Europe is a recipe for a horrendous trip. You will be walking a long way no matter how you travel, so come prepared. Whatever you choose to wear – Birkenstocks, running shoes, stiletto heels, whatever – make sure that they will last at least another few months and are properly broken in. Take at least one five-mile walk in them and see how they feel at the end of it. Put new laces on them before you go. Yes, I know it's obvious, but it still bears repeating. The largest blister I've ever seen was on an American traveler in Munich who came to Europe wearing a brand new pair of shoes.

Rain gear

Gore-Tex rules here, if you can afford the stuff. My favorite traveling companion is a 'tex jacket that has a separate liner that can be zipped in or out, depending on the temperature. Get a jacket with a removable hood if you can. Unless you are traveling in winter, or are going to be spending most of your time in Ireland, Scotland, or Scandinavia, or are planning on some serious hiking elsewhere, you probably won't need a full-length raincoat or Gore-Tex pants. For serious trekkers, a knee-length waterproof coat with a hood is advisable. For all travelers, a small, high-quality umbrella is very handy to have in one's daypack, especially in the countries just mentioned.

Other essential gear

There are any number of other things you should probably have with you, and to save your having to rack your brains for them all, I've included a list of the most likely items here.

Money belt or neck wallet

This kind of thing is as mandatory a piece of gear as I can think of. The security section (Chapter 11, "Crime, safety, and sleaze") details why. Actually, "money belt" is a bit of a misnomer; they're really small, flat pouches large enough to hold a passport, money, and other necessary documents, with elastic belts attached. Neck wallets are a bit smaller, hang on a line around the neck, and are more suited for emergency supplies of cash or credit cards, as they can't hold much else. The money belts made by Eagle Creek are industry standard; they are available from the suppliers listed in Basics #7.

Padlock and chain or cable

This combination is essential, especially for solo travelers. The lock is needed for lockers in hostels, and, with the cable, can be used to secure your pack to train luggage racks, another pack, etc. Those old reliable Master combination padlocks from junior high are perfect. Avoid keys for obvious reasons. For the cable, try to get something at least 48 inches long and a quarter-inch thick, or the same length of solid chain. The cables sold at bike shops that are curled up like a slinky and coated with plastic are perfect. If your hostel or pension doesn't have any lockers, chaining your pack to a bed, pipe, or other solid object, by the shoulder straps, is a good idea. Obviously, a determined thief could cut the straps, but that would leave him with a ruined, awkward-to-carry backpack. Really, you're just trying to deter the opportunistic thief, or at least make him pick somebody else's bag.

First-aid kit

I'm always surprised at how much I use my first-aid kit, and how useful it proves to other people. If nothing else, it will save you the time and expense of buying a whole box of Band-Aids when you only need one. Above all, you should realize that it is far cheaper and better to assemble your own kit than to pay big bucks for the false security that most prepackaged kits on the market provide. Mine includes a bunch of Band-Aids, including some large square ones for scrapes, a roll of gauze, twenty iodine wipes, a tube of antiseptic ointment, a roll of athletic tape, moleskin for blister relief, five needles and a lighter to sterilize them, forty aspirin, a pair of tweezers, and an airline bottle of Scotch for use on sore throats. It weighs about eight ounces. A more elaborate kit is essential for hikers.

Swiss Army knife

Even if you're not camping, you should bring a Swiss Army knife, but you don't need to go for the giant versions that include the chain saw and the frying pan. The bottle opener is handy (twist-offs are less common in Europe), as are scissors. Remember, these will need to be checked, and can't be taken on board a plane as hand luggage.

Sewing/repair kit

A small sewing kit can be worth its weight in platinum. Once again, you can put together your own. Include at least six needles, including some big ones for repairing your pack, as well as some dental floss and some serious wire for the same purpose. Also include thread, several safety pins, some buttons, and whatever else you can think of. The athletic tape in a first-aid kit is useful for repairs as well, as is a small roll of duct tape.

Flashlight

A flashlight is surprisingly useful while traveling, and is vital for campers; in fact, campers should have at least two each. A mini Maglight is just about the right size and weight. Those not camping can get by with a little "squeeze to light" flashlight on a key ring. You'll use it all the time, in dimly lit hotel hallways, dark hostel rooms, and while looking at maps at night.

Sunscreen, sunglasses, lip balm

One 4oz bottle of factor fifteen sunscreen or better should be enough unless you plan on spending a lot of time at the beach. As with any other liquids, keep them in sealed plastic bags with the caps taped on until needed. Trust me on this one. Sunglasses should be sturdy and inexpensive, but not cheap. Bring a pair with real lenses, not just frames with colored glass, which can be worse than nothing. Sunglasses and sunscreen cost a bundle in touristy areas, so bring a lot if you plan on some major beach time. A lip balm that includes sunscreen is best.

Watch with alarm or travel clock

Modern travel alarm clocks can be tiny – no bigger than a cassette tape. A moderately priced digital watch with an alarm and dual time (for timing those phone calls home) will also work if the alarm will wake you reliably – the sound is often not loud enough to stir a deep sleeper. You will have some early trains to catch, and buying a loud, reliable alarm clock is probably going to be money well spent. Make sure you have a spare battery so that the clock doesn't die on you at the worst possible time.

Sleep sack

Sleep sacks are usually required in hostels, and they serve as bed linen, which some hostels do not provide or provide with a charge. A sleep sack is essentially a sleeping bag made from sheets, with a pillowcase attached. They are available direct from Hosteling International and discount travel agencies for about fifteen dollars, but you should skip those and make your own. Perfectly good ones can be made in less than an hour. Just fold a sheet over, sew up the long side and one of the short sides, flip inside out, and sew on a pillowcase – much cheaper than buying one, and a neat reminder of home.

Towel

This is a pet peeve of mine. You are much better off with a small, regular-weight bath towel than with one of those miserable little "travel towels" that soak up about as much water as a tissue and shed like a sheep dog. Sew a couple of solid cloth loops (old belt loops work well) to your towel so you can hang it from your backpack and let it dry while you're on the move.

Camera and film

Obviously a personal choice, but if you're buying a camera for your trip, as with packs and shoes, going cheap is a recipe for heartache. As I write this, a 35mm point-and-shoot, which I bought for its low price of $60, is sitting in front of me. It broke after about three months, and ruined a roll of pictures that were worth more to me than the camera. Again, it's a good idea to buy quality; you won't regret it. On the other hand, a $1000 Nikon will be a constant worry, so don't go to the opposite extreme. I've found that the ideal camera for me is a pocket-sized point-and-shoot 35mm with a built-in zoom. These cameras are small, easy to carry, and run about $150–200. Also, their small size and concealability makes one look a bit less like a camera-toting tourist.

As far as film goes, it's much cheaper to buy it at home. Bring more than you think you'll need, and don't be surprised if you use it all. An extra battery is a good idea as well if yours is a bit old. If you don't use it, store it – and unused film – in the refrigerator when you get home.

For those going digital, bring enough memory for no less than ten pictures a day

Plastic bags

Three or four plastic bags for separating dirty clothes, wrapping wet things, and so on, can be a godsend. They're also good for separating out things you won't need until a later part of your trip, and keeping them out of the way. Taking five ziplock bags is also a good idea for safely storing small or potentially messy items.

Toilet paper

Don't laugh. In my scrapbook, I have several sheets of a gray substance. When asked to identify it, my friends guess that it is a type of mild abrasive, or perhaps tire-patching material. It is neither of these. It is, in fact, toilet paper from a Polish train station, and even today looking at it makes me cringe. But even this hellish stuff is superior to no paper at all, which is not uncommon in some bathrooms, particularly in public places. A good-sized wad of tissue at the bottom of a pocket or a daypack may some day save you from an unpleasant and undignified predicament. Remember, when others, less prepared than you, are in desperation, bargain mercilessly, especially if you've got the downy-soft product from home.

Bathroom kit

Avoid "travel size" bathroom amenities, as they will run out and you will just have to buy more in Europe. An exception to this are small cans of shaving cream or gel, which hold a surprising amount. Just tape the lids on tight, or you may be in for a surprise.

Contact lens stuff/glasses

The nightly chemical process familiar to contact-lens wearers is a mystery to me, but I did meet one guy who had spent two days searching for a particular type of solution in France. Even though the odds are good that gallons of whatever you need are no farther than the nearest pharmacy, brands may differ, and finding exactly what you're used to may be difficult. For simplicity, bring plenty of whatever solutions you need, and you may end up helping others.

When Theodore Roosevelt went charging up San Juan Hill with the Rough Riders, he had a dozen pairs of glasses: one in every possible pocket. This kind of planning is not a bad idea if you wear glasses. I would say three pairs are optimal, since it allows you to break one, lose one, and still keep going. Contact-lens wearers – bring more lenses than you think you will need. Or, bring a supply of disposables and skip the nightly cleaning ritual entirely.

Earplugs

Earplugs can be a sanity-saver for light sleepers in crowded hostels. The soft, yellow, foamy type work well (try at a pharmacy), and you can sometimes get these free on your flight over the Atlantic. Try

out your earplugs before leaving, because they can take some getting used to, and bring several pairs.

The ever-popular universal drain plug

Every year hundreds of retired tennis and racket balls are reincarnated as these devices, used to plug stopper-less sinks for laundry and other chores. Just cut a tennis ball in half, and trim to the size desired. Use with smooth side down.

Maps

Spend a bit more on the best maps you can find and you won't regret it. As I said earlier, tourist offices are a good start but they're only a start. Any large bookstore will also have a map section. Don't rely solely on the maps included in guidebooks, as they just can't do the job properly in such a small space.

The best planning map for rail travelers on the go is the *Rail Map of Europe* by Thomas Cook. Though it's a bit too large for everyday use, this map shows every railroad from Moscow to Gibraltar, along with a wealth of other detail. It's also handy to spot out-of-the-way places where trains don't go. There's also the Eurail train map that comes free with a pass, but this tends to start falling apart after about a week, so get two or three of these if you can. If you can't, reinforce the folds of the one you get with tape, and get a new one from a Eurail Aid office while on the move. These offices are found in many large train stations, and their locations are listed on the Eurail map. This map has some good information on its reverse side that is well worth reading – stuff like language tips, details on train station facilities, Eurail discounts, and so on.

Documents

You should carry your passport with you at all times, because you may be asked to show it as identification. A passport is also necessary to cash travelers' checks, and may be needed to buy airline tickets.

If you lose your passport or if it is stolen, contact the nearest embassy immediately. They can issue you a temporary replacement. This process is much easier if you have a photocopy of the picture page of your passport. Carry at least one copy with you in a very safe place, like in a money belt, and have one copy at home in a very obvious place, like taped to a friend's refrigerator door. If your passport gets lost, you will have a copy of the relevant information with you to take to your embassy. If the copy gets lost as well, the home front can fax you a copy of that same information.

You can do the same for credit cards, but don't carry this copy with you in Europe unless it is absolutely necessary. If your credit cards get stolen, they can be canceled by the person in your home country. Other things you might want to copy and leave behind are travelers' check serial numbers, airline tickets, train passes, and any other documents you may lose.

You will be juggling a number of documents during your trip: a passport or identity card, train passes, airline tickets, and so on. If you don't need something day to day (like airline tickets or backup credit cards), I recommend keeping it out of the way as much as possible, preferably in some kind of folder or cover that is tied to the inside of your main pack – an old checkbook cover is good for this.

Youth Hostel membership cards

Youth Hostel membership can be obtained along the way, but why not buy a card before you go and get one tiny worry off your mind?

They're available from student travel offices or direct from the national organizations themselves (see box below). If possible, get a card, add a photo, and then laminate them together, as an extra form of photo identification.

Student and other identity cards

In Europe, students receive a discount on anything that might be considered "educational," and on many things that aren't. Museums, tours, and other cultural attractions, often have discounted admissions or fares for those bearing an International Student Identification Card (ISIC). Non-students under 26 and teachers can get most of the same discounts with their own respective cards (the "GO 25" card and the International Teachers' Identity card). These are highly worth obtaining and can save you megabucks on an incredible number of things. Teachers, for example, get into Paris museums for nothing. Any student-oriented travel agent, such as Council Travel or Travel CUTS in the States, can either issue an ISIC on the spot or tell you where you can get one. You'll need a small photograph and proof that you're a full-time student. If you are a teacher or "youth," the same agencies can issue you your respective card. For seniors, proof that you are over 50 will get you discounts all over Europe.

When in Europe, and when buying tickets to get there, you should get into the habit of chanting "Is there a student discount?" every time you pull out some cash. This includes airlines, trains, ferries, museums, theaters, funeral parlors – everything, really. When in doubt, ask, and you will be amazed at the money you save.

If you are eligible for one of these cards and don't get one, you will kick yourself all across Europe. In the States, call ☎ 1-800/ GET-AN-ID for more information, or ask at any budget travel agent.

Extra "passport" photos

There are photo booths in seemingly every train station in Europe, so you can buy a set of photos when you get there, or just bring an extra set with you, as they weigh nothing and may be needed for city travel passes and such. You may also need some to give to that lovely European you meet during your travels. Sadly, I still have all four of mine. Regular photo booth pictures are fine; don't pay those death-dealing passport photo places for more pictures than you have to.

International driver's license

You can drive in most countries in Europe on your home country's driver's license. However, in some countries you need an international driver's license, so if you think you might be driving while in Europe, one of these is worth obtaining. For North Americans, they're available from the AAA for ten bucks; you'll need a passport-sized photo and your (valid) driver's license. The process takes all of about ten minutes, and your license will be good for a year. Aussies should try their state RAC, while South Africans and Kiwis should call their local AA. Brits should be fine with their domestic UK license.

Train timetables

The free timetable booklet that comes with your Eurail pass is adequate if you are planning primarily to go to major cities. For those not buying a pass, you can still get a timetable for free or for a nominal charge from any travel agent that sells rail passes. Don't ignore the printed information in this booklet, because some of it is very useful. These tables are quite flimsy, so replacing them when you're in a train station that has a Eurail Aid office is a good idea. Also be advised that this booklet does not list all the trains that are available to you. If you're desperate to leave a city or to get to a destination, go to the station and ask, even if you don't see a train listed. A good rail clerk can find ways of getting you places that aren't listed in this timetable.

The Thomas Cook Railroad Timetable, which gives information on seemingly every object that moves on any rail track in Europe, is of questionable value considering its weight and price ($33). However, if you are going in a group of two or more, you might get one for the group. Also, if you are planning to visit small towns and villages, you might want to invest in one. It certainly has tons of information; just make sure you need it all before buying it.

Hosteling guides

Hosteling International puts out a book that gives details on every hostel in Europe, along with a map that shows their location. These two items are cheap, useful, and are absolutely essential for hostelers. They are especially useful for finding accommodations and/or planning trips off the beaten track, and for finding a hostel near a major city when all of the city accommodations are full. Both the book and the map should be available at any HI hostel in Europe. See Chapter 7, "Accommodations," for more on hosteling.

Finally. . . a journal, and some pens

Bringing a book in which you can keep some sort of journal is a must. I guarantee you that you will be very glad you did after your trip, because the memories do fade. Use a journal not just for recording memories of your trip, but for recording good advice you get from other travelers, phone numbers, addresses, and so on. You should probably leave your address book at home, and take all the addresses you need in one of these. A small bound book will outlast a notebook by centuries, and may even end up amusing your grandchildren. Bound blank volumes are available at any office supply store or college bookstore.

Guidebooks

This may seem an obvious item to bring, but I have met several people who didn't take a guidebook to Europe. They weren't sure if they would need one and were sure that they could buy one easily in Europe if they did. Generally, I met them when they tried to buy my guidebook.

Needless to say, you should bring one. I have traveled both with and without a guidebook, and it is much easier and simpler to have one with you. If you lose yours, you can fake it for a while by using tourist offices to locate places to stay, major sights, and so on, but if you get an opportunity to buy another, you should. There are some travelers who disagree with me, who say guidebooks can become law books, and travelers tend to follow them as if they contained mandatory statutes on what to see and where to stay. There is some truth in this, and it is indeed possible to follow your book too slavishly. However, if that becomes a problem, just stick your book in the bottom of your pack and forget about it until you really need it. On the other hand, if you do need a guide and don't have one, you will be out of luck.

There are an incredible number of guidebooks available for every possible tiny corner of Europe – the amount is truly unbelievable. Some thoughts on this literary tidal wave:

- A typical one-volume guide to Europe has around 100 pages on Italy. A decent guide to Italy covers the same territory in about 800–900 pages. For someone who is going to spend a week in Italy, 100 pages or so is about enough to cover the very basics, and point the way to some of the highlights of Rome, Florence, and Venice. For someone planning on spending a month, wandering from Milan to Palermo and on to Sardinia, 800–900 pages would be a wise investment.
- The book you choose will be a very important part of your trip, and you will use it just about every day. Check a few out of the library, or at least take an hour or two in a bookstore to compare the various options. There are marked differences among the guides available.
- Always use the most up-to-date version of the guidebook you prefer. Trying to save a few dollars by using an old version is a very poor idea.
- All of the books described below, whether I care for them or not, represent a huge amount of work and information gathering. Before going, no matter what book you buy, sit down and read all the opening pages and the section on the first country you will visit. You will find an astounding amount of useful information that you might never have suspected was in there. As always, I learned that the hard way. If you have a question, try your guidebook and see if it is answered somewhere.
- Which is the best guidebook? As always, I can only report from my experiences; whether they are applicable to you is for you to decide. Please note that dishing dirt on another author's work is a tender issue when writing a book, and most authors simply praise

one another in a never-ending circle. As I write this, nobody has raved about me yet, so I don't feel the obligation to rave about anybody else. Let me state at the outset that this book is published by Rough Guides, so you might want to take that into account. They certainly haven't put the heat on me to push their books (and wouldn't succeed if they did), but you should know the facts.

Frommer's

Frommer's is the granddaddy of budget travel guides; Arthur Frommer pretty much invented low-cost travel in Europe for non-Europeans with his revolutionary *Europe on Five Dollars a Day*. The current version is entitled *Frommer's Europe from $70 a Day*, which is a statement in itself on what has happened to budget travel over the years. This guide, however, only covers 31 major cities and the areas around them and, like the rest of the series, has been somewhat overtaken among budget travelers by other, younger series. The information is not particularly budget-oriented, and the presentation is poor. Basically, there are better guides, especially for travelers on a tight budget, but for those with a short itinerary and a little more money, Frommer's may be worth a look.

Let's Go

Let's Go Europe is the guidebook of choice for the majority of young Americans and Canadians traveling in Europe. Let's Go is written by Harvard undergraduate students, so consider the source when opinions are expressed about politics and countries. Let's Go also publishes a number of single-country guides.

Let's Go Europe has a useful color section of metro and city maps; it is partially updated every year; and, if you want to meet your compatriots abroad, remember that more young Americans and Canadians have this book than all others combined. On the downside, it covers 31 countries in one book, and so covers each country without very much depth. Also, Let's Go sell so many books that they can often have a serious impact on the places they write about. If it's mentioned in Let's Go, you may rest assured that other travelers will have been there before, and that prices may have risen as a result.

Lonely Planet

Lonely Planet publishes guides to nearly every country in the world. Originally specializing in Asia and relatively remote areas, they now publish five different multi-country guides to Europe, as well as large single-country guides, and the comprehensive *Europe on a Shoestring* guide. As for their strengths, they include maps of major cities, with places to stay, banks, post offices, etc, shown; they include mini language dictionaries in the country information sections, as well as brief but interesting histories and background articles.

Rick Steves

Rick Steves publishes guidebooks that supposedly take the traveler off the beaten track to "back doors" in Europe. But, just like Let's Go, Steves sells enough books to ensure that any place mentioned in one of his books is automatically moved onto that very beaten track. On the plus side, Steves has traveled in Europe a lot, and if you like his style (I don't), his books are fairly readable, but they are less practical than most of the alternatives.

Rough Guides

Rough Guides is a British company, and therein lies its major

Read your guidebook – how I learned

It was late, I was in Munich, and every hostel was full. My only option was "The Tent" – two big circus-type tents, one with beds and one for those who wanted to save 3 marks by sleeping on the floor. (This place is an experience, by the way; a throwback to the Sixties in many ways.) I needed to phone for directions, so I bought a banana to get change (70 pfennigs). I called the number given in my guidebook (30 pfennigs), got a recording giving those directions, but wasn't ready to copy them. I wandered around the station, bought some candy (50 pfennigs), and got some more change. Back at the phone, I wickedly tried to use a foreign coin which looked like it might work in the phone (10 pence). It didn't. In exasperation I threw a whole 1 mark coin in, only to have it get stuck behind the 10 pence (1 mark). I went to get more change (50 pfennigs) and changed phones. I called again (1 mark) and got my directions, half-an-hour after I started. As I was closing my book, I noticed the directions to "The Tent" – in my guidebook, right under the phone number.

strength as far as Europe goes. It has a home field advantage over other guidebooks, as continental Europe is only a ferry ride away. They publish individual guides to most European countries, as well as a 32-country Europe guide. Most books are updated every two years, some every three – though the comprehensive Europe guide is an annual publication. I really can't say much more about Rough Guides that you would believe; as I said, they publish this book.

If you are looking for a one-book guide to Europe, you should compare the Rough Guide to the Let's Go, and Lonely Planet. In my mind Let's Go is handicapped by the fact that nearly everyone has one. But consider the guides yourself, and then choose whichever you think will be best for you.

Ultra-lightweight trips

In 1994, in Pamplona, Spain I met a woman whom I now suspect was the goddess of lightweight travelers disguised as a human. Helen the Australian had been traveling Europe for months, and her "backpack" was smaller than my daypack. I don't know what it weighed, but I could pick it up with my left pinky – certainly less than five pounds. Maybe you can't get that light, but if you want to try, here are some ideas and a loading list for an ultra-lightweight trip. By ultra-lightweight, I mean 10 pounds or less – a backpack you can wear all day if necessary. The only way you can do this is by minimizing your clothes. Bring no more than the following:

One pair of very lightweight long pants, preferably a pair that can be converted into shorts, and definitely dark in color. Nylon travel pants are perfect.

Three shirts – any kind you like as long as they don't weigh much.

One pair of shorts.

Three pairs of socks and underwear.

One pair of shoes.

A Gore-Tex jacket.

A hat with a brim.

And that's it for clothes – I said ultra-lightweight. Of course, you can get by with this amount of stuff only on summer trips in Southern Europe. As for the rest of your gear, treat it like a mountain-climbing trip – every ounce counts. Bring only one guidebook, a small lock with a lightweight chain, a small sleep sack – at the end of the day, all of those will add up to a large weight savings. Bring the same essentials as on any other trip – if you look at the list in Basics #10, those essentials don't weigh very much.

Optional gear

The following equipment is optional, and most of it relates to camping. Don't make the mistake of bringing camping gear to give yourself "the option of camping." This stuff weighs a lot. Decide before you go if you're going to hostel or camp. This advice does not apply to those who are driving and thus less constrained by weight. In that case, by all means bring camping gear even if you intend to sleep indoors for much of your trip.

Sleeping bag

Obviously, a sleeping bag is mandatory if you are camping, and nice to have if sleeping indoors in rural areas and cool climates, as central heating has not made it to much of Europe's countryside. A sleeping bag is only necessary if you will be spending time in the mountains, Northern Europe/Scandinavia, or other cold areas. For the big cities and for Southern Europe in the summer, a sleeping bag is not needed. Don't forget your sleep sack – many hostels will not allow you to use sleeping bags instead of sleep sacks on beds.

Cooking gear

Some sort of cooking gear can be useful, and not just for campers. Many hostels have fully stocked kitchens, however, so go very light on what you bring. One small mess kit for two people should be fine. Some plastic utensils will also come in handy – I recommend bringing at least a spoon. Cooking is work, but you'll probably eat better, and definitely eat cheaper, cooking for yourself.

Washing liquid, clothes pins, a line

Washing liquid is a necessary evil, since you'll need to wash things fairly regularly. Buy it in Europe. A few clothes pins are also useful,

as is a solid piece of line about twenty feet long that can be used for other things. I guarantee you will find other uses for it.

Tent ✓

A tent is obviously essential for campers, but unnecessary for hostelers. A tent weighs so much and takes up so much space that it is difficult to combine hostels and camping without cursing the damn tent every time you sleep in a hostel. If you are getting around in a car, on the other hand, a tent is a very nice thing to have with you, just in case.

For campers, unless you are planning a serious back-country European trip, you probably won't need the same equipment you would in the mountains of the States or Canada. Your biggest problem will be rain, not cold, and a rain fly is essential, especially in Britain or Scandinavia – at any time of year. Also, remember that you will be spending a much longer time living in your tent than on a typical camping trip. A small tent for two or three people can be very unpleasant. Go for a larger volume than is absolutely necessary. If you have the option, bring a freestanding tent and leave the stakes and guy lines at home. Campgrounds can get crowded, and also those little bits and pieces can get lost very easily. For more information on tents, see the book by Harvey Manning mentioned on p.44.

Sleeping pad

Campers should bring a thick sleeping pad, as much for insulation as for padding. A self-inflating type will be welcome in the mountains or in cold areas. If your pad of choice inflates in any way, bring a patch kit.

Stove

The "Gaz" butane/propane stove is the king of the European campgrounds, and its little blue cylinders can be purchased all over Europe. If you have one of these stoves, remember that the airlines will go berserk if you put one of those little propane bomblets in your luggage. The same thing goes for the bottle of gas for liquid stoves. Open fires are prohibited in most, if not all, European campgrounds, so if you're camping, you'll definitely need a stove. Note that stoves are for campers only; you won't need one if hosteling.

Compass

Absolutely essential for long-distance walkers, a compass is also surprisingly useful in large cities. Unless you have a gyroscope in your head, it is very easy to come out of a subway station disoriented, or to get lost in the maze of streets found in some old cities. A quick glance at your magic compass solves this problem, and will greatly impress your fellow travelers. Get one with a little mirror and a case, for both the protective case and the cute little mirror.

Personal stereo

Only you know whether a personal stereo is essential for you. If it is, be careful where you use it – people wearing headphones are generally less aware of their surroundings, and thieves know this. The right music, though, can be a sure cure for homesickness.

Whistle

A whistle is essential for long-distance walkers and campers who head off the beaten track. Also not a bad idea for single women, as part of a key chain or on a necklace, just in case.

Calculator

Some sort of calculator is useful mainly for quick currency conversions. It doesn't have to be anything special: the smaller and cheaper the better.

Deck of cards

Cards are a great conversation-starter and time-passer on long train rides, rainy days, quiet nights, or when you just can't face another museum.

Bug repellent

If you're visiting rural Scotland (midges) or the countryside in Holland or Scandinavia (saber-toothed mosquitoes), you absolutely must have some sort of bug repellent; and it's handy to have when camping out or walking about in the countryside of any country. When buying this stuff, check the label for the amount of active ingredients: anything under about 25 percent will be ineffective. Creams and liquids such as Cutter or Jungle Juice are better than sprays. Be very careful with some of the more potent liquids (Jungle Juice, for example): they can melt plastics and ruin cameras, packs, and other things they leak onto. For camping trips to Scotland and

Scandinavia, a head net (like beekeepers wear) weighs next to nothing and may save your sanity. Even if you don't expect this to be a problem, bring a small bottle or tube of repellent, just in case.

Lou's Travel Key Chain

My own invention, tried and tested. The idea is that the best equipment is the stuff you have with you when you need it – everything else is worthless at that time. So, the key chain includes a micro Swiss Army knife, a tiny flashlight, a bottle opener, an army surplus mini can opener, and a small spoon. Truly pocket-sized and incredibly useful. I carry one everywhere, and I'd patent it if I could.

Pictures from home

These are good to show to new friends, especially those whose ideas about America may have come from episodes of *Dallas*, *Dynasty*, or *Baywatch*; Canadians might want to consider bringing some postcards of Toronto, for those expecting to see whale meat roasting in front of an igloo. South Africans can amaze those Europeans expecting elephants in Cape Town, and for those Down Under here's your chance to show the world your country is not just kangaroos, koalas, kiwis, and sheep.

What not to bring

There are always things that you wish you hadn't taken – usually too late, when you're schlepping up to the eighth floor of your pension. Rather than having to go through the agonies of offloading stuff halfway through your trip, here are some pointers about what you really might not need.

Too much paper

Maybe it's just me, but I've found this a perennial problem. Those glossy brochures that I mentioned earlier are also given out by tourist offices in many of the countries you will visit, and are just as hard to part with. As before, copy any relevant information into a notebook, and then return the brochure or leave it at a hostel for others to read.

If you should minimize brochures, you should ultra-minimize books. The paper in books is magically transformed into lead when enclosed in a backpack and hoisted to your shoulders. One guide-book per person (preferably different books if in a group), then maybe one book more. If you want to bring something to read in spare moments, bring cheap paperbacks that you can trade or give away.

Electrical items

I'm sure you've heard the stories about melting clock radios, and the hair dryer that blacked out Paris when it was plugged in. Don't bother with this stuff. A battery-operated alarm clock is great, but hair dryers, electric razors, and other items will only be a pain. If you do bring electrical items, you must also bring an adaptor, because European countries use 220-volt current (which may fry items designed for 115-volt operation). And even if you use 220 in your home country, the design of electrical outlets varies from

A final packing idea courtesy of Ahn-uld

The movie *Total Recall*, while disgustingly violent, did contain one very good idea for the European traveler. If you remember, Arnold Schwarzenegger had left himself a briefcase full of money, guns, explosives, disguises, and other handy stuff in case he got into trouble. Well, so can you – sort of. As insurance against a total disaster, such as a stolen backpack, why not put together a box of essentials like a change of clothes, back-up credit cards, an old camera, and anything you might need if a backpack or some of its contents were to be stolen or lost. Leave this box, unsealed, in the hands of someone reliable who can ship it to you should you need any or all of its contents. Nearly everything is more expensive in Europe than in North America, and if you have to do some heavy-duty replacement, the ability to quickly ship your sister's backpack, some clothes, mom's camera, a five-dollar watch, shoes, and so on, could save you a fortune. Why pay European prices to buy things you will only need for a few weeks? Antipodeans are, unfortunately, out of luck here.

At the very least, as mentioned earlier, you should leave a photocopy of the picture page of your passport, and also a copy of any credit cards you have, in case they need to be canceled. Also, if you are unsure that you can really travel as light as I recommend, why not put some of the things you think you might need in a box? If you ultimately do need them you can curse my stupid advice and send for them. I doubt if you will, though.

nation to nation in Europe, and you may need to carry plug adaptors. If you simply must have an electrical item with you, or are planning a very long stay, consider buying what you need after you arrive, and selling it before you leave. If you bring an electrical item with you, be sure to also buy the plug adaptors and so on before you leave for Europe. There is not much of a market for Australian and American adaptors in Europe and hence they can be impossible to find. (Your best bet is at the airport.)

4

Getting there

Okay, guys, this is where some money is going to be saved if you work at it. That airline ticket is going to be a major chunk of your budget, and, as we all know, airline fares are determined by some form of black magic unknown to the flying public. If you are smart and patient, you can pay about half of what the guy on your left is paying for the same flight, and a third of that woman on your right.

I am old enough to barely remember when airlines were really airlines, and planes were airliners, and travel by air was something special. It was more expensive then, but a hell of a lot more gracious and enjoyable. Traveling by air today is a contact sport, bordering on open warfare. Fares are raised for no discernible reason, discounted the next week, and always jacked up ruthlessly before Thanksgiving and Christmas. The reason for all this volatility is, of course, greed. The airlines figure that anyone who has to travel with less than two weeks' notice is probably on business so they can nail them for a much higher fare. They throw a bone to vacationers by giving them cheaper fares at times when they aren't able to fill their planes with business traveler cash cows.

The long and short of it is that flying today is often miserable, and if you're going to be miserable for that day it takes you to make the hop across North America and/or the Atlantic and/or Pacific, you may as well go cheaply. Doing this is going to take some looking around well before you go – like three months before, if possible. That's the time to start if you're serious, and read the travel section of your local paper, or the nearest big city daily, to keep an eye on things.

The factors you will be juggling are the following:

- Price
- Changeability
- Refundability
- How long a stay
- Standby or reserved
- Point of entry to Europe
- Point of exit from Europe
- Which airline
- Arrival time in Europe
- Other restrictions

First steps

The first step is to figure out where you want to fly out of and where you want to start out in Europe. For Americans, Los Angeles, San Francisco, Chicago, Dallas–Fort Worth, Atlanta, Boston, and New York, either JFK or Newark, will usually be cheapest, especially JFK/Newark. It may be worth bumming a ride to one of these places, even from a good distance. Those arriving from other countries don't have as much of a choice. Montreal, Toronto, Auckland, Sydney, Melbourne, and Johannesburg are by far the largest gateways. The major, and probably the cheapest, points of entry to Europe are London, Paris, Amsterdam, and Frankfurt. Those wishing to fly to Rome will probably have to go through Milan.

A word of advice on where to arrive. On a first trip, the first day overseas can be overwhelming, especially if you are alone. Flying into a country where you speak the language will make things less stressful. Despite the long lines and despotic immigration officers, London might not be a bad place to start. London is also a good place to start for the cheap flights available to Greece or points beyond the European continent. Also, since Eurail passes are not valid in Britain, many people go to London first or last to avoid wasting valuable pass time during their time spent there. But if your dream of going to Europe has always included getting on a plane and then getting off in Paris or Rome, then by all means fly to those airports and show 'em who's boss. It's your trip.

After you've chosen where to leave from and fly into, the next step is to establish an upper limit on your fare. This is easily done by calling major airlines on their toll-free numbers, and waiting until their overworked operators answer. When they do answer, ask for the price of the cheapest fare from your exit point to your initial destination, and inquire about any restrictions, advance purchase requirements, etc. Then ask if there is anything cheaper to any other city in Europe you are willing to fly into, and/or from any other city you are willing to fly out of. It pays to be nice to the operator, by the way. He or she will have access to tons of information and may go to greater lengths for you with just a little courtesy on your part.

Barring a fare war or major sale, what you will get from the airlines is their published, economy-class, two-week advance purchase fare. This is now your upper limit. Anybody can get these just by phoning an airline and asking. You are now working down from that price – if someone offers you a "special deal" that costs more than that, hang up. You should find all of the airlines to be very close, if not identical, on the price of these fares. A warning for older travelers: one discount that isn't is the "senior citizen's fare" on airlines. This is usually a ten percent savings on fares sold directly by the airline. But as you will soon see, tickets from budget travel agents can cost hundreds of dollars less than these senior "discount" fares.

The next stop is the Sunday travel section of the nearest large metropolitan newspaper, and the local "alternative" newspaper, if any. Some resources in the US include New York's *Village Voice*, the *LA Weekly*, and the *San Francisco Bay Guardian*; in London, check out the *Evening Standard*, *Time Out*, and *TNT* magazine; and in Australia, try *TNT*. If you're near a major university, you might want to check out a copy of the school paper. In all of these, you should see many small ads for unbelievably priced tickets. Since they are so unbelievable, you should not believe them. What they are good for, however, is a lower limit; you probably won't be able to beat the fares advertised unless you are very fortunate. So there you have it – your fare should lie between the two extremes. The challenge now, of course, is to get as close to the bottom as possible. Your next stop should probably be a travel agent, consolidator, or the Web.

Some companies, consolidators, and agencies, because of their relationships with certain airlines or ticket brokers, can offer better deals than others. Your job, of course, is to find the company, consolidator, or agency with the best deal to get you where you want to go, and when you want to get there.

Travel agents

Travel agents connect those who have some form of "travel product," such as an airline seat, a hotel room or a space on a tour, with the potential buyer. A travel agent is a resource that you should at least consider; they can provide you with far more information than you could possibly gather on your own and, barring a major fare war, you'll never find the cheapest airfare without using some kind of agent. The price structure for agents is set up so that using an agent will not cost you more than booking a ticket yourself.

Travel agents can be a blessing or a curse, and it is up to you, if you choose to go this route, to find one that you feel comfortable with. They can always make travel easier for you, and they can usually make it cheaper, but it is up to you to make decisions based on the information they provide. Your agent should assist you, not direct you.

As with any major purchase, shop around. Don't simply go to the local travel bureau and assume that they will give you the best service and get you the best price. Go with one that deals with budget travel and/or students regularly, preferably daily. Any agent will be happy to fly you to Europe, but if they're used to booking ten-thousand-

dollar/one-month luxury trips they may not be able to serve your needs. You certainly don't want them to reinvent the budget travel wheel in booking your trip. Some agents deal almost exclusively with students and/or budget travelers, and with these places the distinction between travel agency and consolidator (see below) can sometimes become blurry. If you are booking an ultra-cheap seat somewhere, you should be prepared to give the budget/student agent you use the same scrutiny that I advise in the next paragraph.

Before going to an agent, you should have at least a basic idea of where and when you want to go. Don't just walk in and say: "I want to go to Europe, but I don't know where." Make it easy on them by deciding when you want to leave, where you want to start out in Europe, and how long you want to stay. Then work out a rough itinerary. Once you have these issues decided, you and your agent can take it from there. Basics #5 has a list of recommended travel agents.

Consolidators

We all know what a travel agent is; a consolidator is similar. These places, also known as bucket shops, deal in seats the airlines don't think they can sell at normal prices. Rather than sell these seats in their own name, which would irritate customers paying full fare, airlines release blocks of them to consolidators for resale. The consolidators then sell them to travelers who are willing to take the time and effort to seek them out.

Consolidators are the people advertising those unbelievable prices, and even if they are almost never as low as advertised, they can still be very cheap. They can be cheap for a number of reasons: student discounts, lower than expected bookings, inconvenient times, off-season departures, flying on strange airlines, flying into smaller or more inconvenient airports (like London Gatwick instead of London Heathrow), long delays in changing planes, a mandatory stopover in Angola, whatever. If you are persistent, you will probably be able to find something where you want to go, when you want to go, at a couple of hundred dollars below the airline's published fare. So get on the phone and start calling the places in the paper, and see what they can do for you. Do a lot of calling around, write down whatever they tell you in great detail (you'll definitely forget some of what they say if you don't), and don't be afraid to ask questions. Some pointers for dealing with agents or consolidators:

- If you are a student, with an ISIC card, mention that up front.
- Round-trip tickets are almost always cheaper than two one-way tickets. In fact, because most single fares are based on half of the full-price round-trip fare, they can cost more than some discount round trips. Hard to believe, but often true. Don't get a one-way from home and expect to get a cheap single out of London. Get your return ticket from Europe before you go, unless you have no firm date of return.
- Never be pressured into buying a ticket right away, even if they tell you it is "the last one left in the world." If that were the case, they wouldn't need to pressure you to buy it. Don't be rushed into anything. On the other hand, don't get an excellent deal that works perfectly for you and then wait a week for no reason.
- When offered a ticket, keep in mind the ten factors mentioned earlier (see p.72). Ask if it is refundable (it probably won't be if it's cheap). Ask how long it is valid for. Ask how much it would cost to change the European departure city and the day of departure. And ask about any restrictions they may have "forgotten" to tell you about.
- One possibility to consider is a stopover flight, where you stop for a few days in another European city on the way to your final destination. These are usually found on the big European national carriers, and can sometimes be done at no extra charge, or for as little as $50–100 per stop. As an example, Icelandair does a three-day stopover in Iceland on its way to continental Europe.
- Never pay cash if you can avoid it. Use a credit card, and after you have the ticket in hand, call the airline and see if it is a valid ticket (check destination, date, one way or round trip, price, etc). As I write this, the radio is reporting on a group of teachers from California who went to Zimbabwe, only to discover that their "round-trip" tickets were actually one-way. Not one of them checked. Don't make the same mistake. If the ticket is bogus in some way, cancel the charge, and call the police. If you don't have a credit card, and can't use someone else's, be up front. Tell your agent that you want to confirm your ticket with the airline, and get all the details they would use to get the ticket. Then call the airline and ask if the ticket could be issued at the price you're paying. An hour of wariness could save you hundreds of dollars and weeks of headaches.
- Walk out of any place that demands cash in advance. Don't even look back.

- Don't buy a ticket over the phone if you can possibly go to the office itself. If the office is a basement with two phone lines and a desk, it may not be there when something goes wrong with your ticket in three months.
- Ideally, you want to arrive in Europe early in the day. You definitely do not want to get off a plane and then have to look for somewhere to stay in the middle of the night. Remember that you will have to clear customs and immigration upon arrival; it may take as much as two or three hours from your landing time for you to get to your accommodations. Take this into account when planning your arrival time.
- Be aware of the different travel seasons airlines work by. Flights will be cheapest between the end of October and the end of March – the low season. They will be moderately expensive in the so-called "shoulder seasons" of April/May and September/October; and they will be most expensive during the June–August period. As the spring/summer travel season approaches, expect the available seats to dry up. Start poking around in February. If you are reading this in May, get to work now.
- The more shops you visit or call, the more comfortable you will be with the whole process. Start early, have your plans together, don't let yourself be pressured, and you will be fine.
- When booking a ticket, be careful if you are making a connecting flight either to or from Europe. It can take a long time to get through the arrival procedures in any airport. For example, let's say you're flying back to Toronto, and then catching a connecting flight to Winnipeg. To schedule that next flight, include the time needed to empty a 747, claim your bags, clear immigration, clear customs, and get to the other plane – about three hours. If you are changing airports, such as going from JFK to Newark in the States, allow at least four hours. The same applies if you are connecting to another flight after your first landing in Europe: allow *at least* three hours between your takeoff and landing times. Call the airlines involved to get their minimum times required to check in and make your connection, but do not allow less than three hours, no matter what they say is possible.

Buying your ticket online

When updating the last edition of this book my editor thought that online ticket sellers were the one and only future of the travel industry. Yeah, right. Basically, an online ticket vendor is no different from a consolidator or an agent that specializes in budget travel. They can only sell tickets at a low price if they buy tickets at a low price, and they can only do that if they have business relationships with the airlines or with ticket brokers. Sound familiar? All those places promising dirt-cheap tickets online are only doing for the general public what consolidators had been doing all along for smart travelers. The online crowd simply used the "Internet-is-the-Future" frenzy of the late 1990s to market themselves as the be-all and end-all of travel.

The types of websites and online services out there are endless and almost all seem to offer the "deal of the century." What service is best for you mostly depends on how flexible you can be in terms of when you leave, where to and from, and what airline you prefer. If you are willing to sacrifice your freedom in any and all of these, you may just find that deal. However, you don't need to give up too much to find some alternatives on the Web.

Some of the most alluring travel websites are those promoting last-minute deals. I'd say stay away, as you should be planning well in advance for your trip anyway. Other sites are more like online consolidators, dumping tickets for major airlines. Still, these discount agent and consolidator sites often have better-than-average deals and are worth checking out before buying a ticket elsewhere. There are also the somewhat dodgy "name-your-own-price" services. Basically, if you do name your own price and they match it, then you have just bought your ticket, without getting to review the airline times, number of stops, and routes involved. On mainstream and well-known sites, such as Travelocity, Expedia, and Yahoo, or that of any major airline, true low-cost deals can be few and far between, but they are there.

The advantage to surfing for a ticket online is your ability to research and play around with prices, itineraries, and destinations at your own pace, in the privacy of your own home (or work station). There's less pressure to buy, since it's an anonymous process – though that can also be a strike against, as there is no one there to answer your questions, and deals can come and go quite quickly. Keep in mind, too, that the information you are accessing is basically the same a consolidator is getting hold of; you're not getting an exclusive deal just because you found it online. Also, cheap seats often come with many restrictions. Moral: always read the fine print.

Online ticket agencies

Online agents
Ⓦ www.biztravel.com
Ⓦ www.travelocity.com

Ⓦ www.expedia.com
Ⓦ www.travelselect.co.uk

Discount specialists
Ⓦ www.air-fare.com
Ⓦ www.cheaptickets.com (US)
Ⓦ www.lowestfare.com
Ⓦ www.travelzoo.com

Ⓦ www.cheapflights.co.uk (UK)
Ⓦ www.itravel.com
Ⓦ www.travelscape.com

Last-minute deals
Ⓦ www.bargainholidays.com (UK)
Ⓦ www.lastminute.com (UK)

Ⓦ www.bestfares.com
Ⓦ www.lastminutetravel.com

If buying a ticket online is still too foreign a concept for you, that's okay; you needn't feel compelled to catch the latest wave. Think of the Internet instead as a research tool and use it to compare prices quoted to you by agents or to find out more about that mysterious airline the consolidator swears can get you to Amsterdam for $300 less than any major airline. If you are nervous about releasing your credit card number into the wilds of cyberspace, rest assured that pretty much every booking site is secure (encoded during transport from your computer to the ticketing company).

Finally, if you have an email account you check often, sign up for the daily or weekly airfare and travel-related updates certain websites offer. The site Ⓦwww.travelzoo.com, for instance, sends out weekly emails of the twenty best airfare, car rental, hotel, and package deals going.

Charters, courier flights, and other options

During your search for a seat you may hear rumors, or see ads, for incredible deals based on courier flights or charters. Beware. In the travel industry, as elsewhere, there is no free lunch. Courier flights match travelers who want to go somewhere with companies or individuals who need something, usually documents, transported by air. The courier company sells you a cheap ticket in exchange for you sacrificing some or all of your luggage allowance. The amount of these discounts, in accordance with supply and demand, dries up during early and late summer, when many students are happy to save a small amount. Also, most courier flights require a return trip within a certain length of time, usually a few weeks. If this interests you, search the Web and small ads. Be sure to get a firm commitment from a courier company before gambling your trip on this option.

Charters are great when they work, and absolute hell when they don't. Expect older planes packed to the rafters with people, and poor in-flight service. (Actually, that doesn't sound a whole lot different from the major airlines, does it?) At any rate, the big worry with charters is whether or not they will leave as scheduled. The difference between a plane 95 percent full and one that's 99 percent full may be the difference between profit and loss for the charter operator, and a flight may be delayed for "maintenance" while the last few seats are sold. Some charter companies are as reliable as the major airlines, whereas others are operating at the edge of bankruptcy and may disappear with your money without trace. Get a neutral opinion, such as from a travel agent who is not selling you something, on the reliability of a charter company before you hand them several hundred dollars. This is most necessary during the summer, and with flights between popular tourist destinations and London.

Round-the-world tickets

You will notice, once in Europe, the large number of Aussies and Kiwis who seem to be traveling on a perpetual tour of the world for next to nothing. This is not just perception – the relative isolation of those two countries makes a quick trip to and from Europe out of the financial question. However, quirks of the airline industry can make it cheaper to travel around the world than simply back and forth to Europe. For example, a Qantas round-trip ticket from Sydney to London costs around Aus$3000, bought directly from the airline. Meanwhile, an itinerary of London–Nairobi–Delhi–surface travel to Kathmandu–Bangkok–Singapore–Bali–Perth–surface travel to Melbourne–Auckland–Los Angeles–London is about the same price, excluding the cost of surface travel. No wonder so many from Down Under travel this way. Travelers from other countries should consider this option too – some round-the-world (RTW) tickets may be had for as little as US$1000. Why not return to America via Hong Kong? Many of the student and budget travel agencies listed in Basics #5 can put together an RTW trip or refer you to someone who can.

If you're planning an RTW trip from Down Under that hits the United States before Europe and other points east, be aware of another money-saver. Backpacks, camping equipment, hiking boots, and other gear are much cheaper in the States. Besides seeing the spectacular beauty of my homeland, you can save about fifty percent on such items by buying them here. Get catalogs from the suppliers listed in Basics #7 for some comparison shopping.

Package deals

One option that many overlook are package deals, often because they are associated with tours and itineraries that might dictate where you stay and for how long. Most travel agents and airlines can, however, put together flexible deals which can be cheaper than organizing things when you arrive, especially with car rental, which in Europe can be very expensive on the spot. Or you may find a deal that's too good not to take – especially one that might involve accommodation in cities like London or Paris.

There is a sea of options, ranging from fly-drive deals, sun-and-sea packages, and coach tours to special-interest plans. As always read the fine print no matter who you deal with (brochures make everything sound great), and try, if you're coming from the States, to use an operator that is a member of the US Tour Operator Association (USTOA) or approved by the American Society of Travel Agents (ASTA).

5

(Almost) being there

fter all the planning and purchasing, it's finally getting close to departure time, and there are only a few last-minute details to consider. I will also belabor you with some personal advice in this chapter. Heading out for Europe can be a stressful process, and I hope this advice makes the trip as smooth as possible.

- On international flights you should call your airline within 72 hours of your departure time to confirm that you will indeed be going and to check for any schedule changes. Some airlines may offer your seat for sale if you don't, although this supposedly is rare.
- One point to be careful with. If you miss or no-show at one portion of your airline trip, the rest of the trip is canceled. I'll repeat this in the section on going home.
- Definitely call ahead and make a room reservation for your first few nights in Europe. The last thing you want to do on arrival is look for housing. Also, you'll probably be wiped out from the trip. A room in a small pension or cheap hotel, as opposed to a dorm bed in a hostel, might make for a quicker recovery. See Chapter 10, "Communications," for details on making international calls.
- When you make your reservation, get explicit directions to the place you will be staying, including metro stops, cross streets,

prominent landmarks in the area, etc. Once again, make it easy for yourself on that first day.

- If you plan on meeting another traveler while in Europe, be aware that this can be difficult. Try and pick a very specific location (such as "touching the statue of Goya outside the Prado in Madrid" and not "at the Eiffel Tower.") Don't plan to meet outdoors at night or in a place that charges admission. Also, it's a good idea to have a number, even one at home, that both of you can call to leave messages, in case plans change or you miss each other. Another small fruit of bitter experience. . .

- If you live alone, don't forget all of the standard "going-on-a-trip" things to do: empty the refrigerator, stop the paper, make arrangements for plants and pets, put a vacation hold on your mail at the post office, etc. As a personal request, please take special care with pets. Never, ever, just lock a cat out (let alone a dog), with a few pounds of dry food in a bowl.

- If you have a car, especially an old one, you might want to fill the gas tank and disconnect the battery before letting it sit for two months. Or have someone drive it every week or so, if you trust your friend not to take your faithful sled on a road trip.

- Get completely packed, down to your toothbrush, the day before you leave. Trust me on this one. Don't leave any packing for the day of your trip. If you pack on the day you depart, you will, without fail, forget something.

- Remember to leave the penknives off your key ring and/or take them out of your daypack and check them. Those wise souls among you who are not checking anything will have to buy a knife in Europe, or mail one ahead.

- Arrive at the airport at least two hours prior to your takeoff time, especially if you are taking a non-US airline or a charter. New security regulations have increased the time needed for check-in. A frantic dash to the airport, let alone a missed flight, is a poor way to start any trip. Better to get the lines over with and relax.

- Parking at most airports is very expensive and not very secure. If at all possible, get a ride from someone.

- Practice your money-changing skills by purchasing about fifty dollars' worth of the currency of the first country you will visit. That way you can skip the line at the airport change counter in Europe and avoid its lousy exchange rate; it's also a good backup should you turn up and find everything closed. Just like in Europe, try a major bank first. As a last resort, try the change booth at your home airport.

- You may not know this, but airport food is expensive poison, designed to weaken your system so the dreaded airline food can finish you off. Bring your own food with you, and you'll eat much better and much cheaper.

- On long flights, especially long night flights, airplane cabins can get cold enough to grow icicles off your nose. Veteran travelers usually carry an extra pair of socks. For keeping the rest of you warm and comfortable, I recommend traveling in sweats, especially on long flights.

- The air you breathe while on an airplane is drier than any air found naturally anywhere on earth. As a result, it is very easy to become dehydrated on long flights, which can cause headaches, nausea, and other discomforts. Bring a big bottle of water with you, and drink it all during the flight. You'll need it. It's also a good idea to steer clear of alcohol and carbonated drinks.

- If you wear contacts, take them out for your transatlantic flight. The dry air I mentioned previously will suck the life out of your contacts, and they will feel like sandpaper after a few hours. Falling asleep with them on is even worse. (Thanks to Denise Reich, who wrote after her vision had returned.)

- When flying into London Heathrow, if you can, sit on the right (starboard) side of the plane, for a great view of the center of London when you land.

- In most European airports, notably Heathrow, you cannot simply go to your departure gate on a connecting flight, even if you have tickets in hand. Even though you are already past security and so forth, you must check in at the "further clearance" or "further travel" desk, which may be difficult to find.

Upon arrival in Europe, hit the bathroom, and get a drink before getting in the endless customs line upon arrival, or even before commencing the sometimes endless wait at the carousel for your luggage if you've checked it. This, of course, is another reason for packing light, as those with only carry-on items will be able to skip the luggage claim area and go directly to customs, leaving the heavy packers fuming as the customs lines grow longer.

● When and if you get to England, obvious as it may seem, slow down and actively practice looking both ways when crossing streets. The British habit of driving on the left runs counter to years of ingrained habits for most tourists, and every year several are hit by cars. Near misses abound, including several that involved me. Though Brits may snigger at this advice, this is not a matter of intelligence. Winston Churchill, on a visit to New York, was nailed by a taxi after looking the wrong way. Some time ago some genius had the brilliant idea of painting signs on the crosswalks telling you which way to look. Follow these directions; they saved my life once.

● Finally, the best way to deal with the inevitable jet lag is to try to get in synch with the time difference as soon as possible. For example, if you arrive at midday local time, you should attempt to stay awake until reasonably late in the evening rather than taking a nap in the afternoon.

A micro course in European culture

A number of guidebooks list some of the customs and social idiosyncrasies of the various European countries, to help travelers avoid offending their hosts. In general, this is a good idea, but I sincerely doubt that many travelers will be able to pull a particular custom out of their memory when the occasion demands. The following advice should work in all European countries, and all countries in the world, for that matter. Ninety-nine percent of it is common sense, but it does bear repeating. I apologize for any tone of self-righteousness, and I admit that I have violated many of these rules myself.

● Never simply speak English to someone and expect them to answer you in English. I find this extremely rude. How would you react if someone visiting your hometown started talking to you in Swedish and expected to be answered? Always ask, in the local language, if a person speaks English. If they don't, say "Thank you" in the local language before moving on.

- Beginning a sentence with "please" will work wonders. "Please, where is the train station?" sounds a whole lot better than "Where is the train station?"

- If you are holding a conversation in English, it is a nice gesture to thank the person for speaking your language, and thereby making the conversation possible. Whenever I have done this it has been appreciated greatly by the person I thanked.

- Handshakes are very common in continental Europe, particularly in southern European countries. Shaking hands on meeting and departing, even when you see someone several times a day, is common.

- Greeting a storekeeper on entry, and saying goodbye on exit, is standard all over Europe.

- Canadians will not face the occasional scrutiny that some Americans will receive from some Europeans, other than the occasional questioning as to just why their government requires them to wear maple leaves when they travel. Australians may find the image of "Crocodile" Dundee has preceded them, while Kiwis may find that no image has preceded them, and may wish to carry a world map to point out the location of the "Land of the Silver Fern."

- In my experience, Americans (and Australians) are perceived in Europe as friendly, monolingual, a bit loud, and usually in a hurry. There are reasons for all of these perceptions. If I could give advice, it would be the following: try to blend in wherever you happen to be. Try not to change the place you are visiting with your presence, as with, for example, a loud conversation in English in a cathedral or museum. Slow down a bit when dealing with the people and especially in restaurants, as most Europeans expect to be left alone for long periods while eating. Trying to hurry someone or making a scene never helps a situation. There are some countries in Europe, which I won't name, whose traveling citizens could benefit from this advice as well.

- If you are an American, you may be called upon to justify American military action, or even to explain some obscure regulation such as our terribly high tariffs on Danish ham. Don't argue with people who treat you as if you make American foreign policy.

- Wherever you hail from, you are, whether you like it or not, a representative of your country when you are abroad. Treat the people you meet with respect and sensitivity, don't condescend, and you will be fine.

- Far more important than any language skill or knowledge of local customs is a positive, friendly attitude, and, especially, a smile. In every culture on earth a smile means the same thing, and cannot be taken for anything but an expression of friendship. In every culture I've been exposed to, it has worked wonders.

Over to you . . .

At this point, the planning, packing, and buying are over (and so is the cultural sermon). You've got your passport, tickets, and rail pass in hand, your stuff is all packed, your plans are more or less made, and you're ready to go. There's a 747 out there with your name on it, and Europe is yours for the taking. The rest of this book concerns the practical things you need to know about travel in Europe, because that's where you're going. Congratulations.

6

Getting around

So here you are, in Europe at last. I hope that this chapter includes all you need to know to get around easily. You have a major ally in doing so – the local tourist authority. Most European cities and countries benefit greatly from the tourist trade, and they have spent large amounts of money to make things easy on you. Most countries have a large network of tourist offices, sometimes in the smallest town or village, and this is usually an incredibly valuable resource. They can do a lot more for you than simply hand you a map and direct you to a hostel, but to get full value you must ask. The office in the main train station may be a bit crowded in August, so be prepared with some questions, such as (1) are there any festivals or celebrations planned in the local area any time soon, or any planned in the region in the next week or so? (2) is anything on the normal tourist trail closed? (3) is there any attraction that you personally recommend I see, perhaps something off the tourist trail? Be nice to these people – they are often severely overworked during the summer.

Along with tourist offices, there are also train information offices that can help you tremendously in your traveling around. If a question is not answered in this chapter, or you have a question about a specific trip or service, ask at one of these offices, and I guarantee that you will be helped on your way. Since you will probably be taking public transportation from the airport to wherever you are staying, information on getting around cities will be presented first, followed by information on intercity and international travel.

City transportation

The great news is that you are finally in Europe. The not-so-great news is that you are now in an airport. Obviously you need to get out of there as fast as you can, and head for whatever accommodations you have reserved. I have to say that very few issues seem to worry prospective travelers more than moving around foreign cities on public transport. It really should not. Remember that you are not the first person to come to Paris without knowing how to speak French. If only for their own convenience, transportation authorities all over Europe do their best to help foreign visitors. Read the section below and with a little practice you will be well on your way to becoming an expert.

One of the really nice aspects of traveling in Europe is the incredible public transportation that is available in the major cities. Most European cities have combinations of subways (metros), streetcars (trams), and buses that shame the best in the United States, or anywhere else in the world for that matter. Paris and London, in particular, have extremely convenient subway and bus systems. Since most of the famous sights, museums, and monuments are usually clustered in the centers of the larger cities, walking, combined with riding the bus or metro, is an easy way to see a multitude of attractions quickly.

All this convenience comes at a price, however, and intracity transport can be a surprisingly large expense. Buying tickets one at a time is almost never the cheapest way to travel. In major cities like London, Rome, Madrid, and Paris, take a serious look at how much moving around you are going to do, and see if a day or week pass makes sense. In Central London, for example, a one-way trip on the tube costs £1.90, at least in the central zone, while an all-day, unlimited travel pass for Central London costs £5.30 (or £4.10 if you buy it off-peak). Even though, at over $8, the day pass is expensive, it is a good deal for someone who is planning on packing a lot into a day, especially those who want to go out in the morning and afternoon, come back to where they're staying, and then go back out in the evening. A weekly pass, which requires a small photo, at £19.30 is even cheaper per day. If you're staying a week and aiming to see a lot of the city, it may make the most sense.

Other metros sell books of ten tickets at a huge discount versus the cost of single tickets. (Paris, for example, sells one-shots at €1.3 each − $1.30 − or ten tickets for €9). As a general rule, you can expect a weekly pass in a major European city to pay for itself in a five-day stay, or after four days of hard use. The usual tip parade on city transport:

- Metros (subways) can be confusing at first, but will be a piece of cake in a few days. Lines are either named (as in London), designated by a letter or number, or simply named according to the final stop on the line. Usually the various lines are also color-coded. Trains run back and forth on each colored line, and never change colors. To get from one line to another you must stop at a station that serves both lines, walk to another platform and grab another train. Trains are generally named, and announced in the stations, according to the name of the last station on their line in the direction they are going; in most cities trains carry signs showing the name of this last station in their front window. When in doubt about how to get somewhere, ask somebody. Most locals, as well as your fellow travelers, will be glad to help you.
- If you're not sure whether you're going in the right direction, watch as the stations go by. It should be obvious what direction you're going in very quickly. Don't start reading a newspaper and end up across town in Berlin, as I have done.
- Metro tickets can usually be purchased at the station itself. Bus and tram tickets, often one and the same, are usually sold at news

kiosks and tobacco shops, and not by the bus drivers themselves. Most drivers, also, cannot change large bills. Tourist offices sometimes sell daily and weekly passes, and if they don't they can always tell you where to get one.

● Most European buses, trams, and some metros operate on the honor system; you're supposed to cancel your own ticket, often with little punching machines in each car or bus. If you don't see locals doing this, it's because they have monthly passes. From time to time you may be asked to produce your ticket by an inspector. Failure to show a canceled ticket (for that day) can result in a stiff fine on the spot ($15–40, depending on the city) and rude comments from the inspector concerning your morality. The most ferocious inspectors are in Germany and Hungary. In Budapest, especially, take care to get things right, as dozens of thick-necked policemen roam the subways in packs, mercilessly fining tourists by the score.

● Because of the system described above, you often do not have to enter a bus or tram through the front door. Enter anywhere, stamp your ticket, and you're good to go.

● Within a given city there are usually myriad metro/bus/tram transfer privileges. Your guidebook should detail these, but an inquiry at the tourist office is advisable as well.

● Most metro systems give out free pocket-sized maps, which can save pulling out your guidebook or unfolding a city map every few minutes.

● Though buses and trams are slower than metros, they offer a much better view, and give you a feel for the cities that contain all those museums, stores, cafés, and monuments you want to visit.

Moped and bicycle rental

Almost every European city and town has a bicycle rental agency somewhere, which should be listed in your guidebook. Some of these places allow bikes to be dropped off at any of their offices throughout a city or region, allowing some great day-trips. In Holland, Belgium, and France it is often possible to rent bikes at train stations. As I said in Chapter 1, "Planning Your Trip," be careful about using bikes in cities, even if you see the locals doing so, and try to get a helmet. For those who don't want to bring a hard shell helmet with them, the kind made from several flexible tubes is better than nothing, although not by much.

Where you should be careful with a bicycle, you should treat a moped as if it were a sworn enemy. Mopeds are a ton of fun, but can be very dangerous. Once a friend of mine and I were in Barcelona and noticed a large number of beautiful women wearing neck braces and large bandages on their arms and legs. Our waiter explained that these were the result of Spanish vacationers using mopeds during their holidays. Renting a moped is easy, while renting a helmet (or a safe helmet) can be difficult. Consider the risks carefully, and watch out for the other guy.

Taxis

For some reason, a large percentage of taxi drivers everywhere, with the notable exception of London, are scheming, lying crooks who see impoverished travelers as little more than walking piggy banks to be emptied as quickly as possible. This is particularly true in France, Italy, Greece, and especially in Prague, where cabbies have a reputation for thieving and violence akin to that of the Mafia in Sicily. Most of us poor travelers will go months without seeing the inside of a cab, but here's the scoop if one becomes necessary.

- Single women, as always, beware. Don't just get in a cab and tune out your surroundings. Follow the progress of your driver, and if it looks as if he's going somewhere other than where you told him, speak up or get out at a stop. Silence is the best response to suggestive comments.
- At airports there is almost always public transport available. If someone, especially a taxi driver, tells you there isn't, look for yourself. Don't let yourself be pushed toward the taxi stand by a "helpful" porter or airport employee – he may be getting a cut of your fare.
- No meter, no ride. Avoid cabs with no meter, or one that is "broken." In Eastern Europe this may be difficult. In these countries, and especially in Russia, almost anyone with a car is willing to negotiate a ride for a fee. Just make sure you agree on the fee in advance; write it down if necessary. Again, if you can't do this, then don't take the ride. Be especially wary of taking taxis in Prague,

where the industry is totally unregulated and cabbies charge anything they like for a ride, however short.

- Find out what a cab ride should cost from someone who knows, if possible, and offer a bit less than this if the cabbie refuses to use the meter and you absolutely have to use his cab.
- If you agree on a fare, and the cabbie tries to charge you more at the end of your ride, hand him or her the amount you agreed on and walk away. This is less likely to happen if you were firm and clear in stating the fare at the beginning.
- Your average cabbie speaks bits and pieces of more languages than your average diplomat. If s/he pretends not to be able to agree on a fare because of a lack of English, beware.
- If the taxis in an area seem a bit sleazy, don't put anything in the trunk if you can avoid it. If you have to use the trunk, get your things out first, then pay the driver.
- Don't sacrifice safety to stay on a budget. If you arrive after dark, especially in a big city, don't walk the streets with a backpack just to save a couple of bucks. This is especially true for women traveling alone. A taxi is a bargain in this situation.

A taxi to the rescue

When I arrived at the train station in Bergen, Norway, at about 10pm, it was absolutely pouring rain, and darker than the inside of a cow. I covered my backpack with a plastic bag, put on my raincoat, and set off grimly toward the local hostel. After fifteen minutes of hard walking I was soaked, as was everything I had with me. After fifteen more minutes I was completely lost. I managed to wade my way back to the train station, where a chap in a Mercedes cab was sitting, dry as a bone in the Sahara, reading a newspaper. Ten minutes later I stepped out of his cab at the hostel. It cost seven dollars. It was money well spent.

- I feel I should repeat my previous warning about taxis in Prague. Use a cab only when absolutely necessary in that city, and have your hotel or pension call you one rather than pick one up at the taxi ranks.
- Finally, don't leave London without riding in a Black Cab. There's enough room in those things to house (or start) a small family.

Trains

Riding the trains of Europe during the summer puts you squarely in the middle of a giant mass of people on the move. It really can be great fun, and trains are one of the best places to meet people and to exchange information about traveling. I can recall being in a six-person compartment and sharing it with travelers from four different countries. When a young woman claimed the last seat, we asked her where she was from, and she cheerfully replied, "Zimbabwe."

Some train basics follow. These will make much more sense if you read Basics #2 first.

- European trains run on "military time," that is, the 24-hour clock, so get used to 2pm being written as 1400, 10pm as 2200, and so on. Just subtract twelve and add a "pm" to convert. Also, dates are written in the order of day, month, year. June 12, 2001, would be written numerically as 12-6-01. Be careful with this when entering Flexi pass dates. I always write out the month, to avoid confusion.
- Many European cities have more than one train station. Paris, for example, has six mainline stations. Make sure that you know where you must leave from, and don't assume that it is the same station that you came into, or even where you may have bought your ticket. Similarly, when planning an arrival, make sure of which station you will be coming into, since some of the others may be a good distance from your intended destination.
- When traveling to or from large cities, try to get on your train early, or make a seat reservation. Some trains do fill up, especially in southern Italy, on weekends and holidays, and throughout late July and August all over Europe. Standing for five hours is never fun. Reservations usually cost a few dollars and can be made when you buy your ticket (or, if you have a pass, any time you happen to be at a station). If you know how long you want to stay in a place, making your outbound reservation when you arrive is a good idea.
- Reservations are also needed for couchettes, which are bunks for sleeping on night trains. (Sleeping on trains is covered in more detail in Chapter 7, "Accommodations"). Night trains leave a city

in the evening, and adjust their speed to arrive early the following day, regardless of the distance involved.

● There are typically several different kinds of trains in every country, ranging from slow-poke local services that stop at every village to express trains that hit major cities only. The faster trains are usually marked in your timetables – trains marked as "EC" or "IC" for "Eurocities" and "Intercities" are most common. Even with a train pass, you can expect to pay a supplement and/or be required to make a reservation on trains like these. This supplement is usually not very much (about $10), especially considering the time saved, but it can be a surprise when you thought the trip would be free. For details on this, see the first page of your free Eurail timetable, or your InterRail bumph.

● One of the more welcome developments in European travel over the last ten years has been the spread of ultra-high-speed train routes throughout the continent. These trains, such as the TGV (in France), AVE (in Spain), and Pendolino (in Italy), are as much symbols of national pride as they are means of transportation, and are usually much newer and run much more efficiently than their slower cousins. There is often a surcharge for passholders to ride on these trains, but it is usually minimal ($5–10) and the time saved can be well worth it. At 120 to 150 mph, you can cover a lot of ground. The most extensive networks of these trains can be found in France, Germany and, surprisingly, Italy. (Actually, considering how the Italians drive, maybe it's not such a surprise that they like fast trains.) Since high- and ultra-high-speed train tickets are well within the buying power of even the smallest budget, don't just jump on a train that leaves at a convenient time. A faster train might allow you to sleep in and still get you to your destination several hours earlier, for only a few dollars more.

● If you are looking at a long train ride, buy plenty of food and water before heading for the station. Station food is expensive, and train food is even more so.

The French TGV system

Somehow or other, probably through massive government subsidies, the French high-speed train system has grown into a truly marvelous transportation network; one that can get you from one end of France to the other in only a few hours. With hundreds of trains a day out of Paris and other French cities, blazing along the tracks at 300 km/hour, the speed and convenience of the TGV system is nothing less than incredible (Paris to Marseille in three hours, for example). The only way it could be any better is if they used black holes and teleportation.

Copenhagen - Roskilde = €7 (single)

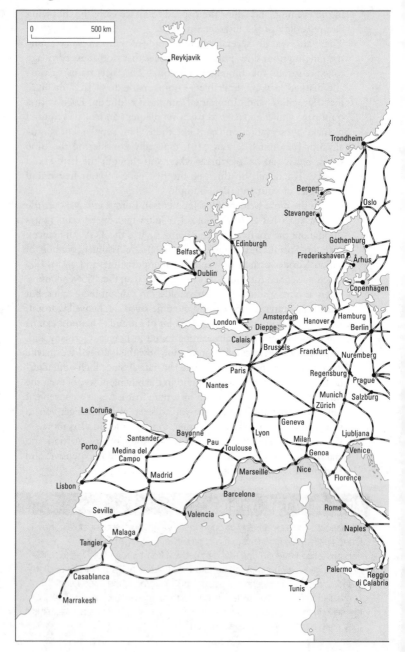

Milan - Naples = €40 (single) / €80 (return)

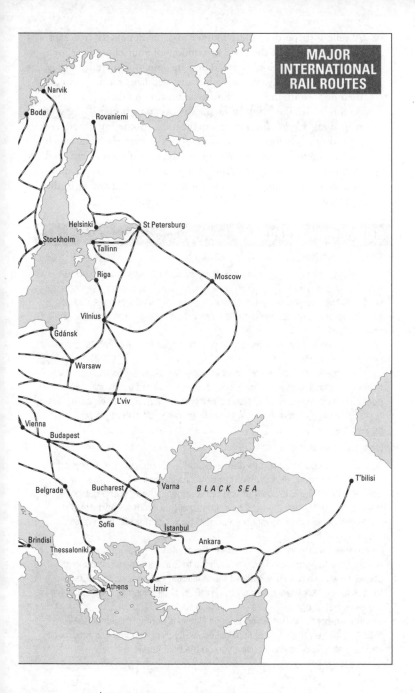

MAJOR
INTERNATIONAL
RAIL ROUTES

- A yellow stripe over the windows of a car designates first class. Also, always check the door or window of your chosen car for a destination sign. Sometimes trains are split up in mid-journey. Usually, but not always, individual cars will have metal signs near their doors with the car's ultimate destination on them (they don't do this in Britain). Make sure that the car you get into is going to your destination, especially on night trains. Sometimes there are signs on the platforms with diagrams of the train showing which cars are going where. If there are no signs visible anywhere, find a conductor, point to the floor of the car, and state your destination in a questioning tone. They'll let you know if you're in the right car.

British railway logic

Okay, here's a test.

You are in London. In a fit of madness you decide that you want to go to Edinburgh to see what Scotsmen wear under their kilts. Eurail passes are not valid in Britain, so you go to the station and find out that a one-way ticket from London to Edinburgh costs £80. How much do you think a round-trip ticket costs?

Why, £81 pounds of course. Eighty pounds to get to Edinburgh, and one pound to get back.

I think I speak for most travelers when I say "What the *hell* is this company thinking?" I don't know, but that's how it works. A round trip is only one pound more than a one-way, *if and only if you buy a round-trip ticket*. If you go to Edinburgh on a one-way, a single ticket back to London will cost you no less than £80.

Here's another test.

You decide to go to Devon for the weekend, and turn up at Paddington Station in London on Friday night to buy a round-trip ticket. How much does it cost? Over £120. What you don't know is that if you'd caught a train earlier in the day it would have cost half that amount, and if you'd booked far enough in advance you could have got a ticket for a bargain £25.

Both these situations are good examples of planning ahead, and knowing as much as you can before you actually go to Europe. I'm sure thousands of non-Britons have not known about these ticketing idiosyncrasies, and paid for that lack of knowledge. As always, plan and call ahead and *always* ask if there is a better price.

(For the record, the best thing to do in Britain is contact National Rail – ☎08457/484 950, ⊛www.nationalrail.co.uk – well before you want to travel, and they should be able to advise you on the best fare.)

- The first few pages of the Eurail timetable contain some useful information, including a train user's dictionary in five languages. These few pages are well worth reading. At the back of the timetable there is a list of the standard pictorial symbols used for services in train stations, such as left-luggage, lockers, etc. Once again, remember that not all trains are listed in your Eurail timetable, and that's especially true for trains which stay inside single countries. The best and most current information is available at the station.
- The free Eurail map has tons of useful information on the back side. This too is well worth reading, and it lists free transportation and discounts you will not find listed anywhere else, as well as pass-abuse penalties. Don't ignore this information.
- The same map lists Eurail Aid offices next to the map itself. These offices can issue new maps or timetables and can deal with pass problems. InterRail passholders can use InterRail centers in London, Copenhagen, Oslo, and Trondheim, some of which even provide accommodations as well as food and somewhere to get cleaned up.
- Once in Europe, travelers without train passes who are under 26 can take advantage of large discounts on a certain type of rail ticket. Known as BIJ tickets, these are available from student and youth travel agencies and can save as much as a third on the price of a regular rail ticket. They're valid for two months and you can stop off wherever you like as long as you keep going in one direction – no backtracking is allowed. These tickets are useful if you want to make one long specific journey and don't need a rail pass.

When in Roma . . .

When in the station or using a timetable, remember that some European cities are spelled differently in English than in their native languages. A friend of mine, a professor at UC Berkeley no less, was once astounded to find that no trains went to "Florence" (Duh, Steve). A short list of the most important cities:

Belgrade	Beograd	Lisbon	Lisboa
Brussels	Bruxelles	Milan	Milano
Cologne	Köln	Munich	München
Copenhagen	København	Naples	Napoli
Florence	Firenze	Prague	Praha
Geneva	Genève	Rome	Roma
Genoa	Genova	Turin	Torino
Gothenburg	Göteborg	Venice	Venezia
The Hague	Den Haag	Vienna	Wien

Train stations

One of the nice things about train travel is that a number of travel necessities can be taken care of upon arrival at the train station. Some recommendations:

- Virtually every train station in Europe offers some form of luggage storage, either in lockers or at a left-luggage office. These are especially useful for those who bring too much and want to drop off their main pack to live out of a daypack for a while. Old-style lockers have a key, while new lockers print out a combination for you. *Be warned that some of the new-style lockers will simply open after the time you have paid for has run out.* Make very sure whether or not you have to pay in advance for all the time you use. I prefer the left-luggage office myself, although it may not be open 24 hours. One idea if you happen to remember: when you check a bag, leave a photo ID that you won't need in the bag. That way, if you lose your claim check, you can easily prove that the stuff is yours.
- Luggage storage facilities in France may be scarce, depending on the current situation with regards to Algerian terrorism. Yet another reason to travel light.
- Plan your exit from a city upon arrival. Check the departure times and platforms for the trains going to your next destination. Make a reservation if necessary, or book a couchette if taking a night train. It is very unpleasant to check out of your room planning to take a night train and find that there are no more couchettes, or that there is no space at all.
- Buy a phone card if necessary – they're usually available from tobacco or newspaper kiosks. There's more on phone cards in Chapter 10, "Communications."
- Hit the tourist office for maps, the dates of any festivals or events coming up in the local area, and any places in the city to avoid after dark (or altogether).

Train pass conservation strategies

You just paid a lot of money for a Eurail or InterRail pass, and I guarantee that on some of those long train trips you will think long and hard about how to get the most out of it. Once again, most of these will make more sense if you read Basics #2 first.

- If you have a first-class Eurail pass, you can always buy second-class reservations on high-speed trains such as the AVE or the Thalys.

This can save you anywhere from five to twenty dollars, and all you miss in second class is a hideous meal that makes airline food look good. (For some reason, the Thalys is especially expensive, and the food served on it would be disgraceful if served in a prison.) Also, the Channel Tunnel is much cheaper in second than first class. Second is perfectly comfortable, and the ride is over in three hours anyhow.

- To save some travel days or time on a Flexi Eurailpass, or time on an unlimited pass, don't validate your pass until you are ready to really start traveling. For example, if you fly into Madrid, and then intend to go to Pamplona to run with the bulls for a week or so, it is worth buying a ticket from Madrid to Pamplona (for about $35), rather than starting up your unlimited pass, or starting up and using a day on a Flexi pass. Try to plan any long city stays on either end of your trip, for the same reason. If you want to spend two weeks in Paris, don't do it in the middle of your trip while your pass is activated. Balance this, though, with the possible need to take a break mid-trip. If you aren't enjoying your trip because of too much go-go-go, don't keep pushing simply to "get the most" out of a pass.

- Don't forget that even though a Flexi pass works off travel days used, it too has a one- or two-month clock ticking, just like an unlimited pass.

- When taking a night train, if you leave after 7pm (1900) you will only be charged one Flexi Eurailpass day, for travel up to midnight on the next day (29 hours later). You can cover a lot of ground in 29 hours. *Just remember to enter the next day's date on your Flexi pass or you'll be charged for two days.*

- Most night trains do indeed leave after 7pm. Once, though, I had to take a night train from Oostende that left at about 6.15pm, so I bought a $10 ticket to Ghent, where the train arrived just after 7pm. From Ghent onward I used my pass, and only had to use one day to get all the way from Ghent to Copenhagen. The conductors nodded their heads in admiration at this bit of chicanery, and labeled me the "Clever American."

- If you want to make a short- to medium-length trip, it may be worth buying a train or bus ticket rather than using a Flexi pass day, especially if you are running out of days.

- Remember that England, Scotland, Wales, and Northern Ireland are not Eurail or InterRail countries. Go to these places first or last.

- Every May and June sales of erasable pens soar in college bookstores across the nation, as thousands of students prepare to swindle the Flexi pass system. Yes, wicked as it may seem, erasing days and changing numbers is rampant among holders of these passes. It happens, and you know it happens, and they know it happens. Officially, conductors should stamp, with a date, every entry you make in your travel day boxes. In reality, they sometimes don't bother, and this opens the door to such originality on the part of passholders. Fines and penalties are stiff if you are caught; a description of them is included with your pass and is printed on the free map.

● Don't let the goal of getting the absolutely, positively last dime out of your pass impact your trip. Above all, don't get so caught up in cheap travel that you skip a trip somewhere interesting just because you might have to buy a train ticket to save a "Flexi day." You've spent quite a bit of money to get to Europe. Money spent to go places while you're there is usually money well spent.

WARNING: Some of the "free" things offered with your Eurail pass, such as a Rhine cruise, require you to use a day or validate your pass. Typically if something is given free to passholders, it will cost you a validation and/or a day. If something is merely discounted, it usually will not cost you a day, with the possible exception of the Channel Tunnel (detailed below). Using a Flexi pass day to get a "free" boat ride that would only cost fifteen dollars to buy outright is a waste. Thanks and a tip of the hat to Brian at the Forsyth Travel Library for this information.

Ferries and the Channel Tunnel

Two ferry crossings that many travelers will make are the English Channel and the infamous Brindisi to Patras crossing to Greece, which can be similar to the trip described on p.14. This is, incidentally, "free" to holders of the right InterRail pass. Apart from the Channel ferries and those between Italy and Greece, others that you might want to consider are those between France and Ireland, which are "free" with a Eurail pass. Your Eurail map will show discounted and "free" ferry routes, as will your InterRail information.

"Free" ferry lines will almost always have some way of squeezing money out of you, however. "Summer supplements" and port or departure taxes are common tactics. Don't be surprised if your "free" trip ends up costing you twenty or thirty dollars and a Flexi pass day. This is especially true on the Italy to Greece run.

When taking an overnight ferry, you will usually have several price-dependent seating choices. The cheapest option is "deck," which allows you to find a place on deck or on a bench to camp out. Most ferries also offer airline-type seats for a bit more, but expect clouds of smoke. A bunk in a cabin is the most expensive option, but even that can be cheap enough to fit into a very tight budget. You don't have to pay for the whole room – bunks are usually sold individually. That ten bucks you could save by sleeping on deck may not be worth it.

Ferry food is very expensive and rarely appealing. Bring enough food and water to last the journey. Coins from all countries served are accepted on almost all ferries. Finally, when you get on a ferry, think of the time zone change. Crossing the English Channel, crossing from Italy to Greece, and crossing from Sweden to Finland each involve a one-hour shift. Be especially careful if you have a connecting train or flight to catch.

Channel crossings

The English Channel is crisscrossed by hundreds of ferries, hovercraft, jetfoils, and other craft, and there are dozens of ways to get from England to the rest of Europe. The shortest crossing, not surprisingly, is at the closest point between France and England (Dover to Calais) and some Eurailers opt for this. Others choose similar trips from one of the nearby ports such as Oostende in Belgium, on which there is a Eurail discount, or Boulogne. There are fifty percent discounts on many Channel crossings for InterRail under-26 passholders, although those with the 26+ pass will find the selection much less extensive. Most of the vessels crossing the Channel are car and passenger ferries, although some routes are covered by hovercraft and jetfoils. These make the trip across the Channel in less than half the time of a ferry, but you can't get out on deck and walk around. Some things to remember about crossing the Channel:

- Since England is not a Eurail country, you will have to pay for your rail ticket between London and the port in Britain (about $30 from London to Dover, for example). You also have to pay with an InterRail pass, although discounts are available.
- Even though the boats are slower, they do allow you to get a beautiful view of the white cliffs of Dover when approaching or leaving England. You can't get this on the jetfoil, and the cliffs really are worth seeing at least once.
- Money-changing facilities on the ferry or at the port will cost you your eyeteeth, so change money before leaving for the ferry. Traveling to Britain from the continent, you should remember this because you'll need money to buy an onward ticket to London when you arrive since your pass won't work in Britain. Or you could buy this ticket at wherever you're setting out from, although this may cost a small amount extra.
- There is a decent (35 percent) Eurail discount on ferries and jetfoils from Oostende to Ramsgate and Dover, with the jetfoil service costing slightly more. InterRail passes usually give 50 percent, and on a wider variety of routes.
- Since England is still not a Eurail country, your Eurail timetable lists the channel port city rather than London as the destination. For example, if you're traveling to London from Paris using the boats and jetfoils that operate out of Oostende, look up "Oostende" as the destination to reach from Paris. Then check the Oostende ferry schedule (also in your timetable) to see if there will be a ferry or jetfoil to meet your train from Paris. The ferry/jetfoil and train terminal in Oostende are one and the same, and for some trains from Paris there is only a ten-minute wait for a departure to England. Typically, trains will also meet ferries and other crafts on both sides of the Channel, but check before you choose your ferry, in case there is a lengthy wait.
- British readers finally face a challenge at this point: finding the best combination of ferry and/or land transportation to get from their homes to the continent. Call a travel agent for information on when and where ferries leave your area, then prepare to juggle prices, discounts, arrival times, etc. Compare your best options

Flying within Europe

Consider the following example for a situation when flying makes sense. Greece is a very common destination for first-time travelers in Europe. Let's say you are in London, and want to go to the island of Ios and party yourself into a hospital bed. Ios is good for that. With a Eurail pass you would pay to cross the Channel (Eurail is not valid in England) by either Channel Tunnel train, ferry and train, bus, or whatever. You would then proceed, probably via Paris, to Rome, and on to the hellhole port of Brindisi, to catch a ferry to Athens. The train ride from Paris to Brindisi will take roughly eighteen hours. You then get on the ferry in Brindisi, pay a port tax and summer supplement (even with a ferry that takes Eurail passes), and then spend the night sleeping either on the deck or in a room full of smoke. The next morning you arrive in Patras on the west coast of Greece, and pay for a bus, or wait for a train, to Piraeus, the port of Athens, which will probably involve a transfer. At the port you pay full price for a ferry, and spend another night on deck on the way to Ios, where you arrive the next morning.

Sounds great, doesn't it? I've done it and it stinks. It's less painful if you start from Rome, but it's still eight hours from Rome to Brindisi. And you have to do the whole process in reverse to get back. The total cost, if you have a train pass, including couchettes, port taxes, etc, is around $120. Flying out of London to Athens, on the other hand, will cost about $200 round trip (or much less if you get a cheap flight with a no-frills airline), and you will arrive feeling like a human being instead of a piece of raw meat. The cost of flying is about $80 more than the cost of taking the train, but you avoid five days of almost constant and very unpleasant travel. Also, if you've got a Flexi Eurailpass, you save a whopping five travel days, at a cost of roughly $40 per day. With an unlimited pass, flying saves you time and misery. With a Flexi pass, it saves you time, misery, and big, big bucks. Even better, if you can get a flight from London directly to one of the larger islands, rather than to Athens, you don't need to think about the cost and hassle of the ferry. The pleasure of sitting on a beach sipping a beer while others are cursing their lives in Brindisi is worth it. And when you're ready to leave, you get on the plane and you get off a few hours later in London.

Other than Greece, the really incredible deals out of London are to Turkey, Egypt, and Israel – and to smaller European cities on the no-frills airlines. Check and see what deals are available when you arrive in London, and plan ahead if you are coming back and can take advantage of something. I recommend flying into Portugal almost as much as Greece – even at this date Portugal is quite isolated from the rest of Europe, and getting there from London will take several days of train travel.

Also, no matter how you get to one of these exotic locales, you may be able to get a cheap charter back to London. Don't count on this, though, if you have to catch a flight home on the day after your charter is due to arrive. Charter companies vary in their reliability and may leave you in the lurch.

with the expense of traveling to Ramsgate or Dover and leaving from there. Don't expect companies to give a full range of options – most will claim never to have even heard of their competitors. Also consider the availability of onward transport from your ferry's destination. A cheap ferry into an industrial port miles from the nearest train station won't seem like such a good deal after a long walk or taxi ride.

● When ferrying out of England, don't just think France. Ferries also go to Norway, Sweden, Germany, the Netherlands, and Spain. If your main destination is Scandinavia, consider one long ferry trip straight there rather than a short ferry ride followed by a long train journey. For someone going from London to, say, Oslo, a ferry would be competitive in terms of price and time with a train. And, again, there are good discounts for holders of InterRail and Eurail passes.

● Watch out for that one-hour cross-Channel time change.

The Channel Tunnel

The Channel Tunnel offers three-hour trips between London and Paris, and a two-hour forty-minute service between London and Brussels. Over twenty Eurostar trains per day run between London and Paris, and ten per day between London and Brussels. Any type of seventeen-country Eurail pass, a Selectpass that includes France, a France RailPass, Brit RailPass, or Benelux pass will get you a discount.

● Having taken the Channel Tunnel a number of times, I would describe it as an engineering marvel administered by a bunch of drooling idiots. In order to maximize profits, the fare structure for the Chunnel trains is set up exactly like those stupid airfares already mentioned. For the round-trip London to Paris run, there are no less than seventeen different fares, varying in price from as much as $658 to as little as $150 – though special offers can bring this down to $70. All of the worst parts of airfare pricing, such as mid-week fares, Saturday stay-over requirements and nonrefundable/nonchangeable fares, can be found here. What a shame. The passholder discount is about 30 percent. To get this discount you must activate your pass, but it will not cost a travel day for those with Flexi or Selectpasses.

● A regular train between London and Paris will cost a passholder about $70 and a train-pass travel day, and it takes about eight hours, making the tunnel a good idea despite the complicated fare structure. Just remember to treat the Channel Tunnel services as you would if you were traveling by plane: call as soon as you know when you want to travel, and watch those restrictions. For those on two- or three-week trips, it is definitely worth the price to save a day in Paris or London. Again, there are full details in Basics #2.

Creative transportation

If your train pass has run out or if you want to conserve one, or you never had one, you might want to consider one of the following ways of getting around.

Ride-sharing

Ride-sharing is highly recommended if you have more time than money, and is always worth an inquiry, unless you have an unlimited Eurail pass. Ride-share is also perfect if you lose your rail pass, or if the money you've budgeted for transportation is diverted to other and more gratifying uses. Ride-share is a sort of an organized hitch-hiking service, whereby drivers with extra room offer seats for sale through an agency. The agency then tries to match the empty seats with travelers going to the drivers' destinations. Most European countries have one or more of these agencies. As an example, Munich to Hamburg cost me €45 in total – dirt cheap compared with a train or bus ticket. The big disadvantage of this mode of travel is the uncertainty of finding someone going both where you want to go and when you want to go there. However, for someone who has no fixed schedule, who is happy to wander all over Europe wherever the next driver takes him, or someone who is trying to conserve Flexi pass days, this way of getting around is fantastic. I suppose other disadvantages could include being stuck for hours in a car with a cigar-smoking loudmouth possessed of a five-gallon bladder, but that hasn't happened to me yet. Also, even though ride-sharing is much safer than hitchhiking for women, if you are female and are uncomfortable getting into a car with a particular person, don't accept the ride. Or, you can ask only for rides from women, to be on the ultra-safe side. Enquire about ride-sharing services at tourist offices and hostels. Big cities are good, and big cities with universities are better. If you are near a university, you could always check out the college notice boards. Otherwise, consult the list on p.108, which is by no means comprehensive but covers the major national services I've been able to find.

Ride-share services

Austria – Mitfahrzentrale, Vienna ⓣ22/242 72 74.

Belgium – Taxi-Stop, Brussels ⓣ02 223 2310.

Denmark – Use It Center, Copenhagen ⓣ01.15.65.18; Interstop-Kor-Med-Centralen, Copenhagen ⓣ01.23.24.40.

England – Freewheelers: Bristol ⓣ01272/351 435; London ⓣ020/7738 6861; Newcastle ⓣ0191/222 0090.

France – Allostop-Provoya, Paris ⓣ01.53.20.42.42.

Germany – Mitfahrzentrale: Berlin ⓣ030/19444; Hamburg ⓣ040/19444; Hanover ⓣ0511/19444; Heidelberg ⓣ06221/19444; Munich ⓣ089/19444; Stuttgart ⓣ0711/603 885.

Greece – Salonik Allo-Stop, Thessaloniki ⓣ031/545 749.

Italy – Viavai, Bologna ⓣ051/495.523; Auto-Stop Firenze, Florence ⓣ055/280.626; Allonsanfan, Florence ⓣ055/655.0717; Immagine C.A.R., Milan ⓣ039/2266.5246.

Netherlands – Liftcentrale, Rotterdam ⓣ010/422 4835, ⓔinfo@liftcentrale.nl, ⓦwww.liftcentrale.nl.

Spain – Barnastop, Barcelona ⓣ93 443 06 32; Iberstop, Granada ⓣ95 829 29 20; Iberstop, Malaga ⓣ95 225 45 84; Dedo Express, Salamanca ⓣ92 326 72 88; MFZ, San Sebastian ⓣ94 327 83 51; Comparte Coche, Seville ⓣ95 490 75 82.

Sweden – Hitch Hiking, Stockholm ⓣ08/84 20 72.

Switzerland – Allostop, Geneva ⓣ022/329 65 88.

Ride-sharing and the Web are made for each other. Go to ⓦwww.liftcentrale.net or ⓦwww.hitchhikers.org, or try ⓦwww.allostop.com and click on the "Europe" link, or directly to ⓦwww.allostop.com/english/default.htm, for even more listings than those below. Be aware, however, that these services do come and go, and don't give up if the sites or numbers don't work. If they don't work, call the local tourist office and see if they can help you.

Hitchhiking

I've done it, but I don't recommend it, for obvious reasons. I once met a five-foot, ninety-pound, 16-year-old Polish girl who had hitchhiked, from Warsaw to Rome, alone. When she told me that I actually felt my skin crawl. If you do wish to hitch, remember that while the violent crime rate in most of Europe is relatively low, such crime does happen. Women should not hitchhike, alone or in groups. Period. Some tips for those who insist on hitching:

- Using a sign, especially for women, can be dangerous. Don't use one, and when someone stops, ask where they are going. That way the driver cannot lie about his destination to get you into his car.

- If at all possible, keep your luggage with you rather than in the trunk, and pull it out of the back seat before getting out of the car. If you put it in the trunk, you may get out at your destination only to watch your backpack disappear down the road in a squeal of tires. The same thing goes for gas and bathroom stops.
- Some hitchhikers use a flag to appeal to their traveling compatriots.
- Most student-oriented guidebooks usually have a few sentences on where to hitch out of major cities.
- Women who hitch (although I'm advising against this) will have rapid success in groups of three or less. Men in groups of one or more will be waiting a long time.
- Finally, if you are hitching, be very, very careful. If it feels wrong, it probably is wrong. A long walk or a bed for the night is better than a ride that ends up in robbery or worse.

I shoulda' gone by train

Once, when hitching in Italy, I had spent an entire morning baking in the sun and sucking exhaust fumes. At first, I found relief in profanity. When that failed me, I used blasphemy. As I stood there, a young woman came out of a nearby store, and began walking toward the road. Before she even got to the shoulder a Mercedes slammed on its brakes and pulled over in front of her. Without breaking stride she pulled the door open. She then asked a few questions, jumped in the front seat, and roared off, leaving me standing there. Such is the lot of the male hitchhiker.

Buses

If you do not have a rail pass, and need to get to a specific destination at a specific time, then buses are hard to beat for a cheap ride – and, believe me, they can be incredibly cheap.

Unfortunately, buses are also hard to beat for inflicting pain, and few experiences are as agonizing as a long or overnight ride on a crowded bus. Basically, you're paying for the low price with discomfort. This discomfort is somewhat mitigated if you are comfortable enough with your seat partner to sleep sprawled all over each other. I recommend buses if you have the specific time/place/need mentioned, and especially if the alternative is a long, expensive train ride. I once took a bus from Copenhagen to London. Yes, I was a pitiful, whimpering wreck by the end of the nineteen-hour trip, but it saved about $120 over a train ticket. For that kind of money, I can be miserable for one night.

7

Accommodations

Most travelers automatically think of hostels when they think of budget accommodations. Hostels usually are the cheapest and best way to go if you're on a tight budget, but there are exceptions, especially if you are traveling in a couple or a group. Two or more people can often find a room in a hotel or pension for about the same price as an equivalent number of hostel beds, and often with much better amenities. So, especially if you are in a group, don't simply march to the nearest hostel and ignore all other possibilities. Shopping around can save you time, keep you away from packed and noisy dorms, and maybe even save you money. This is where Commandments One, Two, and Three rear their happy heads in triplicate. If you are traveling light, it's much easier to spend some time going around to several places before choosing one. If you've arrived early, you have more options than someone who shows up as night is falling. And if you've planned ahead, you have a reservation somewhere, so you're not searching out of desperation.

After sleeping everywhere from plush resorts to rooftops, I can say that there is often no correlation between the quality of the experience you have in a place you stay and the price you pay to stay there. I have slept in very cheap places that were spacious, bright, and immaculately clean, and I have stayed in hotels that cost four times as much and were shabby, dark, and depressing. In the words of an old German traveler I met in Italy: "What I look for are clean bathrooms and friendly people. With those two, everything else I can live with."

One handy tip, which I will try and repeat elsewhere: Europeans like to travel too. Since they can get to major tourist attractions and major cities on weekends, they do this a lot. (At Neuschwanstein Castle in Bavaria, the most touristy of places, at least two-thirds of the crowd on the day I went chose the tour given in German.) Try and time your arrival at major cities, and your visits to major attractions, for days other than Friday, Saturday, and holidays.

In general, the price of accommodations declines as you move south and east. Don't go only to hostels in Portugal, Spain, Greece, and especially in Eastern Europe. In Scandinavia, on the other hand, hostels and camping are usually the only accommodations that are reasonably affordable, especially for solo travelers. In other countries, the size of the city may make the difference. For example, a hostel in a village in England I once went to charged £12 for breakfast and a bed in a very large, but very clean, dorm. In the same town, a beautiful little bed and breakfast charged £13 for a single room that looked like something out of *House and Garden*. The sweet old woman who owned the place made me sandwiches when I showed up after the local pub had closed, and proudly showed me pictures of her son, the Police Constable. It was worth the extra "quid," believe me.

The accommodation hunt

The cheapest, simplest, and most efficient way to hunt for accommodation is not to hunt at all. Ideally, you should avoid everything covered on the next few pages by taking a few minutes and finding your next accommodation before you leave the current place you're staying. The best way to do this is to ask around where you're staying and see if anyone knows a good place in your next destination. (A notice on the bulletin board can also work.) Remember, a guidebook's information is a year old, at best (although good places don't change too quickly). Another traveler can give you real-time information and first-hand experience.

If you do not have a room reservation when you arrive in town, prepare to play "Who's got a room?" No matter how you arrive in a city, even with your own transport, use the phone to search for a place, either out of your guidebook or from a tourist office. Using the tourist office can make your bed-hunting easier: they should have the latest information on local accommodation, they should know which places are full and which are not, and can often make a booking for you (they may charge a small fee for this). If the tourist office can't call for you, get a phone card and call around before heading out to look at places. Obvious? Of course. But you'd be surprised how many fall into the temptation of "This one's only five minutes away – let's just go there." Also, don't quit calling if the first place has beds. If it's a pit when you get there, you'll have to hike back to the station and start over. Find two or three places with rooms, start with the one that sounded closest, best, friendliest, cheapest, whatever you want, and go take a look. (It's a lot easier "to go take a look" if you're traveling light.)

When you arrive, ask a few questions. (1) Always ask to see the room you will be renting. Consider how noisy it will be at night. (2) Always ask how much the room will cost in total, with all taxes, fees, charges for breakfast and the like included, to avoid nasty surprises when you check out. (3) Take a good look at your fellow lodgers. A bunch of men with pencil-thin mustaches picking their teeth with stilettos is usually a bad sign. (4) If possible, ask someone staying there if they like it and if there is anything you should know. (5) Owners and staff may not show you the cheapest room first. If that is important to you, ask up front for the cheapest available, and then work up in price if you don't like it. (6) If you ask for a room and the person

behind the desk asks how long you will be staying, "three days" is probably the answer they're looking for (whether you plan to or not). If you're staying longer than three days, especially if the place isn't crowded, ask for a discount. You may get it. (7) If you are alone, and only doubles are available, ask if you can share with a single person who comes later. Or you may

A tale of two room hunts

Person A arrives in Paris at 8pm. He buys a phone card, and calls the first hostel listed in *Let's Go*. He gets an answering machine. He calls another hostel. It's full. He calls another hostel. Full again. He calls a fourth hostel, and is told that it doesn't take reservations, and that he will have to come by in person. Our traveler (wisely) checks his backpack into a locker and gets on the Metro. He arrives at the hostel at 9pm, only to find that it's now full. He parks himself by the phone at that hostel and (wisely) borrows a different guidebook and starts calling. Eight calls later he finds a place on the edge of Paris called the *Bugbite Bed and Breakfast*. He rides the Metro as close as he can, and arrives at the *Bugbite* at 10.30pm. When he gets there, he's told that he can only stay for one night – they're full the rest of the week.

Person B is in Bayeux on Monday, and wants to go to Paris on Thursday, so he can arrive before the weekend rush. He asks around at his hostel in Bayeux and is told that the *Posh Palace* is a fine place to stay. He calls the *Palace* to make a reservation. They're full. Is he dismayed? Au contraire, mi amigo! He calls around from the comfort of his hostel's common room, not really caring when the first six places he calls are full. (When you're not alone in a phone booth in a train station at night, you don't have to care as much.) Finally he finds a place called the *Dewdrop Inn* that is cheap, centrally located, and will take a reservation. He arrives in Paris and takes a taxi to his inn, paying with the money he saved by calling around. On the way, his taxi splashes water all over Person A, who is walking back to the station on his way out of Paris.

have to find a roommate yourself if you really want/need that room. Note that all these points imply that you have a choice of going somewhere else. If every place is packed except the one you're at, however, your choice will be easy.

If there is no tourist office in your town and nothing about that town in your guidebook, you're probably well off the beaten track. Good for you. To look for housing, ask some of the station staff if they know of a cheap place to stay. Taxi drivers are also potential sources of information, although they may not offer anything which does not involve a taxi ride. Hotels tend to cluster around train stations: even if they are out of your price range (and they may not be – station areas are often home to the cheapest places), they may be able to direct you somewhere else.

If the first place you go to is full, don't panic. First off, ask the owner/staff of the place that's full if they know of any place that isn't; you can be sure that he knows his local competition. Also ask if you can call from there, and potentially save yourself a long walk. If the owner can't help you at all, or if everything is full, return to the train station and start the whole process over. (This is when you will be blessing your light backpacks, and swearing to call me and thank me for harping on the idea of going light. You will forget as soon as you find a bed, but that's only human.) You may have to adjust the maximum amount you're willing to pay if things get really bad.

In a large city, one option to consider before paying a lot more is "commuting": staying outside of that city and traveling in by train each day. The accommodations you find in a suburb or small town will probably be cheaper, nicer, and less crowded than in the city center, and the money you save will probably offset the cost of the commute, especially if you have an unlimited rail pass that you can use

Agents and "touts"

When you arrive at train stations, especially if you are wearing a backpack, you may be approached by a bed agent or "tout" who tries to sell you on staying at his or her hostel, hotel, or private apartment. These people are rarely criminals, but they can represent all levels of accommodation, from the vile and bug-infested to the surprisingly nice. (Bugs outnumber nice surprises by about ten to one.) Most of the time they represent places the guidebooks have passed over, either accidentally or for a reason. Single women should be careful with these guys, just in case. Other travelers may want to give these places a look, but only after first grilling the tout (on the spot) about every aspect of the place. How much does it cost? How many beds per room? What floor of the building is it on? Are there lockers or a guarded luggage room? Is there a lock-out during the day for cleaning? Is there a curfew? How close is it to the metro/bus/tram stop? Is someone at the front desk all night? Can we get a room together? Are the dorms co-ed? How many beds per room was that again? Are there laundry facilities? And the one question that's sure to bring forth a lie: "How far is it from here?" "Five minutes" is the universal answer to that question – if you get there in ten, you're doing well. If you decide to go and look, when you get there, ask to see the room you will be staying in, take a long look at the bathrooms, and give the rest of the place the once-over. If it looks good, then consider it. In the Greek Islands, touts will usually meet you at the boat, and will sometimes be aggressive – though they'll just as often be sweet little old ladies with a room to let. If they don't meet you, you've got a problem. Start looking hard.

In Eastern Europe, especially in smaller towns, the "tout" may also be a grandmother offering a bed in her apartment, although these days she may have been replaced by a cellphone-wielding shark. These apartments are often a good deal, and can offer a glimpse into the realities of life after forty years of the Communist paradise. Ask the same questions before going to have a look, but don't give some nice old woman the third degree, and don't be too hard-nosed over a dollar or two.

for the daily round trip. If you're hosteling, you may find yourself doing this anyway, as hostels are often situated outside of city centers.

In a city or a small town, if it really looks as if you may not find any accommodation at all, and you can't commute, before you spend another five hours looking, give yourself an out. Check the train schedules. Find one going to a place listed in your guidebook. Call ahead to make a reservation. At least that way there is a bed somewhere with your name on it. If your search for a bed does come up empty, you can always get on a train and go to your reservation. And if all else fails, you can always catch a night train, with or without couchette.

Please be reassured that situations like this are rare, except in cases of late arrival in major cities or tourist centers, or if there is a major event taking place in the area (such as Easter in Nice, Oktoberfest in Munich, etc). In almost every case spending more money will guarantee finding a room. Rooms in the nicer hotels in a town will still be available long after all hostel and budget rooms in a city have sold out. If it comes to this, call around to the local hotels first. Don't expect a discount if you go in person; once you're in the lobby, the hotel knows they've got you.

Hostels

Because you will probably be spending a large amount of your time staying in hostels, I think they are worth a fairly long look. Starting at the beginning: hostels are shared accommodation, usually sex-segregated, consisting of five or ten to occasionally as many as forty beds per room or dormitory. Bathroom facilities are also shared. Usually there are some smaller rooms for families or couples, but these fill up fast. The actual building housing all of these beds can vary from spartan to highly elaborate: some hostels are little more than barracks, whereas others are in castles, beautiful old houses, or rustic farm buildings. Facilities you can expect in most hostels include luggage storage, lockers, a kitchen for those cooking for themselves, some kind of common room, and usually laundry facilities. Many places serve breakfast, and some, not many, serve dinner. Some hostels, especially those in Scandinavia, shut down from October 15 through April 1. And at least half of those open during the winter close their doors from December 20 through January 10.

The majority of hostels are part of the long-established Hosteling International group (formerly the International Youth Hostels Association), and their affiliated hostels are normally of a high standard – very clean, very well equipped, and in large cities, often very full. However, with the boom in budget travel more and more "private" hostels have opened, particularly in larger cities, and these can be as basic or as elaborate or as clean or as dirty as the owner chooses.

Other than always choosing an HI-affiliated hostel, there is no way to predict what your hostel will be like with certainty, especially since the other people staying there, especially in your room, will be a large part of your hostel experience. Your guidebook might have some information. In general, though, the older, smaller, and more isolated the hostel is, the better. Small towns are better than big cities, and the attitude of the hostel staff can make a huge difference. Having said that, one of the best nights of my life was spent in a large, full, private hostel in the center of Rome, which had a staff that genuinely hated humanity. The people who were staying there with me made all the difference, as did my willingness to get out and meet them. The hostel was terrible, the people were great.

Older hostelers

The term "Youth Hostel" has probably discouraged millions of somewhat older people from staying in hostels or from taking trips altogether because of the high cost of accommodations. However, except in Bavaria (where you must be 26 or under), there are no age restrictions in official HI hostels (which is partly why they were renamed), and I can't imagine any private hostels imposing them unless they were full. "Youth" may have priority in some other places, but during several months of traipsing around Europe at the advanced age of 31, and staying, for the most part, in hostels, I was never turned away because of my age. In fact, there were a number of times when I was the youngest person staying in a hostel, and once when I was the only one in the place below 50. While the clientele of most hostels does tend toward the young and the restless, you will find plenty of older travelers, especially Europeans, hosteling away happily into their 60s and/or 70s. Don't let the feeling that you may be "too old" stop you from traveling or staying in hostels. Uncouth youths who do not respect their elders can usually be silenced by reminiscing about seeing Jimi Hendrix or Jim Morrison live in concert, whether you did or not.

Modern hostels

Back in the Dark Ages, hostels were different than they are today. They were exclusively for the young, they closed during the day, there was a curfew at night, every guest was assigned chores, and supposedly more than a few were run like prisons by power-crazed wardens. I tell you this because any or all of these quaint features may still be present at the hostel you stay in. Chores have pretty much gone the way of the dodo, as have age restrictions. Some, I would guess maybe half of all hostels, impose some kind of lock-out so they can clean the place – usually from 10am to 3pm – but late-night curfews are getting few and far between, which can be unfortunate, as one drunk can wake up forty other people. Finally, I have yet to meet the proverbial "Attila the Warden."

Prices and reservations

Since all you are paying for in a hostel is a bed and the use of common facilities, they can be very cheap – I've paid as little as $6. In major cities, however, they can cost quite a bit – $28 was the most I've ever paid, although that was in central London. Other cities will fall between those figures, usually in the $16–22 range – dirt cheap compared with a hotel, but not as cheap as you'd like, I'm sure. As we will see in the section on pensions, a hostel may be the cheapest in terms of dollars per bed, but not have the privacy and quiet of a pension or a B&B. Also, crime in hostels does occur, but usually to the unwary or unwise.

Since hostels are the accommodation of choice for most budget travelers, they can fill up quickly, especially in the summer, especially on weekends, and roughly in order of how they're listed in *Let's Go*. If you are planning on staying in a hostel in a major city during June, July, or August, especially in an HI hostel, you *must* call ahead or risk a long hot walk followed by a longer, hotter walk back. Before I found that place I mentioned in Rome, I had metroed, bussed, and walked all the way out to the Ostello de Foro Italico, and waited an hour for the place to open (at the end of a one-hundred-person line). I never even saw the reception desk before they filled up. I should have called ahead. Maybe two weeks ahead.

One way to avoid this situation is to book a room from one hostel to another. Many HI hostels will call ahead for you, take a one-night deposit, and give you a receipt to take to your next place. Other hostels will call ahead to other places for you, especially if the two places are owned by the same person. Always ask other travelers for their recommendations, and if you can't get the numbers of the places they recommend, ask your hostel's staff for help in calling information or in making the calls. As mentioned in Chapter 3, "What to Take," the *HI Guide to Europe* is a good investment at about $12/£8, detailing every official hostel in Europe. Don't forget it, or the map HI sells, as these are essential if you are going to be hosteling a lot.

Hotels

Inexpensive hotels can be found in Europe that are livable and even nice, so don't think that "cheap" automatically means dirty or sleazy. For couples, or anyone who is sick of the hostel scene, there are small, cheap hotels out there that are clean and comfortable, if a bit basic. If you can handle a bathroom down the hall, you increase your choices tremendously. There are, of course, plenty of miserable roach ranches as well, so you may have to do some looking before finding something that matches your budget and standards.

Hotels that cost about the same may vary drastically in terms of cleanliness, comfort, and other amenities. It mostly depends on the owner's attitude. A ten-room hotel that has been run by the same family for two hundred years may lack modern plumbing or central heating, but I'd much rather stay there than at a new two-hundred-room hotel with an absentee owner and a lackadaisical staff. Be aware that traditional European hotels will almost always be cheaper and have more "atmosphere" than those that have been built to "American" standards and designed for tourists.

In Eastern Europe, or somewhere like Turkey, where hostels may be a bit dingy, even a single traveler can afford a hotel, while groups of two or more are good to go. The local hostel will obviously be cheaper, but not always by that much; and the question is really what you are willing to live with – or in. It's usually worth checking the hostel first, as you may get lucky. If it looks bad, move on up the ladder until your money and amenity standards converge.

Pensions

The distinction between a hotel and a pension is a blurry one. In my mind, a pension is run by an owner who lives on-site, and the building wasn't necessarily built to accommodate paying guests. The facilities are usually a bit more extensive than in a bed and breakfast (see opposite), and include things like a common room where the guests can sit and eat together, things that make the place "homier" than a hotel. Like the perfect bed and breakfast (run by the apple-cheeked woman who treats you like family), the perfect pension – full of colorful locals, run by a jovial man named Luigi who makes great pasta – is the Holy Grail of budget travel: much sought-after, rarely found. By definition, these places are almost never in guidebooks; otherwise, they would long ago have been swamped with travelers. When travelers do find places like this, they guard their names and locations as if they were state secrets. The atmosphere in a pension depends greatly on the attitude and personality of the owner. Some of these places fit the dream, others are clip joints full of creepy-crawlies with both two and six legs. In Italy, especially in rural areas, and in France, Spain, and Portugal – somewhere out there that perfect pension exists. But you won't find it in a guidebook.

Bed and breakfasts

There are more bed and breakfasts in Britain and Ireland than you can imagine – they're everywhere. Unlike the States and Canada, where B&Bs have certain snob appeal and can cost a fortune, the $30 B&B is alive and well in rural Britain. This can make rural travel very pleasant: since there are so many B&Bs available, you can blissfully ignore the rule of planning ahead *during the week*. Wander at will until the right place strikes you, settle there for a day or two, get a recommendation on a place in the next town or valley, and move on.

In small towns, in Britain and elsewhere, B&Bs are almost all sidelines: people in houses designed for large families with room to spare. They can be a bit more elaborate in larger cities, and there is an unfortunate tendency for ugly little bathrooms to be jammed into bedrooms to satisfy those too shy to walk down a hallway to the shower, or for extra "stars" in their official ratings. B&Bs are generally more expensive than hostels in cities, closer in price even a few miles away from the tourist hordes, and very competitive in the country, as previously mentioned. Try a rural B&B at least once on your trip if you can.

In other countries, the B&B/pension distinction, as detailed earlier, is not so obvious, nor are there so many per square meter.

Camping

I arbitrarily divide campers into two broad categories: those who are going for a backwoods/wilderness experience, and those who are camping in order to see the cities and countryside of Europe as cheaply as possible. Camping is indeed the cheapest form of accommodation in Europe, but be warned, it is much more enjoyable if you are traveling by car. Taking a train to a city or town and then carrying all of the normal budget traveler load, plus tent, stove, real sleeping bag, and other camping essentials out to a campground is often a daunting prospect. Consider this if you plan to use camping as your primary means of accommodation.

Before you plan on camping your way across Europe, think about how much you will enjoy living out of a tent for two months. Camping in Europe is a bit more settled than in other continents, and campgrounds are generally well equipped with amenities, especially in France. Nevertheless, sixty days in a tent is a long time. If you plan this, try and budget for at least a few nights in a bed. Tips follow for the tenting crowd:

- For the ultra-, ultra-budgeters, hitching rides from campground to campground with Europeans on vacations is sometimes possible, especially if you assure your ride that you won't ask for another one at the next campground.
- One very important piece of advice: expect and plan for rain. For backwoods types, even though you're not in the Rockies or the Sierras, don't underestimate British, and especially Scottish, weather. A change of a few hundred feet in altitude, or a very few minutes, can bring a total change in weather, from sun to blowing, chilly rain. Triple this warning in Scandinavia and in the former Soviet Union.
- Bring a good stove, as very few organized campgrounds allow fires. As mentioned in Chapter 3, "What to take," "Gaz" stoves are the standard unit all over Europe.
- Norway and Sweden allow "free camping," a great institution. Under the law, you have the right to camp anywhere on public or private land as long as you stay no longer than two days, clean up after yourself, and are not within 150m of any buildings. This can be a low-cost lifesaver in these expensive countries. In other countries, a polite inquiry to the local landowner may get you a low-impact, no-fire campsite.
- An International Camping Carnet, which is similar to a hostel membership card, is required at a few campgrounds and ignored in many others. For $35, you may get a discount, priority if the place is full, and, most important, you don't have to leave your passport with the campground office. They are available from Family Campers, 4804 Transit Road, Building 2, Depew, NY 14043, or you can buy them in Europe.
- Good books on camping in Europe are few and far between. Dedicated campers might want to get a copy of *Europa Camping and Caravanning*, available from Recreational Equipment, Inc. (listed in Basics #7), *Camping Your Way Through Europe* (Carol Mickelson, Affordable Adventures, Inc.), or the *Travellers Guide to European Camping* (Mike and Terri Church, Rolling Home Press).

Mooching off friends

Now here is the ideal accommodation if you can find it. Trading addresses and invitations is very common among travelers in Europe, and it may be worth changing your plans to accept an invitation. You will probably end up well off the tourist trail and get a glimpse into the real everyday life of your host's country. If you do accept such hospitality, remember that your hosts will probably be working or going to school and may not have the time to show you around. Plan to arrive on a weekend. It is also a nice gesture to spend some of the money you'll save on accommodation to take your friend(s) out, bring a gift when you arrive, or buy a truckload of beer and throw a party that destroys their apartment. It is considered bad form to be given an invitation and then arrive in town six weeks later and expect to be welcomed immediately. A postcard and/or phone call in the interim to alert your future hosts as to your intentions is both smart and polite.

Other accommodations

Other accommodations are as varied as the imagination: YMCAs, YWCAs, monasteries and convents in Italy (not much partying there), private homes – whatever turns up if you look beyond the guidebook. Even though you will probably be hosteling a lot, I do recommend trying out other options; you may be pleasantly surprised. Your local tourist office is a good start, and don't be shy about asking other travelers about unusual places they have stayed.

One possibility to consider, especially if you want a single room and some peace and quiet, is student housing. These are university residence halls that are opened to travelers when school is out for the summer. Rooms are usually quite small, simple, and clean.

Student housing in Prague

The unquestioned king of student housing opportunities has to be Prague, where a simply enormous complex of dormitories is partially open for business every summer. This is Communist architecture at its finest: concrete slabs and plenty of 'em. Scattered throughout this rabbit warren of about twelve high-rise dormitories are tiny bars, pubs, discos, stores, restaurants, and other facilities, all with incredibly cheap prices. Beer in the pub, for example, is cheaper per liter than soda from the stores.

This complex is also good for a glimpse at how students lived under the old system of government. Amid these bleak, depressing buildings it is still possible to get a tiny feel for what life was like before the "Velvet Revolution" of 1989 brought freedom to what was then Czechoslovakia.

Worth looking into, especially for a couple, or for a hostel break. As a bonus, you can talk to your friends about "your time spent at the London School of Economics." Student housing is usually listed in guidebooks, but you should also check at the tourist office if you're interested.

Sleep-inns and slum hostels

This is one accommodation option that you may only want to try if everything else is unavailable. Genuine sleep-inns, at least in my experience, open only in the summers, and are mainly there to keep people from sleeping on the streets when the local hostels are overrun (Amsterdam's "Sleep-Inn" is an exception and is open year-round). They are aptly named, since there is little to do but sleep in one of these places, and a bed is pretty much all they provide. Expect huge, crowded dorms full to the rafters. Imagine two doors, one saying "Beds 1–75", and the other "Beds 76–150". That's when you pray for the ghost of John Wesley Hardin to make an appearance, and with plenty of ammunition. These places are better than nothing, but are not real hostels – and sometimes they're

not even much of a cost-saver. For example, in Copenhagen, the *Amager* hostel has only two- and five-bed rooms, and charges 120 crowns (about $18) for breakfast and a bed in a five-bed room. It has a kitchen, laundry, playground, TV room, serves a hot dinner, and so on. The *City Public Hostel*, actually a sleep-inn, has the two dorms just mentioned, and a few smaller rooms, and charges 135 crowns ($20), with breakfast. The point is not that sleep-inns are run by bad people; they fill a need as best they can. However, if you end up in one of these places, get out as soon as possible. Don't make the mistake of thinking that all hostels are like this or that once in a place like this, you're stuck.

The same goes for some of the private "hostels" that appear like mushrooms after rain all over congested summertime Europe – slum hostels, basically. Imagine paying €20 (about $18) to sleep in a basement, with forty other people in one room, on dirty mattresses that are either on the floor or thrown on pallets. I don't have to imagine, because I've done it, and every single one of the other beds was full, so a lot of other people have, too. No facilities whatsoever, just a mattress and a bathroom.

These places are opened up, often temporarily, by greedy people who see a need and want to fill it as cheaply and profitably as possible. Their natural prey are those who wait until they arrive in town to find accommodations, and especially those who arrive late in the day, tired, loaded with stuff, and willing to take anything just to end the housing search and keep from sleeping in the train station that night. As I have said before, if you are going to a major city, especially in July or August, plan ahead, make reservations, and you may avoid having to join them.

Sleeping on trains

Sleeping on trains, surprisingly, does not save money so much as time. Especially on a short trip, days wasted sitting in a train are frustrating, and some people recommend traveling almost entirely by night train so the days can be spent sightseeing. If you could get a decent night's sleep, this might be true, but the various noises, stops, border crossings, and other disturbances that occur on any train journey mean this can be difficult for all but the heaviest sleepers. Bear in mind, also, that taking night trains cuts down on some of the best times to see Europe: mornings, and especially at night, when most cities come alive. That said, a night train here and there can be a sensible use of limited time. If you want to sleep on a train, on a budget at least, you have three options: a seat, a reclining seat in a compartment, or a couchette. There are also "hotel trains" and sleepers in first class, but you could charter a plane for the cost of one of those beds.

Sleeping in an upright seat is recommended only if you are Catholic and doing penance – and you must have done something pretty bad to deserve this. Reclining seats are better, especially if you are in a group, and especially if your group has the compartment to itself. However, whether or not you get a train with reclining seats is a matter of luck and simply depends on how the train happens to be constructed. They very rarely cost any extra. Note that the six seats in a compartment usually convert into only three "beds" (the bottom part of the seat pulls out, while the backrest can be pushed down), and you then have a choice of either sleeping foot to head to foot, and smelling feet all night, or head to head to head, and waking up with a person who mistakes you for their spouse or sweetie. Note also that if the train is half full or less, everyone can stretch out, and if it's completely full, nobody can. It is therefore worth your while to get in an empty compartment as early as you can, and then to look as unsavory as possible in the hope of warding off people. Groups of three or more should try to reserve seats in a single compartment for the same reason.

If you're prepared to pay a little extra, couchettes are, in my opinion, the way to go. Couchettes are benches that convert to separate bunks and are grouped four or six per compartment. It is always worth paying a few dollars more for a four-bed compartment. If you're in a large enough group, by all means try to get a compartment to yourselves and whoop it up. Sheets are supplied, and there is a total charge of about twenty dollars for bunk and linen, whether or not you have a train pass. Couchettes are sold without regard to age, sex, or marital status, and I truly believe the reservation agents delight in mixing strange groups together. When you are making a couchette reservation (and you should do so as soon as you know when you're leaving), ask for an upper bunk. These are quieter and a bit less liable to theft, and you don't have people climbing past you at odd hours.

Sleeping out, or in train stations

Before you do either of these, think long and hard about spending more money than normal, or catching a train somewhere else. Sleeping in stations used to be quite popular with penniless student travelers, but it is now less so. It is safer than sleeping in a park, especially if someone in a group stays up to keep an eye on things, but a train station at 3.30am does not attract the most lovable characters. You may be asked by security to show a ticket at some stations these days, especially if you look a bit "alternative". Setting up shop near some business that will stay open all night, or near the security office itself if possible, is a good idea.

Sleeping out – in parks, under bridges, wherever – is taking your personal safety and putting it squarely in the hands of any person who wanders by where you are sleeping at 3am. No thanks. If against all sane advice you choose to do this, leave anything you don't want stolen in a locker, go in a group (with people you know well), and try and find some-place out of sight.

One option to consider before doing either of these things is sleeping at an airport if there is one within public transport range. Airports are always more isolated than train stations, and they don't get the late-night wanderers that train stations attract. However, if you're at this point it's probably time to head home.

Some accommodation basics

It's amazing how easy it is to take certain creature comforts for granted – and also how quickly you can adapt to not having them once you're out on the road for a while. Not every facility will be available to you at your homes away from home – unless you're living in four-star luxury – so it pays to know what you'll be up against.

Laundry

Get used to the idea of washing your socks and underwear in the sink and then hanging them to dry where you can contemplate them as you fall asleep. Laundromats, except in Britain, can be hard to find, and they are expensive everywhere – figure about $6 a load. Yes, laundry is a pain; yes, it's inconvenient and time-consuming; and yes, it's necessary, especially if you're trying to travel as light as possible. However, you may adjust your standards somewhat. Those who are used to washing something after one use usually go through a short process of reassessment in Europe, and after a week have made rules like: "If it's dirty, and I keep it in my backpack for more than 48 hours, it comes out clean." The usual tips:

- If you are staying in hostels, there may be washing machines available at stiff prices. Ask around if you can share a load with someone.
- The best way to dry something, especially in southern Europe, is to put it on you and head out the door. When it's 107 degrees in Seville, a wet T-shirt can be a godsend. Not advisable in muggy climates.
- A small (250ml) bottle of dishwashing liquid with a secure cap is enough for one person (who is not overly fastidious) for about one month. Buy it in Europe, and don't forget to tape the cap down, or else!
- Many pensions and family-owned hotels prohibit the washing and drying of laundry in rooms, although this rule is violated all over Europe. You shouldn't be too brazen, though, putting wet clothes on wood furniture, slopping water around, and so on. If you're clean and discreet, they probably won't mind. If they make a specific point of telling you not to do laundry, don't. At most hostels you could dry clothes on the flagpole and they'd hardly notice.

Showers

You will occasionally see some hostels or other places advertising "24-hour hot showers". They advertise them for a good reason: Some places only permit the use of showers, or provide hot water, at certain times. The reason for this is cost, since it is expensive to keep a tank of hot water heated during the day, when nobody is likely to use it. So, sensibly, the heat is turned on in the morning and evening, and off during the day and night.

Sometimes you are the person who turns on the heat. If you have a shower with an individual hot-water heater in your room, look for a switch, hit it, and then wait for about twenty minutes. Some places, but not many, may charge per shower. On the same subject, late risers in many hostels and small hotels can expect freezing showers that make glacial snowmelt feel warm and toasty. It usually pays to be the first one to the bathroom in the morning.

Eurotoilets

How can I put this? There are "facilities" in Europe that the average traveler is not familiar with, and may have to face at a time of desperate, diarrhea-induced panic. These are the bidet, and the two-footed "straight shot".

A bidet is that funny-looking oval porcelain thing with the faucet that shoots straight up. In the words of Crocodile Dundee, it is for "washing off your backside," and is also a primitive form of birth control. It is not for laundry, nor is it for washing dishes, nor is it normally used for an ice tub to cool off beers and grapes, although I have seen it used for all of those things. Unless you are extremely and justifiably angry at your hosts,

The shower from heaven

A few years ago, November found me and three traveling companions boarding the Hurtigruten, the Norwegian coastal steamer, on a trip to the Lofoten Islands. After we had shaken the snow off our clothes and laid claim to a corner of the forward lounge, one of the guys announced that he was going to go look for the ship's shower. His announcement was met with dubious grunts in three languages; after weeks of dribbling showers in freezing Scandinavian bathrooms, we didn't expect anything different on the boat. Our friend returned an hour later, all pink and wrinkled. "That was the best shower of my life," he murmured with a glazed expression of bliss. "You must try it." A few minutes later I walked into the shower room, a bare steel compartment with a shower head sticking straight down out of the ceiling. Without much hope I turned the knob, and was instantly buried under a cataract of wonderfully hot water that came thundering out of that innocent-looking shower. The water was heated by the ship's engines, and was in almost unlimited supply, which was a very good thing for the other passengers. For the next three days my friends and I were without question the cleanest backpackers in Europe, as the trip quickly turned into a series of snowball fights, snow-covered Norwegian port towns, and refuge from the cold in the shower from heaven.

defecating in bidets is not a good idea. The French love these things, for some reason.

A "straight shot" usually comes as an unpleasant surprise to most tourists. The door opens, to reveal not a lovely porcelain throne, but a very shallow basin about three feet square, with a couple of raised places to stand upon, and a small, evil-smelling hole leading to a seething troll-infested pit too horrible to contemplate. Evidence of the aiming ability, kidney function, and recent diet of the last five or six users can be all too apparent. Toilet paper may be only an ancient memory.

These facilities (the norm for most of the world, by the way) are most common in France and southern Europe. They may make an appearance in public toilets anywhere, however, as they are cheap, easy to clean and maintain, and difficult to vandalize. If you don't like them, realize that the other option would probably be no facilities at all. Call it a cultural experience, and mind your aim. Using one of these while drunk and balance-impaired can have disastrous consequences.

One final thought . . .

No matter where you stay, write down the name and address of the place, and take it with you when you head out for the first few times. As ridiculous as it may sound, it is very easy to forget exactly where you are staying, since many hostels have similar names and may be packed into the same general area. If alcohol is involved, it is even easier. Yes, I have done this, and it's finally funny now . . . twelve years later.

Money matters

There are three perennial issues concerning money while traveling in Europe: how much do I need, in what form should I carry it, and how can I best exchange the different currencies still used in Europe? These three subjects, and particularly the last two, can cause no end of headaches and extra expense. For example, if the first place you trade money is in a hotel and you get into the habit of doing so, it will cost you big, big bucks by the end of your trip. "How much should I take?" was dealt with in Chapter 2, "Budgeting"; now it's time to fight it out with the other two issues.

Changing money

When changing money you will lose value in any one of four different ways:

- With a percentage of the total amount changed.
- With a flat fee.
- With a minimum fee.
- With the exchange rate itself.

Here's an example:
Bank A is offering a rate of 1.6 Swiss francs per dollar, with a 3-franc minimum fee or a 1-percent commission.

The euro has landed

After decades of talking about it, most of Western Europe has a common currency. A little history, before the practical details.

The euro was designed to be a common medium of exchange that, ultimately, would be used by all members of the European Union. Not only would that eliminate the problems of changing money, but it would unite the countries of Europe against the rest of the world economically, allow cross-border banking and borrowing, and ultimately, tie the individual countries of Europe tighter to the bloated EU bureaucracy. Those most in favor of the euro even saw it competing with the US dollar as an international medium of exchange.

Well, that was the plan, at least. When the euro was introduced on New Year's Day, 1999, it was worth $1.17, and "experts" predicted it would rise after introduction. Instead, to the delight of dollar-bearing travelers, the euro's value against the dollar promptly dropped like a lead balloon. Six months after introduction a euro was worth $1.03, and it eventually plunged to about $0.87. The gold rush days of the Amazing Falling Euro are now over, unfortunately, and the euro is back up to almost exactly one American dollar. Also, the idea of one currency has not caught on completely, as the table below shows:

Euro Nations		Non-Euro Nations
Austria	Ireland	Britain
Belgium	Italy	Denmark
Finland	Luxembourg	Norway
France	The Netherlands	Sweden
Germany	Portugal	Switzerland
Greece	Spain	All Eastern European countries

The euro was a first step towards European integration, for better or for worse, and will have profound effects on the future of Europe. For the traveler, however, the euro is purely good. As you will see it the next section, few travel issues can be as irritating and annoying as changing money, and while the exchange booth and the hidden commission aren't gone entirely, it really is a joy to travel from Lisbon to Hamburg or Athens to Amsterdam and only use one currency, instead of ten.

The advice which follows on changing money is necessary for two reasons: (1) you will still have to buy euros at least once during your trip, and (2) odds are good you will need to buy other currencies as well. You might want to drink an espresso or two before reading further.

Bank B is offering a rate of 1.65 Swiss francs per dollar, with a 2-percent commission or a 1-franc minimum fee.

Which is the better deal for changing $50?

The answer is that Bank B is the winner. Bank A will charge its minimum fee of 3 francs, since the commission of 0.8 francs (1 percent of 50 x 1.6) is less than its minimum fee. Bank B will charge 1.65 francs (2 percent of 50 x 1.65) since 1.65 is greater than its minimum fee. So for $50, Bank B is better. Be careful, though. To change $500, Bank A is better, and will only charge 8 francs, while Bank B will charge 16.5 francs. For large amounts, Bank A wins by a mile.

I'll bet 95 percent of you just had your eyes glaze over. Seems like those miserable word problems you thought you left behind in high school doesn't it?

Who needs this on vacation? You arrive at a train station tired, hot, and sweaty, and you've got to deal with this nonsense, and when you do, you still have the feeling that you've been taken. So remember the following:

- Banks, the larger the better, are almost always the best places to change money. They may not be in the train station with flashing rate boards, but they will have the lowest fees and the best rates. It is worth your while leaving the train station to find one, especially for changing large amounts. (Holland is a notable exception to this rule, where all medium- to large-sized train stations have change booths that charge the same as any bank.)
- When trying to compare two money-changing facilities, forget about the advertised rates. Ask the question: "If I give you this many dollars, how many francs, marks, pounds, etc, will you give me after all of your fees and commissions?" That's the bottom line.
- Money-changing facilities at airports and at borders almost always have very poor rates and/or high fees. If you have to use them, try to find one with low fees and only exchange enough money to get you through your first night, or to a bank.
- In general, for a small amount, like $20, look for low or no fees. For large amounts, look for a good exchange rate and a flat fee, not a percentage.
- Change bureaux are much more slippery and hard to pin down than banks. Beware of large minimum fees: a £2 minimum will cost you more than 30 percent of your money if you only change $10.

- Hotels and hostels almost always have the worst rates, but may not charge a fee at all, and can be good if you have only a small amount to change. Just don't use them too much.
- It is always better to change $100 than to change $50 on two separate occasions. If you are traveling in a group, change all your money together, and only pay the fee once.
- Larger denomination dollar bills and travelers' checks – one hundreds and occasionally fifties – sometimes get a slightly better rate than smaller amounts.

WARNING: Once you have crossed a border, coins almost always become unexchangeable scrap metal. If you are coming back to a country, save enough to make a few phone calls on your return. If you are not coming back, change all your coins in the country that issued them, or spend them before leaving. International ferries will accept coins from both countries they serve, but other than this coins can almost never be exchanged once a border is crossed. You might be able to exchange larger-denomination coins at major international airports, but it's not worth taking the chance. A pocketful of useless change can be an expensive lesson for the novice traveler, especially with Danish twenty-krone pieces (worth about $3) and British two-pound coins (worth a whopping $3.20 each). These make lousy souvenirs.

Carrying and accessing money

Travelers' checks

In my opinion, travelers' checks are damn near obsolete, a holdover from the time before electronic banking. Back then it was impossible for banks to efficiently communicate information about the validity of a person's personal check across continents. Since nobody wanted to carry big wads of cash, travelers' check companies could sell their guaranteed checks as a kind of universal currency. Well, we don't use rotary phones and typewriters very much anymore, and that's how I feel about travelers' checks. It is far simpler and more convenient to walk up to an ATM and pull out a few hundred bucks in local currency than it is to find someone willing to cash a travelers' check for a fee. Travelers' checks also have the drawback that you pay a commission twice: once when you buy them, and then again when you cash them – though this may be avoidable (see below). In any case, ATMs are sprouting up everywhere, even in small towns.

The one good thing about travelers' checks is that they can be replaced if lost or stolen, although this is not nearly as fast, simple, or easy as commonly believed. Generally, you will need the serial numbers of the checks that were lost/stolen, and the date and place of purchase. If you do get travelers' checks, keep at least one list with you (separate from the checks, of course) and keep another list at home in an obvious spot. Study the refund procedures for your specific company very thoroughly before leaving, as they can sometimes be complicated. You can't just pick up a phone, say "I lost my checks," and expect replacements to be delivered to you in an hour. No way.

I would use travelers' checks as backups: bring about two hundred American dollars in checks and hang on to them for emergencies. By the way, if you're going to get checks as a backup, get American Express. Other types of checks are far less widely accepted than Amex, and Amex has plenty of offices overseas. Although Thomas Cook is a widely recognized name in the world of travelers' checks, be aware that they may deny you a refund on lost or stolen checks if they think you weren't careful enough with them. When cashing checks of any kind, you will need your passport for identification. And finally, it's "check," not "cheque," or I'll hit you in the neque.

ATM cards

One of the most beautiful short train journeys in the world is the Flåm railway in Norway, which winds off a main rail line down a canyon to the tiny town of Flåm, which sits at the head of one of

the most majestic fjords in Norway. After rattling past waterfalls, massive granite cliffs, and little postcard farms, the train let me off near the ferry landing in Flåm. Near the dock was a little glassed-in hut with a foot of grass growing off its roof. Inside the hut was an ATM. Out of curiosity I walked in, stuck in my card, and walked out one minute later with a couple of hundred Norwegian crowns which would later be debited from my checking account back in Florida, at an exchange rate better than any I had seen in Norway.

Needless to say, ATMs can be pretty darn convenient; in fact, they're my primary means of obtaining money while in Europe. Some tips on ATMs:

- Check that your current card, or a new one you obtain for your trip, is connected to systems worldwide. Obviously this is essential. Connecting your card to the Cirrus or Plus system, or both, is a good start.
- Try to get a card from your bank that does not have a transaction fee. Almost all credit cards can also be used as a debit card but will charge a hefty fee or percentage when you use it as such.
- The obvious weakness of ATM cards is that you are extremely dependent on that little piece of plastic. For that reason, don't rely on them completely; always have at least one hundred, and probably two hundred, dollars in cash or travelers' checks on hand. If you have this much, and lose your card, you can survive until you get another one sent from home. That said, you could avoid such an emergency by bringing at least two cards that can access your account, and only carrying one at a time.
- Visit ATMs during the day, and keep an eye out even then. Don't get fixated on the little buttons and forget to watch your back.

Credit and charge cards

Credit cards can be very, very handy for those with, uh, cash flow problems. I strongly recommend getting one before you go, even if it's only one of those Citibank cards that are handed out like party favors in student unions all over the country. The whole problem of credit cards as a way to get sucked into debt slavery is not the issue here; if you are in trouble in Europe, these can be a lifesaver. As a last-ditch disaster aid, a credit card is the next best thing to a hundred-dollar bill in your shoe. For an example of this, rent the movie *The Sure Thing*.

- If you lose a credit card, only look for an hour or two before calling the company and beginning the cancellation/reissue procedures. If you know one has been stolen, call immediately. Credit card companies are a lot better about taking your money than refunding it.
- Many credit cards can be used to withdraw money from ATM machines. Just request a PIN from your credit card company and you have another way to get hold of cash in an emergency. Expect to get nailed with hefty fees when you withdraw this way, however.
- To avoid coming home to overdue bills, leave some stamped envelopes with credit card payments with someone reliable, who can mail them off during your trip.
- Note that an American Express card, with a passport as further identification, can be used to convert personal checks into local currency at some Amex offices in large cities. This can be quite useful for those willing to pay $75 a year for a card. Card holders can also use some Amex offices as mail pick-up points.
- Some people pay for most of their trip with plastic and avoid cash as much as possible. If you do this, remember that the exchange rate may change between the day that you charge and the day you get your bill, and may cost, or save, you some money, depending on which way your home currency goes. Also, if you use a credit card authorization for a deposit, make sure that the authorization is taken off your account as soon as possible, preferably while you watch. For example, if you rent a moped a $300 fee may be placed on your card until you return the moped. It's up to you to make sure that when you do return it, the authorization is removed. If you don't, it will stay charged against your account and reduce your available credit until taken off.

Cash

Money talks, in no uncertain terms, with no accent, in the local language, everywhere in the world. Always keep at least some of this wonderful stuff on hand. Generations of travelers have been frightened into thinking that carrying cash while traveling is something evil by years of American Express commercials. Nonsense. Carry some cash beyond your daily needs, but don't carry too much. How much is too much? I guess the answer to that is another question: how much can you afford to lose? Changing anything much below a hundred dollars at a time, though, will force you to the bank or ATM machine endlessly, and make you spend a great deal more in commissions than you need to. Also, a hundred-dollar bill, or the equivalent in local currency, stuck in a jacket lining or someplace else where you will not use it day-to-day can come in very handy, and not just in case of disaster. Public holidays, late arrivals, and/or incompatible ATMs can all cause inconvenience. Cash-in-hand is the universal inconvenience remover.

Wiring money

In case of disaster, you might be able to have money "wired" from home in a matter of hours, if you're in a big town or city. Wiring money is simple – someone hands over a wad of cash or a credit card in one office, the company takes a whopping fee, and you get the remainder paid to you in another company office. The fees for doing so are outrageous – as much as five to ten percent, for what amounts, in this modern age, to a phone call.

Western Union is the most famous company that offers this service. Their number in the US and Canada is ☎1-800/325-6000. If Western Union can't help you, try Moneygram at ☎1-800/926-9400, which offers a similar service at similar fees. They might serve locations that Western Union can't, and vice versa.

The State Department Citizens Center for Emergency Services may also be able to help Americans get money while abroad or help out in an emergency. Be advised, however, that this office provided me with the worst phone service of any organization I contacted in writing this book. The most incompetent of the tourist offices I spoke with was light years ahead of the State Department of the United States of America in terms of professionalism and service. How sad. Their number, for what it's worth, is ☎202/647-5225. Other nationalities should contact their embassies and hope for the best.

Value-added tax

Many European countries are expensive in part because of value-added tax, which is like a super-hefty sales tax and averages about 17 percent. If you are buying something expensive and leaving the country afterward, you can often get some of this tax refunded (many countries require a sizeable minimum purchase before you qualify for the refund). But, if you do make a major purchase, this can save big bucks, and can also make something that you couldn't afford without the refund fit into your budget. The procedures for doing this are usually complicated, and should be explained by a tourist office or at a more upscale store. Look for the blue-and-red or blue-and-silver signs that say "Tax Free for Tourists" – these places can give you a check for the amount of tax you have paid on the spot, and this can usually be cashed at the airport or sent in after you get home. If you wait until you get home, don't count on getting your refund right away.

In sickness and in health

Why might you be more likely to get sick while traveling in Europe, you ask? Well, let's see. You're on the move constantly, you're under a fair amount of stress, eating unfamiliar foods at irregular intervals, meeting lots of people, probably drinking more than usual, inhaling mass quantities of secondhand smoke, sleeping less, and when you do sleep it's usually in close proximity to large numbers of other people. Gee, I wonder why you might get some sort of bug after two months of that.

Despite that rather grim, but realistic, review of the situation, traveling for a summer is not equivalent to a death sentence by typhoid. However, recognize that your system will be stressed by a number of things, and plan accordingly. Stay well, rather than get well, is the best policy. Some thoughts on staying well:

- Heat, and staying hydrated, is definitely a concern, particularly in Greece, Portugal, Spain, and Italy. Most of the tourists wandering around Rome or Madrid in July and August seem to be carrying 1.5-liter bottles of water, which is a great idea. When it's hot, one of these bottles per day is an absolute minimum, while two is much better, and three is optimum. When you are moving around, and it's hot, it is difficult to drink too much water. Heat exhaustion and/or dehydration are serious problems, and thirst is not a reliable indicator of either. If you're really burning up, or you have symptoms like headaches, cramps, nausea, or vomiting, don't ignore them. Get to some place air-conditioned, get at least a liter of water and a pinch of salt into you, and start thinking about an emergency-room trip if you don't feel a lot better very soon. If you are older or especially heat-sensitive, this section goes double for you. When it's 103 degrees in Rome, take a taxi rather than walk two miles to the cathedral. Finally, there is a good reason for the tradition of siesta in Southern Europe. During the blazing hours of the afternoon, a cool room, a shady tree near a pond or fountain, or in the fountain itself, are all good places to be.

- Tap water in most European countries tastes like skunk urine. It may be safe, and it is safe everywhere in Western Europe except possibly southern Italy, but it still tastes terrible. Don't trust water in Greece, Turkey, Morocco, Eastern Europe, and Russia. Bottled water is available cheaply everywhere, although it will often be carbonated. To tell the difference, if you can't read the label, squeeze the bottle. Plastic bottles of carbonated water will feel harder than noncarbonated.

- Bring along some vitamin and mineral supplements, and (unlike me) take them regularly. Those in hard tablet form (not soft gel tabs) should be all right without refrigeration; call the number on the bottle to be sure. Also, bring along a supply of any drugs you need, and the prescriptions as well, to satisfy inquiring border guards. Check with your pharmacist on any prescription drug refrigeration requirements.

- The best way to prevent colds and most upper respiratory infections, believe it or not, is to wash your hands often, especially when you are living and eating among large groups of people. This prevents transfer of germs from hands to mouth.

- On one recent trip to Europe I went for an eighteen-mile stroll up and down hills on the third day of my trip. Needless to say, I got a set of blisters that made strong men sick when they saw them. I got them because I was stupid and lazy and didn't prepare for my trip by getting away from my computer and out into the world. Learn from my mistakes. You will be walking a lot on any trip to Europe, even if you're not going hiking: there are literally miles of corridors in the Louvre, for example. Take the time to get out and walk a bit before you go, preferably in the shoes and with the pack you are going to take with you, or you may be hobbling for your entire trip. Once I saw the Uffizi Gallery in Florence with a hole in the front of my right foot exactly the size, shape, and depth of two stacked quarters. It was not fun.

- A blister is a natural sterile dressing for the injured area. If you do get a blister, hard as it may be, leave it alone, and it will eventually take care of itself. Not always possible, I know, but still advisable.

- Sunburn, like blisters, can make your trip utterly miserable if you overdo it at the beginning. Some of the English and Irish tourists you'll see in Spain and Greece look like they've been sprayed Day-Glo pink. An extra hour spent in the sun can result in days of suffering. Sunscreen costs the earth in Europe, so bring a good-sized bottle of factor fifteen or better, and use it, particularly for the first few days.

- The Transylvanian Trots, the Hershey Squirts, Delhi Belly, the Orient Express, the Evacuation of Paris: they all mean diarrhea. Stay close to a bathroom, drink plenty of clean, bottled, or boiled water with a little salt, and/or flat soda (not coffee), and be careful not to get dehydrated. When in doubt as to the severity of an attack, there is no doubt about what to do: swallow your pride and see a doctor. Greasy food, particularly that processed mystery meat cooked on vertical spits, is a prime suspect in this problem, as are salads, and drinks with ice if the local water is suspect. Plain, preferably live, yoghurt can be very soothing to the system if this occurs. If you are going out in the wilderness, especially in Greece, Turkey, Morocco, or Russia, some packets of rehydration salts would be a smart thing to carry, just in case.

- If you are getting sick, admit it to yourself and take a break. Don't catch that twelve-hour night train to Budapest. By taking a break, I mean spend a bit more money, get a single or double room, down a liter or so of orange juice and a couple of packages of yoghurt, get twelve hours' sleep, and then take it easy the next day. Your body will thank you. Don't feel as if you have to keep going to get the most out of your trip. Visiting a museum while sick as a dog is not going to be a very worthwhile experience. Relax for a day or so, then continue the death march through the museums of Europe.

- If you are really sick or injured, your embassy, which should be listed in your guidebook, will be able to recommend an English-speaking doctor. Also, remember that the United States is the home of horrendously expensive health care. In Europe it's cheap by comparison, and may be free, even to travelers, in some countries.

- An insurance policy bought specifically for your trip is usually expensive in relation to the coverage provided, and may or may not be worth it to you. Travelers who are a bit older may wish to consider it more thoroughly. The policies that pay for you to be flown home are in my mind a dubious value. As long as you are in Western Europe, you will get fine medical care should disaster strike. Americans returning to the States may boost their hospital bill by a factor of ten. Before you buy a new policy, check to see if your old policy, if any, has something about evacuation already in it, or if an add-on can be bought for something less than a new policy. The prices on all these policies vary widely, and the coverage is often no better than what the buyers of ISIC cards receive. If you are eligible for any of the cards mentioned previously, buy one first and then see how much more coverage a separate policy will get you. Wade through the pages of fine print to see what you are really buying. For those with something that makes an injury more likely, such as a bad back or a knee that's been operated on, and for those interested in mountain climbing, kayaking, or other more dangerous sports, a policy to get you home may be a good idea.

- No vaccinations are compulsory for traveling in Europe that aren't compulsory in the States or Canada, though you might want to consider tick encephalitis (see below) or hepatitis if traveling in Turkey, Morocco, or the former Soviet Union.

- Not surprisingly, AIDS is as prevalent in Europe as elsewhere in the developed world. Make sure you're as cautious as you would be at home.

WARNING: For those going into the woods – especially in Scandinavia, Central and Eastern Europe, and Russia – be aware of a disease called tick encephalitis (encephalitis is a swelling of the brain). Since it is spread by ticks, take precautions against being bitten, such as long pants, bug repellent, something to cover your head, and so on. Before setting out into the woods, get local advice from a knowledgeable source about the danger in a particular area. There is a vaccine for this disease available in Europe, but not elsewhere. It's probably worth getting if you're planning a camping trip to a high-risk area.

10

Communications

The days of operators, transatlantic cables, telegrams, and all of the old images of communicating with Europe are gone with the wind. In today's information-driven world, Europe is only an electronic microsecond away. The mail can take a while to get through, but, except in some parts of Eastern Europe, it is almost always possible to call home quickly and easily, or keep in touch over cyberspace. It's a small world, and getting smaller.

Phones and international calls

I remember once speaking with a friend who was planning to leave for Europe two weeks later. When I mentioned that she should make a hostel reservation (she was going to start in Paris), she said she was putting it off until she figured out how to call. She had a point: I had never made an international phone call before my first trip to Europe, and I suspect some of you may not have either. So, to make that reservation before you head out, or to call abroad for any other reason, here's an example of dialing abroad to a hostel in Paris from the United States:

☏011–33–1–48–42–04–05.

Stay in Touch & Save!

Visit *www.roughguides.ekit.com*
or call toll-free 1-800-707-0031 in the US

ContactMe   **www.roughguides.ekit.com**

NAME

To leave me a FREE voicemail: Dial 1-800-706-1333

Press ✻ 2 & enter my eKit account #

And leave me a message!

Or send me an email:

Powered by
ekit

ContactMe   **www.roughguides.ekit.com**

NAME

To leave me a FREE voicemail: Dial 1-800-706-1333

Press ✻ 2 & enter my eKit account #

And leave me a message!

Or send me an email:

Powered by
ekit

Carry this card with you!

To a make a call:

1. Dial the access number for the country you are in, from any touchtone phone

2. Enter your eKit account #

   & Press # followed by your PIN

   & Press #

3. Press 2 , then dial the country code, area code and phone number

   Follow instructions for additional options.

Powered by

ROUGH GUIDES

"011" is the international access code for dialing out of the United States to any country. Dialing this prefix puts you on the international lines. Other countries use different prefixes, and these are listed on the inside front cover of this book.

"33" is the country code for France. Each country in the world has a code, and the pertinent European ones are also listed on the inside front cover. No matter what country you're calling from, the country codes remain the same – for example, the code for France is always "33."

"1" is the French area code for Paris. These codes may begin with a "0" if dialed from within the country, but this "0" should always be dropped if dialing internationally. For example, Central London's area code if calling from Oxford is "0207"; if calling from Kansas City, Kenya, or Singapore it's "207." Area codes should be listed with local numbers, or will be in the city information sections of your guidebook. The remainder is the local Paris phone number of the hostel.

Even now it still amazes me that I can pick up a phone and be speaking to someone in Paris or Rome in a matter of five seconds. Don't hesitate to call ahead for that first place to stay. If you don't call, you'll worry about where you're going to sleep all the way across the Atlantic.

Calling internationally within Europe

Calling between countries in Europe is about as easy as calling between states in America or Australia, which makes sense since the distance is usually shorter. The procedure is exactly like the above. Each country has its own international access code (listed at the end of this book); after this you dial the country code of the country you are calling, the area code (dropping the "0" if it is the first digit in the area code), and then the number.

To call that same hostel from London:

☏00-33-1-48-42-04-05.

The *only* difference in calling from England is that the British international access code is "00" instead of "011."

Calling home from Europe

In most of Western Europe you will be able to phone directly home in seconds. In Eastern Europe, some phone systems are more modern than others, and you may need to use an operator, or a direct phone service, if you can't say "please reverse the charges" in Polish. Your guidebook should give the details, as most of the less modern countries are catching up in a hurry. In any country where there is a real problem direct dialing, go to a hotel and ask for help. It may be more expensive, up to twice as much as a regular call, but you will almost surely be able to get through.

To call home cheaply, pay for a call, or call collect only long enough to spit out your phone number for a call back (call at a cheap time for the folks at home to call you). In many countries, you can also buy cheap-rate phone cards. You just dial a given number (from any phone – private or public), type in the PIN given on the back of the card, and then call the number you need; calls to the US and Australia can cost as little as $0.05 per minute. The cards are on sale at shops (typically tobacconists), which generally have various posters up in the window advertising all the different cards and their rates.

To call home, you will need the international access code for that country, the country code ("1" for the United States), and the area code and number, without another "1." To call information in Oakland, California, from Warsaw, you would dial:

☎00-1-510-555-1212.

Direct telephone services

For those with AT&T, Sprint, and MCIWorldCom credit cards, all of these companies offer direct dial services that can be used to phone home to the States or Canada. Those without cards can use these services to call collect. Be warned, though, that the *first one minute of these services will cost you a bundle* – as in five dollars for the first minute, and then about a dollar a minute after that. It is much cheaper to use coins or a card to call home, and then have them call back, or to use one of the cheap-rate phone cards mentioned above. If you just want to leave an answering machine message of "I'm alive and well," a phone card or coins will save you big money over these services. For instance, I once made a forty-second call from Assisi, Italy, to San Francisco, California, on a Sunday afternoon. It cost 1400 lire – about $1 at the time. The same call using AT&T would have cost $4.38.

All these companies use the enormous fees they charge you to take out ads proclaiming how cheap they are compared with the other guys. Should you need an access number, remember that they are advertised in the *International Herald Tribune* almost every day. These companies also give out little wallet-sized cards with their access codes in various countries. And most international operators will look up these codes for you on request. (Thank them profusely when they do.) Phone-home services also exist for those from Australia, South Africa, and New Zealand, but they are VERY expensive. Also, the companies are a bit dodgy, and seem to come and go every few months. The best advice I can give to those who need to call back those countries is to find a compatriot who has been in Europe for a few months and ask their advice on what is best and cheapest.

WARNING: Ignore those stickers promising cheap and easy "phone home" services that you find slapped on the interior of phone booths all over Europe. These aren't instructions from the phone companies – they're from rip-off artists who will charge you upwards of five dollars a minute if you use them. ATT and MCI are bad enough, but the sticker companies are run by con men, pure and simple.

Using your cell phone abroad

Cell phones have become very popular of late in the States, but compared to the vast number of Europeans walking around with these things, it's still not even a close contest. Unfortunately, merely having a mobile phone doesn't necessarily mean it will be of use to you on your trip, though the situation is much better if you're coming from Britain or the continent, because all European wireless companies use the same digital technology, GSM, or global system for mobile communication. Just sign up with a network provider that offers international roaming, like T-Mobile (more on the monthly plans they offer can be found at ®www.t-mobile.co.uk).

North American companies, on the other hand, use frequencies which aren't compatible with GSM, rendering pretty much all US and Canadian mobile phones useless abroad. If you think you can't do without one (believe me, you can), try International Mobile Communications (☎1-888/967-5323, ⊛www.worldcell.com) or Nextel Communications (☎1-800/639-8359, ⊛www.nextel.com/worldwide); the former rents cell phones and has accounts you can set up for international calling, while the latter has paired with Motorola to come up with a service that works on the GSM frequency. Prices for both, however, are exorbitant, whether it's in rental fees or per-minute rates.

You could also check into renting a mobile phone while in Europe, which would be less expensive, though still likely an unnecessary hassle. Phones with prepaid cards are available at sales offices affiliated with GSM throughout the continent: see ⊛www.gsm.org for a comprehensive list of stores.

Time zones

When making all of these intercontinental connections, remember your time zones: the Atlantic is five hours wide, from the East Coast of North America to Great Britain, Iceland, Ireland, and Portugal. To everywhere else in Europe, add one more hour, except for Finland, Greece, Romania, and Bulgaria, where you add two more; for Russia you should add three hours. Australians should think of the bulk of Europe as being nine hours behind Sydney, adding on an extra hour for Britain, etc, and losing one for Greece and the rest. For all travelers, especially those from Down Under who deal with the confusing International Date Line, a dual-time watch will make the issue much simpler – leave one on home time, set one to local, and you're good to go. Finally, remember to add or subtract an hour to that watch crossing the English Channel; it's easy to forget, given the short distance you're traveling. As always, a picture says it better than a paragraph, so have a look at the map on p.150–151.

European payphones

European coin phones are usually a bit more sophisticated than their North American counterparts. For example, they allow more than one call per coin, which allows you to make a series of calls using one large coin, rather than having to scrounge for a bunch of little ones. If you have finished a call and want to make another, and still have credit showing in the read-out, press the button marked FC (Follow-on Call), or follow the multilingual instructions found on payphones in most European countries. If there is no such button, or instructions, just flick the lever down and release quickly. You should get a dial tone and keep your credit. Many payphones will return unused coins, but they will not give change.

Once again, the cheapest way to call home is to use a coin or card phone, ring the person you want to talk to, and have them call you back, or use a cheap-rate phone card. This is *much* cheaper and simpler than calling collect.

Phone cards

Phone cards are very useful devices and are used all over Europe. They're little, prepaid phone credit cards that you pop into a slot in the phone rather than fumbling with coins. One of the best things you can do upon arrival in a country is to buy a phone card, and use that to make your calls during your stay. Coin phones (instead of card phones) can be irritatingly hard to find in some major cities, and may swallow coins mercilessly (see my story about "The Tent" on p.63). Phone cards are usually sold through tobacco stands and news kiosks. Some can be quite beautiful and artistic, and when they expire they make neat souvenirs. For some reason, calls made with cards are incredibly cheap in France, and absurdly expensive in Italy, with the rest of Europe somewhere in between. Don't ask me why.

Tokens

Some less modern payphones in less modern countries, especially in Eastern Europe, may still require tokens. The tokens can be bought at the same kiosks and tobacco shops as phone cards. If the phone you are using looks ancient and refuses to accept coins, you may need a token or two.

Email and the Internet

The Internet, and its accessibility via cybercafés scattered around Europe, has made communication unbelievably easy for travelers.

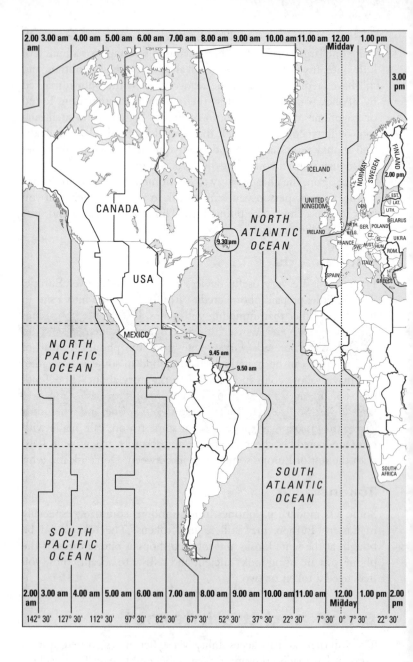

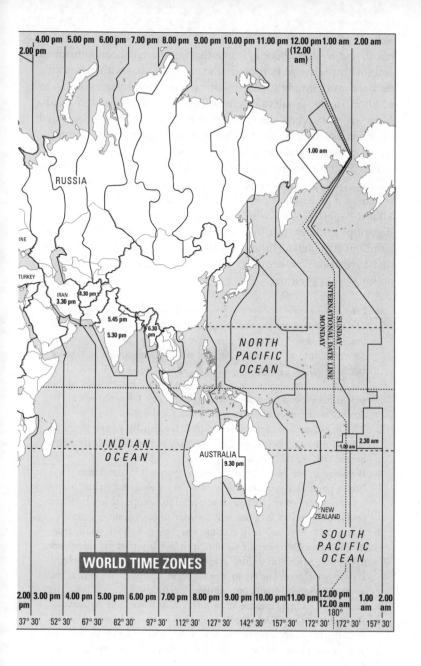

WORLD TIME ZONES

With little effort, you can stay in touch with other travelers, check email, and reassure those at home that you haven't been kidnapped and sold into slavery. For those who are unfamiliar with cybercafés, they are quite simply small bars or cafés offering Internet access in addition to the usual café fare of coffee, sandwiches, and salads. Most of the cybercafés I have visited have slightly outdated machines but they work just fine for receiving and sending email – which is likely what you'll be using them for.

The process is simple enough: walk in, place your money on the counter (you usually pay per hour), log on to their browser, and surf away. The handiest part about these places is that there is always a local expert around who can help maneuver you through the sign-in procedures, just in case you can't translate "enter the password" in Romanian (although a large number of the cafés I've visited have had Web browsers in English). Below are a couple of points about cybercafés:

- Like regular cafés, cybercafés seem to open and close every couple of weeks. I promise you that if ten cafés are listed in your guidebook, three have closed, two no longer have computers, and one has been converted into a fetish bar. The best way to locate a working cyber-café is to ask at your local tourist office, and then CALL FIRST, to see if and when they're open. Had I done that a few months ago, it would have saved me a long cold trek through Copenhagen in the dead of winter to a café that was closed for the day.
- The per-hour charges for computers are usually pretty steep, so write your email before you go, or at least organize your thoughts before starting the meter.
- If you've never done a remote email grab while away from your home computer, you might want to try doing one while across town in your home city before you head to Europe. If you have any problems, you can find out why in your home country/language.
- If you don't have an email account that you can check while away, it's easy enough to get a free one from any Internet provider such as Yahoo!, Microsoft (which is Hotmail), Excite – really anywhere. Before you leave, log on to one of these websites (Ⓦwww.yahoo .com, Ⓦwww.hotmail.com, Ⓦwww.excite.com) and follow the basic steps, which include choosing a user name and a password. Remember to jot your password down somewhere safe – it's amazing how fast you can forget it. Once you've set up an account you can retrieve and send messages to and from anywhere in the world – for free.

Gadgets on the go

I used to think there was nothing more miserable than lugging a laptop around Europe in a backpack, until I went on a trip where I carried both a laptop and a printer. Perhaps I am scarred by that experience, but I definitely recommend that you leave the computer, Palm Pilot, satellite pager, and wristwatch fax at home. If you bring these items you will constantly worry about them being banged up, rained on, melted, or stolen. Why stress yourself out? Remember: you are going to Europe to be in Europe.

At the risk of sounding nostalgic for the days of Morse code and carrier pigeons, it is possible to have too much contact with home. And as someone who is a compulsive email checker, I can tell you that it is indeed possible to survive if you only check your inbox once a week. If you actually need to check your email every day, by all means bring a laptop, modem, adaptor plugs, phone cable adaptors, battery chargers, etc. Better yet, you could just stay home....

- A surprising number of cafés I've visited, especially in Britain, have had AOL. However, if a café does not have AOL you can still retrieve your email account by logging on to ⓦwww.aol.com and clicking on "email retrieval." It's easy enough to follow the steps from there. Still, it's not a bad idea to open a free account (as discussed above) as a backup system.
- European keyboards have been the source of massive amounts of profanity by those from other countries. You'll understand when you use one. A word of advice: use control-alt-9 to get an "@" symbol, or cut and paste from an email.

Faxes

Fax machines are a very popular means of communication in Europe, perhaps due to the high cost of normal phone service, and they are available at many stores, hostels, and businesses. They can be quite useful for making reservations, getting information from embassies, touching base with home, and avoiding confusing phone systems (since someone will likely help you with the fax machine, they'll help you with dialing too).

Mail

One of the great pleasures of traveling in Europe is sending rude postcards back to the poor, pathetic souls who are stuck at home

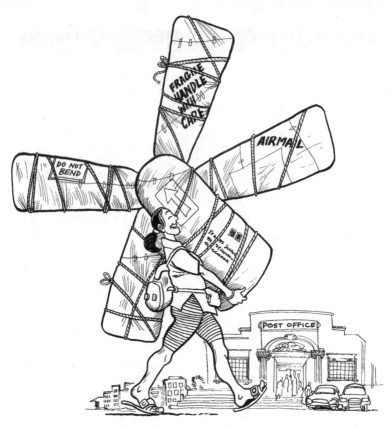

while you travel. If you do this properly, your friends may wish to respond with some photos of your wrecked car – and they can, even if you are moving around. Poste Restante, or General Delivery, is offered all over Europe. Address as below:

Ned Kelly	Abraham Lincoln
Poste Restante	Poste Restante
Roma 1	Madrid 1
Italy	España

The number "1" designates the central post office and may not be necessary in some countries. Use it anyway. Also, check your guidebook for information on mailing to specific countries: France, for example, requires a postal code on everything mailed into the country. Mail may arrive without it, but will probably be delayed. Leave clear instructions for the folks back home. If you know the proper name of the town you're sending mail to (München, for example, rather than Munich; or Firenze rather than Florence), by all means use it. If not, don't worry about it – it probably won't matter a bit.

Officially, letters and packages will be held for two weeks in German postes restante before being sent back, and will be held for at least a month in other countries. (In Italy they may be there until doomsday.) Unless letters are sent to a specific post office with a street address included, they will normally go to the central post office in the city, to the "Poste Restante" window or desk. When picking up your mail, bring your passport, expect to pay a nominal fee, and don't forget to ask the clerk to look under your first name, your last name, and "M" for Mr, Mrs, etc, if your bills or junk mail are being forwarded.

If you have an American Express card or travelers' checks, some American Express offices will hold letters for up to thirty days. They won't accept packages, though, because they claim to be afraid of bombs. Call American Express for a little booklet listing their overseas offices that accept client mail.

The unclaimed package storeroom: where time has no meaning

I went to a post office in Rome expecting a package to be waiting for me. It wasn't. The clerk helpfully pointed me outside and toward another door in the side of the building. When I entered, I thought I had mistakenly walked into the employees' lounge. Two men were playing chess, one was dozing in his chair, two others were reading quietly. After smiles of welcome and some Spanish/Italian/English communication, I realized that I was in the unclaimed package storeroom. I mentioned my search and was politely invited to sit down and relax. The warm air in the office was heavy and still, smelling of paper and ink . . . the chair was actually quite comfortable . . . the clock in the office was broken, but that really didn't matter much. Time seemed irrelevant in that room. I became mildly interested in the chess game. All was quiet, as if sound was somehow muffled. When I woke up, I was almost sorry to see one of my new friends standing there with my package in hand. Had he not found it, I might still be in that room. I signed an old ledger the size of a dictionary, waved goodbye, and stepped back into the real world. Outside, the traffic was flowing and the usual horde of mopeds was running like salmon. But inside the unclaimed package storeroom, in the Italian post office near the Spanish Steps, there was no hurry at all, and I don't think there ever will be.

Mailing things home

Sending packages home is certainly possible, but can be expensive if you want them to get there within a week. Normal mail takes from one to three weeks and is relatively inexpensive. Sending things by boat can be remarkably inexpensive, but can take several months. When planning to do this, expect to spend some time in the post office, as customs formalities can take a while. However, typically, if you keep the weight of your package to under two kilograms you can avoid customs. (Thanks to Sandi Sakiyabu for this tip.) Remember, the box or envelope you send will be beaten and battered on its journey. Use the strongest box you can find and tape it up very thoroughly. Wait until you get to the post office to do this, as they may need to look inside.

For those postcards and letters you send home, make sure you have enough postage – postcards are more expensive abroad, and do not necessarily use the cheapest possible stamp. Ask at the post office for the correct amount to get your card home, and remember to use the cute little blue "Par Avion" stickers. These stickers, and stamps, can be purchased at tobacco shops in most countries.

Express mail and courier services

For that emergency package I mentioned before, you might want to use some sort of express mail service. UPS and Federal Express can ship things to Europe, at varying rates of speed for varying rates of pay: $125 for a twenty-pound box of stuff, Oakland to Munich, in two business days, is a rough baseline figure. An eight-ounce letter will cost roughly $30 for the same service. The best services are Federal Express (☎1-800/247-4747) and UPS (☎1-800/742-5877).

Newspapers and magazines

Both *USA Today* and the *International Herald Tribune* are widely available in continental Europe, for those who need a daily news fix. At roughly $2 a copy, the cost can add up, though. Try the *Herald Tribune*, which has a certain snob appeal. It also has a decent crossword puzzle, whose difficulty varies at random from idiot-proof to impossible. Also, *The European*, an English-language newspaper that focuses on the affairs of Europe, is widely available, as are European editions of various British papers. While in Britain, definitely check out its wide selection of papers; to get both ends of the spectrum try the *Times* and the *Daily Sport*. Also in London, look out for the numerous maga-

zines and newspapers aimed at expatriates. *Southern Cross*, South Africa *UK News*, and so on, serve the needs of their homesick ex-colonials, and are well worth a look for travelers from other countries. You can pick them up free from bins all over the city.

A blizzard of magazines in English can be found all over Europe, with *Time* and *Newsweek* on sale pretty much everywhere. Also, try the foreign versions of well-known magazines from home and note the differences. For example, British *Cosmopolitan* is so brainless and sex-obsessed that it makes the American version look like something written by Dickens.

"Listings" magazines and tourist publications

Listings magazines, written in English, are designed to alert tourists (and residents for that matter) to what's happening during a given week or month in a particular city. *Time Out* in London is the granddaddy of these, and is about as complete a guide to a city as you're likely to find (it also publishes a version in Amsterdam, and an English supplement in Paris). Other cities usually have some sort of tourist publication, varying from full-sized magazines to small pamphlets, often titled "What's On . . . " (Munich, Copenhagen, etc). They can be useful for spotting events and for getting an up-to-date list of nightspots, and are usually worth a look. Most of them are distributed to hotels and hostels or can be found at tourist information centers. In addition, most accommodations have the dreaded "tacky brochure rack," full of amazing attractions ("See the World's Largest Mayonnaise Factory! Free Samples for All"). Kidding aside, these displays are well worth a look to see if something strikes your fancy.

11

Crime, safety, and sleaze

urope is extremely safe on the whole – probably much safer than home if you come from a big American city and a world away from South Africa. Nevertheless, petty crime against tourists does happen, has happened to me several times, and has increased greatly in only the last few years. You should know that the odds of having your purse or daypack snatched or your pocket picked are fairly high. Crime is something you should be aware of but not afraid of; be prepared, but not paranoid. Rather than gloss over the problem for fear of frightening you, I'll give you all of the gory details. In all cases, an ounce of prevention is worth a kilogram of cure.

Notice how many of the problems discussed below are prevented by using a money belt or neck wallet inside your clothes. This is your first line of defense, and it is very effective. To avoid having to snake-charm your way into your money belt every time you buy a drink on the street, carry a cheap wallet with ten or twenty dollars in it in a front pocket. This prevents you from having to flash the location of your cash in public places.

Theft on trains

Robbery on trains happens fairly often, especially in Italy and Eastern Europe, and especially on night trains. Once, when getting off a night train to Naples one morning, I saw five people lined up at the police office to report stolen daypacks. Prevention is the key to this problem:

- Never sleep in a compartment alone if you can avoid it. This goes for both men and women.
- Always lock or chain your backpack to the luggage rack, even during the day, by as many straps as possible. That may be just enough to make a potential thief look for easier prey.
- Thieves prefer daypacks because that's where the small, easily sold valuables tend to be kept. When sleeping, put your passport, documents, money, and camera in bed with you, and lock your daypack inside your main bag.
- Don't be shy about locking your train compartment. If someone wants to come in and sit, fine – let them knock and wake you up first. If there's no lock on the door, use your own, or use wire or rope to tie the door shut. Once, on a night train in Poland, I thought about doing that and didn't bother. The next morning I woke up in Germany to find my daypack was gone. What the hell was I going to do about it? The train crew had changed at the border, and I was in a different country. By the way, I was a classic target: alone in a compartment on a night train, with the door unlocked. Don't repeat my mistake.
- If you are in a group and you can't lock your door, consider having someone stay awake at night, especially in Eastern Europe.
- Top bunks are a bit more secure than bottom bunks.
- Be very wary in and around train stations, especially if you have just arrived in town, are a bit confused, and are loaded down with stuff. Distracted and unaware people are a pickpocket's dream.
- Never, ever, allow someone you just met to "help" you put stuff in a locker at a train station. You will be putting it into a locker to which this person has a key or combination, and five minutes after your back is turned your stuff will be cleaned out.
- If you are in a group of two or more, and you leave someone at the train station with all the large packs while everyone else looks for accommodation, changes money, and so on, tie all of the bags together, or better yet, lock them all to something solid. The person watching them should keep a sharp eye on both the bags and

their surroundings. I once saw a girl guarding four large packs. Had someone grabbed one and started running, she could either have left the other three or just watched him go. (Yet another reason to travel light.)

● If you are riding a bus and put your bag in the luggage bins, keep your daypack with you, and if you are traveling with someone else, lock your bags together. It's better to use the luggage storage area inside the bus, but beware. Sit as close as possible to the storage area, and when the bus makes stops, keep an eye on your stuff. Once, in Portugal, I watched as a man got up to leave my bus, and grabbed my bag along with his. I had noticed the guy when he got on, and probably knew he was going to steal my bag before he did. When he picked up my bag, I was in his face before he could turn around. Like most thieves, he was also a coward. When caught, he started whimpering that he was "helping me take my bag off the bus." Yeah, right.

I'm sure you've heard the stories about gangs of professional thieves using "sleeping gas" to knock out and rob whole compartments (or even whole cars) full of passengers. Don't worry very much about stuff like that – it's neither very likely nor very preventable (although I guess opening the window couldn't hurt). Worry instead about the teenaged punk looking for a bag to snatch just before the train reaches a station, or the pickpocket looking for someone who has just arrived and is wandering around lost. Simply by taking the precautions just listed, as well as those to follow, you will be a much harder target.

Pickpockets

Here's my first pickpocket story, which has a number of lessons in it. Getting on the Metro in Madrid one day, I found the train door blocked by two men who just stood there rather than getting on the train. As I moved around them another man (who had just gotten on the train) walked out; as he went by he bumped into me rather obviously and kept walking without an apology. Such rudeness is almost unheard of in Spain, and, not being a total nimrod, I felt for my wallet, which I was carrying in the front pocket of my shorts. It was gone. I immediately ran after the guy, got right behind him, and used my Spanish to call him a thief, a son of a whore, and other gross profanities. He kept walking without looking back. This convinced me beyond doubt that he was a thief, as any innocent Spanish man called such things would have fought me on the spot. After a few more seconds of being called a male prostitute, my new friend threw my wallet in one direction and took off in another. When I recovered it, every peseta was in place, and virtue had triumphed over the forces of evil.

All well and good, you may say. Except that I did everything wrong, and could very well have been seriously injured. The whole situation would never have occurred had I been using a money belt – the most obvious of security precautions. Those three guys wouldn't have even considered me as a target. Second, following the thief as closely and insulting him as thoroughly as I did was asking for him to pull a knife. A far better tactic would have been to follow at a good distance and shout for a policeman as loudly as possible. I got lucky. Learn from my mistakes.

- Every serious traveler uses a money belt or neck wallet. Again, highly recommended.
- If you must wear a fanny pack, wear it in front. Three seconds on a crowded bus, train, or street are all a thief needs to slash and empty your pack.
- Unless you really need all of those credit cards, leave them locked up wherever you're staying, or in a money belt – whichever feels safer.
- Be very careful in crowded trains and train stations. Hold wallets and purses (if any) at chest level. Both times my pocket has been picked I was getting on a Metro train. There were people moving around me in both directions, I was looking around for a seat – in other words, I was distracted. Be very careful in this same situation, especially in the middle of large crowds.
- Be exceptionally careful in Barcelona. Theft in that city has exploded recently, and the Spanish authorities aren't doing a whole lot about it. I was in Barcelona very recently, was getting on a Metro train and literally waiting to be pickpocketed when, sure enough, I felt a hand reach into the front pocket of my shorts. (There was nothing in that pocket but some coins, a bag of candy,

and some tissues – I'd learned my lesson.) Well, wallet in hand or not, that pickpocket "had the wrong sow by the ear." I spun around, frothing at the mouth in anger. I was facing two women and a man, who were saved when a transit cop appeared out of nowhere, flashed a badge, and told us that he had seen the whole thing. This same crime probably happened in that city fifty times on that same day, and I'm sure some trips were ruined as a result.

Kids and snatch thieves

I have heard more first-hand stories of robbery by gangs of kids, often gypsies, than any other type of crime. The tactic is simple: five or six small children run up to you, shouting and waving newspapers or pieces of cardboard. As they swarm around and distract you, your wallet/purse and the contents of your fanny/daypack are swiped, and off they run in three different directions. Elapsed time: six seconds. I've seen it happen, most commonly in Italy, less so in France.

If this happens to you, don't just stand there. Move away from the brats, yell at them to get away, and don't be shy about letting loose some slaps or shoves at any kid within range. Remember, these are not innocent tykes. They are professionally trained thieves, who will clean you out before you can blink. As with pickpockets, prevention is the best defense; a money belt inside your clothing is a million times safer than a purse or fanny pack.

Snatch thieves specialize in surprise tactics – grabbing cameras, bags, and packs from the non-alert and from those whom they have deliberately distracted. One woman I met had just gotten on a train when she felt hand cream or suntan lotion splatter on the back of her legs. When she put down her daypack and turned to wipe it off, the thief grabbed her pack and was gone in a flash. Variations on this include moped-riding purse-snatchers, camera thieves, etc.

- In any crowded area, such as on public transportation, carry your daypack in front of you.
- Should you be shoved, distracted, splattered, whatever, grab hold of whatever you have.
- Wear cameras and shoulder bags across your body rather than over a shoulder, and on the side away from the street.
- Don't carry a purse. If you must, and you really shouldn't, don't carry anything important in it. If someone grabs it and starts pulling, scream your lungs out. If the person continues to pull, let go. Don't get into a tug-of-war with someone who is probably angry, frightened, and excited. This is especially the case if the thief is on a moped, motorcycle, or in a car, in which case you should let go

immediately. Don't risk a serious injury for the contents of a purse or shoulder bag. Anything in one should be easily replaceable, or it shouldn't be in there at all.

Theft from cars

Rental cars are viewed by thieves the world over as mobile piggy banks. Tactics for crime prevention with cars are simple:

- Try not to rent or buy a car without a separate, lockable trunk. Be advised that this can be difficult. The smallest and cheapest rental cars are usually hatchbacks.
- Never park a car, especially a rental car, with anything of the slightest value visible inside. It is even worth pulling out the cover to the back of a hatchback to demonstrate its emptiness.
- At night, even though it's a royal pain in the neck, carry everything you can't afford to lose up to your room, lock the rest in the trunk, and leave the glove compartment open and empty.
- On the road, especially in a rental car, beware if someone motions you to pull over, especially if you are female, and especially if two or more males are in the other car. If your car is running well, pull over at the next gas station, if at all.

A tale of automotive woe in Amsterdam

A friend of mine and a person she met while in Europe recently drove into Amsterdam to go to the visitors' bureau. As they got out of their car, her friend said, "Hey, should we take our packs?" She said, "Naw, they weigh a ton, and we'll only be gone a few minutes." Twenty minutes later they returned to find the car cleaned out: both packs, as well as everything else of value, were gone. The most tragic part was that I had loaned her my backpack for the trip! My friend did a number of things right and a number of things wrong that day, and they make for good examples for any traveler.

Wrong . . .
1. Driving a rental car into the center of Amsterdam.
2. Ignoring the windshield sticker that warned (in English!) about leaving things in the car.
3. By not packing light, her backpack was too heavy to carry comfortably, which resulted in her leaving it in the car.

Right . . .
1. Immediately after discovering the theft, the two of them searched the surrounding neighborhood. Thieves will often clean out the money and small valuables, and dump the pack and/or its other contents. Searching is not, however, advisable at night, or in a particularly dangerous area.
2. She reported the theft to the police, who would then be able to contact her in case someone else found her pack. For this reason, she stayed in Amsterdam for a couple of days. She might also have been able to file a claim on her insurance policy, and would have needed the police report.
3. She took her daypack, which included her money, passport, camera, and other small, valuable stuff, with her to the tourist office.
4. She didn't let the theft ruin her trip, and still managed to enjoy herself during her remaining time in Europe (maybe because she was traveling pretty darn light by this time).
5. She bought me a new pack!

Scams and swindles

The days of black market money changing, and Western currencies being worth twice as much on the street as in the official exchange rate have gone the way of the hoop skirt. Money-changing con men, however, have not. Rest assured, there are plenty of people in Europe who would be happy to separate you from your cash. Take this handy quiz:

(1) How do you say "legal tender" in Czech?
(2) How is a Polish 10-zloty note different from a Hungarian 10-forint bill?
(3) How does a magician change a coin into an egg right before your eyes?

If you answered "I don't know" to any one of those three questions, you shouldn't be changing money on the streets of Europe.

The most common scam, especially in Eastern Europe, is very simple. A guy greets you on the street and offers you a terrific rate on changing money, especially dollars. He then gives you worthless bills in exchange, either old notes from before the fall of Communism, or bills from another country entirely. The Polish Zloty (which used to trade at 25,000 to the dollar) is a favorite for this sort of scam, since ten-zloty notes are virtually worthless. If the con man is a bit more skilled, he or she doesn't bother with other currencies – he counts out the real thing, then palms it while you're distracted. Bottom Line: don't trade money on the street or with individuals. Use a bank.

Along with the obvious stuff, like having a purse cleaned out while dancing with "new friends" at a night club, also be careful of "great deals," especially on art work or cultural items such as jewelry, Russian icons, or "antique" anything. As a general rule, anything that seems too good to be true probably is. Anything that requires you to give money to someone to "hold," or "invest," or any venture that requires you to bring something back to your home country, is nothing but trouble. Basically, if you give money to a new acquaintance, consider it gone.

Theft from hostels

Theft from hostels happens occasionally, and is particularly galling because you know that a fellow budget traveler, who should understand your situation, is most likely the thief.

- If lockers are available, use them. Be warned, though, that those little locks that are so handy for locking up a backpack are inadequate for this task, and can be easily broken. Also, the key to someone else's little lock may very well open yours. I found this out when I opened what I thought was my locker and found a nice new camera that definitely wasn't mine. You can bet that thieves are aware of this fact.
- If lockers are not available, chain your backpack to your bed, a pipe, or something of the like. This will not stop a really determined thief, but it may make him pass up your backpack for another.
- *Never* leave a money belt, neck bag, or wallet lying around, even for an instant. Do not let these out of your sight, especially in hostels. Leaving one of these unattended among a group of budget travelers is a guarantee that it will be stolen. Wear yours to the bathroom, take it into the shower stall, and when you sleep either keep it on or put it at the bottom of your sleep sack or sleeping bag. My editor, on her first InterRailing trip, actually left her money belt dangling from the end of her bed while sleeping in a 20-bed dorm, thereby donating £100 to a thief. Clearly, she needed *First-Time Europe*!

Theft in other accommodations

When people stay in hostels, they are usually on their toes, if only because there are so many people about. If you are in a pension or hotel, don't relax your guard completely just because you can lock a door. Never leave valuables lying around your room. Remember, at least one other person has a key. A friend tells the story of entering "her" room at a very nice hotel to find a couple sleeping in "her" bed. It turned out that she was on the wrong floor, but her key worked just as well in that door as her own.

Violent theft

This is much less common in Europe than in the United States, and may even be less prevalent than in Canada. One of the saddest experiences of my life was returning to the States from a long trip, getting on to the Boston metro system, and feeling a prickling sense of unease that I hadn't felt anywhere in Europe, Russia, or the Middle East. Street crime does happen, however, and all the normal precautions apply in Europe. Trust your instincts. If a situation such as walking down a street, walking past a group of men, etc, just doesn't feel right, turn around and walk the other way. Be particularly wary around train stations and red-light districts, and it's always smart to ask in the local tourist office if there are any local areas that are unsafe. ATMs, at home and abroad, are a place to visit during the day or with a friend if you must go at night. On the plus side, muggers armed with handguns, UZIs, and AK-47s are not a major problem in Europe: Los Angeles has more handgun murders in a month than London does in a year.

One final word: if confronted by a punk with a knife, let alone a gun, don't play Rambo. Give the worthless puke what he wants as quickly as possible, and don't end up in a hospital over a camera or a few dollars. Any police officer in any country will advise you to do the same.

After a theft

As mentioned earlier, if something is stolen, even if it's your backpack, don't panic. Yes, it's a hassle, but you will be amazed at how much better things will feel after a few days. Whatever you do, don't give up and go home. In the long run, that will cost you far more than the loss of your bag. The first steps that my friend took after her car was broken into were exactly right: look around the neighborhood, if it's safe to do so, report the theft to the police, and stay in town for a day or so to see if something turns up. Beyond that, there's not much you can do to get your stuff back. If it's not coming back, I can only advise you to let it go, and try not to let it ruin the rest of your vacation. Easy for me to say, I know.

Your difficulties will be greatly magnified if your documents and money or credit cards are taken with your backpack. In that case, you'll need to make a collect call home in order to get your credit cards canceled and to get some money shipped out, followed by a trip to the embassy for a temporary passport (see pp.156 and 138 for info on express mail and wiring money). The embassy can arrange to get money sent to you from someone else, but don't expect any cash from them unless you are really desperate. The next step is to call the airline so they can issue you a new ticket. In this situation, a hundred-dollar bill or fifty-pound note (that you sewed into the lining of your shoe or jacket) would be a major help. I do it.

Lost or stolen passes, pass returns and refunds

If you never validate a pass, you have one year to return it to your vendor for an 85 percent refund. If you validate a pass, you own it. It used to be that if a rail pass was lost or stolen, you might get some sympathy from the rail company. No longer. You should treat your rail pass as if it were several hundred dollars in cash, because if it's lost or stolen, you will definitely have to find some other way of getting around.

Rail Europe does offer "pass protection" insurance for $10, but the refund procedures are a nightmare, and the best you can get, months after you lose your pass, is a partial refund of whatever your pass "should" have been worth on the date you lost it, but only if you buy another pass, or buy rail tickets to get around. (I guess continuing to travel by train "proves" that you still intended to use your pass.) Contact Rail Europe or go to their website (ⓦ www.raileurope.com) for more information.

If you are reading this after your pass was lost or stolen and you didn't have pass protection, it's gone forever. If you did buy pass protection, you need to file a police report within 24 hours and get a copy of that report, then file a claim within 30 days of returning from Europe. As far as getting around Europe for the remainder of your trip, all I can say is that a pass is not a requirement for a great time. You may not get to ten countries, but you can see a whole lot of France for not much money, or spend a month in Rome followed by a month in Vienna and pay very little to get from one to the other (either by ride-share, meeting someone with a car, or by bus). DON'T GIVE UP AND GO HOME! Do like the Marines do: adapt and overcome. Good luck.

If the above situation sounds unpleasant, it is. Remember what I said earlier about having a copy of your passport, credit cards, travelers' checks, and airline tickets taped to the refrigerator at home? In a situation like the one just described, that piece of paper could be faxed to you in half an hour, and make your life much, much easier. Packing a box full of stuff that can be shipped out to you could have you back on the road, ready to travel, in three days. After prevention, it's the best theft insurance I can think of.

Harassment of women

Harassment of women happens, and I'm sorry to say that the worst place for it in Europe is Italy, followed by Greece. Female tourists, especially those who are wearing shorts or skimpy tops, are seen as fair targets for verbal or physical harassment that may not be dangerous, but can be unrelenting, and can spoil a trip to some of the most beautiful places in the world. Obviously, I haven't experienced this first-hand, so my thanks to all of the female travelers who shared their experiences, which are summarized here.

- Traveling (and walking) in groups is better than traveling alone – much better. Walking or traveling in the company of a man works wonders and will cut casual harassment by almost 100 percent.
- Shorts and revealing clothing, especially in smaller towns away from the tourist trail, are like red flags. I know wearing long sleeves or long pants in summer when it's 102 degrees is very unpleasant, but that's the way it is. A long, light peasant skirt is a good alternative to pants.
- Any verbal response by you to a comment, noise, pinch, etc, is seen as a success. Silence, disdain, and a lack of eye contact are the best response to fervent declarations of passion. Sunglasses to prevent eye contact can help. An exception to this rule is the dreaded public transportation groper. In that case, a loud protest is best in order to embarrass your assailant into stopping.
- Do not share tables with men who ask to join you, especially if the café or restaurant is half empty, most especially if you are alone.
- With two women, holding hands or linking arms may help.
- The fake wedding ring trick has been mentioned to me more than once as a way to discourage persistent types.
- Really unpleasant men, guys who get grossly physical, or those who seem dangerous, are a matter for the police. Don't hesitate to call them. Also, an appeal to the nearest group of local women, if you speak the language, or tourists of either sex, might help.
- Don't bring jewelry you cannot afford to lose. Necklaces are especially vulnerable to theft, and the display of any jewelry makes you a more likely target.
- Do not allow anyone you do not know WELL to hold a drink for you in a club or a bar. Avoid setting a drink down and leaving it alone. If someone wants to buy you something, go to the bar with them and personally take the drink from the bartender. The "date rape pill" originated in Europe and is still there today.
- Getting physical may provoke a physical response: Be very careful with this. Women just don't hit men in some countries.

Terrorism

When I first started updating this edition of *First-Time Europe*, several months after the September 11 terrorist attacks on the States, I thought I would have to make some major revisions to this section. However, after re-reading the advice below, I stand by everything I've said over the years, including the assertion that the odds of you being involved in a terrorist incident are roughly equal to that of you winning your state's lottery. Go, enjoy yourself, and don't stress out. I went to Europe for Christmas of 2001, and other than some longer lines at the airports, nothing had changed. Only a few very common-sense tips are necessary now.

- Don't accept packages to carry if flying or crossing a border.
- Don't accept a request to "watch" a stranger's luggage in a public place, especially an airport, train or bus station.
- Move away from unattended packages or luggage and report them to the nearest police officer or public official.
- When you get to an airport, get checked-in and get past the security checkpoint as soon as possible. (I don't know why anybody would want to spend another second in the check-in area than they had to, terrorists or not.)
- Don't give those poor souls at the X-ray machine a hard time. How would you like to get out of bed and have to go do that job?
- If you see a demonstration or protest, resist the (very strong) impulse to go look at it.
- Try to blend in with the locals, and don't make it obvious that you are a foreigner. (This is another of those ideas that is a good thing, terrorists or not.)

Finally, let me offer these words of advice. If you want to go to Europe, and are worried about terrorism, that is the best possible reason to head straight to the airport, if only because it flies in the face of the fear, ignorance and isolation that terrorism thrives on.

Losing things

Now here is a subject that I am truly a world expert on; the kind of expert Albert Einstein was in the field of physics. The result of losing stuff can vary from the mildly irritating – say, a pen – to the trip-halting (a wallet, passport, etc). I know, because during my travels I have generously distributed sunglasses, pens, Swiss Army knives, airline tickets, books, a camera, and other things, all over the world, to the delight of the finders. Even now, some guy in Syria is blessing the stu-

A few years ago I lost my wallet on Stephansplatz, the very center of the city of Vienna. I searched everywhere, retraced my steps, and, following my own advice (without much hope), reported the loss to the police. After I filled out the form, the thick-necked, gray-haired policeman looked at it, looked up and said, "Herr CasaBianca?!?! Moment, Bitte!" He returned with another officer, and a policewoman who looked even tougher than the two guys. Each of them was grinning from ear to ear. The woman produced a sealed envelope, which I ripped open, and found my wallet, safe and sound, with every credit card, dollar, mark, pfennig, and schilling untouched. I don't know who was happier – me or the police. I would like to give a huge, international thank you to the unknown citizen of Vienna, who put honesty ahead of personal gain and did his city proud. And if you, the reader, happen to lose something, don't give up. You might get the kind of help I did.

pid tourist who presented him with a camera worth more than the average Syrian makes in a month. The bitter fruits of my experiences:

- On any long train or plane trip, where you're sitting for several hours, things have a way of climbing out of pockets. Well before your destination, get up, get your things together, and check under, in, and around your seat for anything that might be lying around. Do this if you change seats within the train or plane as well. Account for tickets and passports well before landing or arriving at your station. Don't wait until the last minute and then be forced to dash out – that's a great way to leave something behind.

- Try not to carry more than one bag at a time. Put bags of things you've bought into a daypack rather than carrying them all separately.

- If you are leaving a place, and have this vague feeling that you may have forgotten something, or that you used to have something in your hands that isn't there any more, *listen to that feeling*. Stop for a minute, check to make sure you have everything you came in with, and everything you took out with you in the morning. Believe me, that funny feeling doesn't lie.

● If you've lost something and there's no way of getting it back, forget about it, don't get totally pissed off, and don't let it ruin your day. My friends who read this will howl with laughter, but just because I can't do that doesn't mean you shouldn't.

Sleazy Europe: red-light districts and drugs

There are certain activities, and certain "special economic zones" in some European countries which are illegal elsewhere – hence they are damn near irresistible to some travelers. I have to admit that I sure made a beeline for the red-light district upon my first arrival in Amsterdam. Rather than ignore the presence of such activities and places, here are my opinions on, and experiences of, the seamy side of Europe.

Drugs

No, Virginia, the smoking of hashish is not legal in the city of Amsterdam. It is, however, widely tolerated. Because of this, thousands of people come to this city at least partly to engage in this activity. Perhaps my opinions are biased, but I don't think Amsterdam is currently made any nicer by the presence of decriminalized hashish. What started as a free-spirited Sixties-type scene has gotten a bit rough around the edges. Results include large numbers of burnt-out types hanging around the city, increased crime, as well as some seedy hostels that cater to those who come solely to smoke. Also, the presence of such large amounts of hashish inevitably brings a certain amount of harder drugs in its wake. If you have the desire to see someone shooting heroin into their arm, walk out of the back door of Amsterdam's Centraal Station any time after dark and turn right. All those empty sugar packets were not left there by coffee drinkers.

Be that as it may, if you desperately want to smoke hash in Amsterdam, there is plenty available. It is sold in certain well-marked coffee houses. You should realize that even in Amsterdam, possession of large (in the opinion of the police, mind you) amounts of hashish, drug dealing, and the possession of any amount of cocaine or other "hard" drug, is treated in the same way as in other countries – arrest and possible imprisonment. Also, resale of anything you buy may or may not put you in the drug-dealer category, depending on how the police see it.

In other parts of Europe, except for certain parts of certain major cities, drugs are much less available than in North America. In most countries the standard rule of thumb applies: if you are arrested for drugs overseas, you are in for the most miserable and dehumanizing experience of your life. Consider going into a prison system where you don't speak the language, have no constitutional rights, would be a member of a tiny minority, and might be held for months without even seeing a judge. As far as getting help from the embassy in the event of arrest: not bloody likely, mate. They're barely civil to non-criminals asking for assistance or information. Travelers arrested for drugs are seen as a waste of their time, and treated accordingly. They will check that you are not being abused (by local standards, which are probably hellish), and inform your family of the situation, but that's about it. Anyone who thinks that they will work tirelessly on your behalf because you are a compatriot in need is kidding himself.

Prostitution

Along with tolerated "soft" drugs, Amsterdam also has tolerated and semi-legalized (certainly controlled) prostitution, located in its infamous red-light district. Although there are large numbers of "professional" women here, and plenty of red lights, the district is a major tourist attraction, and it is hard to get any sense of wickedness when tour groups of camera-wielding senior citizens come walking through every hour or so. On a Friday or Saturday night the women sitting in the windows under the red neon lights are outnumbered ten or twenty to one by young men wandering the streets gawking. The whole place is more bizarre and surreal than anything else, but the district is such a part of Amsterdam that it is a virtual must-see. The crime rate here is above that of the rest of the city, but it is still relatively safe.

Hamburg's Reeperbahn District is a bit tougher and seedier than Amsterdam's red-light district, although it is also a major – and advertised – tourist attraction. Instead of quietly sitting in windows, battalions of multilingual women patrol the sidewalks. The district is also the home of many normal dance clubs and bars. There are other, smaller districts all over Europe, but these two are by far the most famous.

If you go out for the night in the Reeperbahn (and you shouldn't go alone), beware: the oldest scam in the world has reached its highest form here. To wit: you are in a bar, or nightclub, and a very sexy but slightly tough-looking woman joins you at your table. She is dressed tastefully, speaks five languages, and is friendly in a way that, well, pleasantly violates your personal space just a little. Her name is Heidi, and she is busty, and she is beautiful. You, being slightly under the influence, decide that this person is attracted to you and only you. When she suggests that you buy her a drink, you do. The bill arrives with it, and you find that you have just paid no less than $200 for a glass of lukewarm champagne. That's not a misprint: $200. This woman's job is to hustle you to buy those drinks, and she gets a cut out of the price you pay. And you are going to pay every euro of that price, because outside the bar is a little tiny placard with drink prices listed, and there at the bottom in teeny-weeny black and white is the price of a glass of champagne. It's completely legal. The police will be on the side of the no-neck bouncer. Call it a cultural experience. Similar scams are run in bars all over Europe, especially in Hungary and the Czech Republic.

Private clubs and private thugs

While we're on the subject of no-neck bouncers, many of the clubs and dance spots in Europe, particular-

ly in France and Germany, are officially private, meaning that you can and will be denied entrance if you are not up to snuff. Most have entry ages of 18 rather than 21; most also charge in the $20–50 range for entry, have a smoke-filled atmosphere that closely resembles a tear-gas attack, and have dress codes beyond the means of a Rockefeller. Entry standards are heavily weighted against men. (Women should breeze through if properly dressed, while the beautiful may get in free.) For rejected and frustrated men, be aware that the bouncers who guard these establishments are often little more than thugs in suits, and that they are happy to demonstrate that fact to you. (Bouncers in France are especially violent.) If you are refused admittance to one of these places, don't get belligerent – just move on to the next place. Don't give these knuckle-dragging throwbacks a reason to get physical.

Police and border patrols

If, for whatever reason, you manage to attract the attention of the local law enforcement authority, innocent or not, do not cop an attitude, raise your voice, or act indignant. Police, like everyone else, respond to courtesy and don't like rude people. The difference with the police is that they can do something about rude people, and you probably won't like it when they do. A smile and a cooperative attitude will work wonders. It is particularly important to remember this when dealing with the Spanish Guardia Civil (the guys with the leather hats), and especially any member of the French police force. If you get indignant ("You can't treat me this way – I'm an American") you're asking for trouble. This is especially the case if alcohol is involved.

Also, realize that, in the relatively law-abiding societies of Europe, what is considered a nothing offense in the United States or Australia may attract police attention. Once, on my way to the train station in Copenhagen, two policemen in a car pulled over and gave me a stern lecture on the evils of jaywalking. Not likely in New York or King's Cross.

At the border

Most of the time, crossing an international border within Europe is a non-event; your passport will be glanced at and you'll be on your way – sometimes, between Holland and Belgium or Spain and Portugal, even that won't happen. Be aware, though – an offense that may be ignored in a large city will probably be taken seriously at a border crossing, especially anything having to do with drugs. If you forget about that little bag of Amsterdam hash until a friendly canine reminds you about it when crossing into Germany, you have just become a drug smuggler. Even drug paraphernalia, used or not, will raise eyebrows if spotted. Border guards, unlike big-city

police, do not deal with or arrest criminals regularly – their main concerns are stamping passports and catching senior citizens with too many cigarettes. Nailing a genuine drug smuggler will most certainly make their day. The absolute best you can expect if drugs are discovered on you is a long delay, a blitzkrieg search through every inch of your things, and denial of entry to the country you're trying to visit. The worst you can get, especially in Spain, Greece, or, God forbid, Turkey, doesn't bear thinking about.

This all may seem obvious, but in London I once met an American girl who cheerfully described how she carried marijuana in her pocket through Heathrow Airport customs. By-the-by, had you been traveling with this person, or even struck up a friendship on the plane, guess who could have been detained had she been caught. This goes double for countries like Greece and Turkey. Yelling "But I just met the girl!!" probably won't convince the border guard who has just arrested your new friend for drugs, and is now pushing you into the back of a van bound for God knows where.

One final border note: entering Britain

One other thing to know about borders, and this goes for everybody. British immigration officials have a very bad and very deserved reputation for refusing entry to those who they feel are coming into Britain to work illegally. They can, and will, on a hunch, refuse entry to anyone. Do not, under any circumstances, bring anything with you that might seem work-related, such as resumés, names of references, want ads from British papers, anything of that sort. I have seen them go through a guy's diary page by page looking for entries about how he was coming to Britain to look for a job. Those who look like Deadheads or are carrying guitars can expect major scrutiny.

This is the drill. When entering Britain you are there for tourism. You have plenty of money and plenty of credit cards. You are leaving in one week to another country. You have a reservation in a hostel in London (really make one, not just for the benefit of the border guards), and you wouldn't dream of sleeping in the parks. Leave it at that. A wad of cash is a good thing to have with you if asked to show means of travel. If you really don't have a whole lot of cash, then a reservation on a train or plane out of England, paid for or not, is a very handy thing to show the officials. Do not kid around with these guys, especially if they start the third degree.

Don't judge all of England by them either; I don't know why they're like this. So many destitute Aussies, Kiwis, and other Commonwealth citizens come to Britain with legitimate work visas that excluding the odd Yank or Canuck is like picking individual stones out of an avalanche. Be that as it may, expect a hard look, and be prepared with a clean appearance, a bright smile, and as much cash and as many credit cards as you can get your hands on. And after you make it through, look at your passport stamp. In case you didn't get the hint, there it is, in black and white: "Employment and recourse to public funds prohibited."

For just these reasons, be very suspicious if someone asks you to carry something for them, especially across a border (refuse immediately and get the hell away from that person), and be careful with the casual traveling partners you pick up. Horror stories of chance acquaintances loading a kilogram of hashish into the luggage of their new friend before crossing a border are not just stories. This applies more to the serious trekker than the summer traveler, but it can't hurt to be aware of the possibility.

Don't be put off!

Please don't let this section frighten you into not going to Europe, or into being overly fearful when you do. The four principal "Amazing True Crime" experiences I just related are the only incidents I personally suffered in multiple trips all over the world totaling somewhere around fifty or sixty months of travel. These trips included a great deal of wandering alone late at night through Naples, Moscow, Cairo, Rome, and other big cities, and never once did I feel unsafe or threatened. Admittedly, I am male, tall, and fairly ugly, but the fact remains that millions of tourists travel in Europe every year without any problems whatsoever. Just be reasonably cautious, don't make obvious mistakes that present easy opportunities for theft or invite harassment, and you will be fine.

Even more so than this, 99 percent of you won't have to worry about any of the drug-related and sex industry problems. Those of you that do will have to decide whether the possible benefits are worth the risks involved. Before you head-butt that bouncer, steal that pub sign, or sally forth in search of your drug of choice, remember that you are a long way from home.

12

What to see

The following are my totally subjective opinions on what I've seen in Europe. I haven't been everywhere, or even come close, but I have seen quite a bit. In every case, no matter where you go, I can give you one piece of advice that will be worth its weight in gold. As I've said before, GO EARLY. For example, at the Uffizi Gallery in Florence one morning, ninety minutes before opening there was one person in line. Sixty minutes prior about one hundred people were in line. Thirty minutes prior, five hundred people were waiting, and, as the doors opened, at least one thousand people were in a line stretching out of sight.

I would advise arriving at major museums about an hour before opening time during the summer. That way you will wait roughly one hour in the cool of the morning, see a relatively uncrowded museum, and be on your way as the crowds begin to get bad. Also, at the Louvre you can go late, during the relatively uncrowded evening hours on Mondays and Wednesdays.

Before you go, here are a few tips to avoid offending your hosts, and to help preserve the marvelous works of art you are going to see. Also, remember that most of the churches and cathedrals you will be visiting are functioning houses of worship and/or hold great religious significance. Behave accordingly.

- Keep the talk to a bare minimum, and whisper. Marble echoes terribly.

- Do NOT take flash photos without prior approval. Make sure that you take a camera which allows you to turn the flash function off. If you happen to enter a church during a mass or service, stand silently in the back. If you wish to stay, walk to a side pew. Don't walk down the center aisle.
- Do your part in art preservation. Refrain from taking flash photos of tapestries, paintings, and frescoes. The intense light of a flash deteriorates paint, and greatly accelerates the aging of other works of art. Even daylight is harmful to some more fragile works, and for this reason many churches keep their artworks in dark chapels, and some are illuminated only on request, or by pressing a button. NEVER use a flash on works displayed in this manner.
- Mosaics and sculptures are usually safe to photograph using a flash, but, as stated, you should ask permission to do so. It really shouldn't be necessary, though. You can find all but the most obscure works of art on postcards, which usually cost less than the price of a photo, and are typically of better quality than any picture you might take.
- If you are desperate to take pictures of paintings, you

Going early pays off big in Rome

The first time I went to the Vatican Museum I followed my own advice and arrived an hour early, with a newspaper and my journal to kill the wait. As I stood in my one-man line, a tour group came up and was admitted to the museum. I followed them in, thinking that my guidebook was wrong about the museum hours. When I got to the ticket desk I found that tour groups were allowed in early so that they could be shepherded through the museum for an hour or so before they were taken to the Sistine Chapel. Standing there alone in front of the desk, as the guard read a newspaper and sipped an espresso, it suddenly occurred to me that I was the only visitor in the museum not on a tour, and therefore would have the Chapel to myself if I could buy a ticket early. A few smiles, some broken Spanish/Italian, and a few thousand lire later I was race-walking to the Chapel, having been admitted by the friendly guard.

I had the Sistine Chapel to myself for the better part of half an hour; no other tourists, no cameras, and, believe it or not, for most of the time, no guards. Completely alone. Even if this was a unique experience, I noticed something else. After the first other tourists came in (about fifteen minutes after the museum opened) there was still about half an hour when fewer than twenty people were in the Chapel itself. It was almost nicer with them there, to see their reactions.

After seeing some of the museum's collection I looked back into the Chapel at about 4pm. The entire floor, every square foot, was packed with a mass of people. Flashbulbs were going off constantly, and the sound of a hundred conversations was echoing off the walls and ceiling. I didn't even go back in.

I guarantee you that the first few people I shared the Sistine Chapel with early that morning had a totally different experience than those who came only a few hours later. It pays to go early.

may do so without a flash by using very high-speed film – 1000 ASA or better. Those who intend to take a number of photos of works of art probably know more about this subject than I do, but I recommend that you bring twice as much film as you think you will need. Some museums, such as the Prado, if I remember correctly, sell this stuff, but it is likely to be old, and you will have to take out a second mortgage to buy more than a few rolls.

Seven "must see" works of art

1. The *Mona Lisa* (the Louvre, Paris)
2. The *Venus de Milo* (the Louvre)
3. The *Winged Victory of Samothrace* (the Louvre)
4. The **Sistine Chapel** (Vatican Museum, Rome)
5. **Michelangelo's** *Pietà* (St Peter's, Rome)
6. **Michelangelo's** *David* (the Accademia, Florence)
7. **Botticelli's** *Birth of Venus* (the Uffizi Gallery, Florence)

All these works are very familiar, almost to the point of being clichéd, especially the *Mona Lisa* (the *Winged Victory* is that stone angel with no head, and *Birth of Venus* is that naked blond girl on the seashell). Since they are so familiar, and their images have been seen so many times, they may disappoint at first. The presence of scores of frenzied, camera-flashing tourists (as is the case at the *Mona Lisa* from dawn till dusk) won't help. If you go to see any of these works, try to be at the head of the line when the museum opens, go directly to them and then move on to the other magnificent works of art to be found in these museums. Do not skip them, however. All these works are surpassingly beautiful, justly famous, and well worth seeing.

Eight favorite works of art and architecture

These are my personal favorites with a brief explanation of each. Totally subjective, by the way, and in no particular order.

1. **Velazquez's** *Las Meniñas* (Museo del Prado, Madrid). The greatest non-fresco painting I've ever seen, and one of the truly

great paintings in all of art. The unquestioned masterpiece of a lifetime by one of the true geniuses of painting. The illusion of depth the artist is able to achieve with a layer of paint on a piece of canvas must be seen to be believed.

2. **Goya's** *Saturn Devouring a Son* (Museo del Prado, Madrid). The work of an artist teetering on the brink of insanity. If you see this painting, you won't have to be told that. There is a painting of the same subject by Rubens, also in the Prado. Compare the two, and you will understand how close Goya was to the edge. He painted this depiction of savagery on the wall of his home, for his eyes only.

3. **Rubens'** *Little Fur* (Kunsthistorisches Museum, Vienna). A portrait of his wife that Rubens painted for himself, and the loving care and skill he put into it are marvelous to see. It hangs in a room with other works by Rubens, and it is so far superior to them that it makes the other paintings look ordinary. A strong contender for the greatest portrait ever painted – the work of a genius, at the peak of his skill.

4. **Leonardo da Vinci's** *Virgin of the Rocks* (National Gallery, London). One of two similar but not identical paintings – the other version hangs in the Louvre. The face of the angel, in particular, is surpassingly beautiful.

5. **The stained-glass windows of the Cathedral at Chartres**. World famous for their astounding blue tones, this is only one aspect of a truly breathtaking cathedral located in a small town southwest of Paris. As my high-school Spanish teacher said to me years ago, "If you are ever in France, please, be kind to yourself, and go to Chartres."

6. **The Medici Chapel** (Florence). Possibly the most overwhelming single room in the world, with four or five Michelangelo statues down the hall as a bonus. Built to house the tombs of the Medici rulers of Florence, and as an expression of their wealth and power. Look closely at the altar; what appears to be paint is actually mosaic inlay.

7. **The double cloister in Jerónimos Monastery in Lisbon, Portugal**. I've seen a lot of churches, and a lot of beautiful buildings, but I've never seen anything like this. This is the one absolute "can't-miss sight" in Lisbon, an open courtyard surrounded by a double tier of carved stone so delicate and detailed that it would look perfectly at home in a temple in Cambodia.

8. **The Tables at the Prado, Madrid**. As mentioned in the section in museums (see below), the Prado has the finest collection of

paintings in the world. Along with the paintings, scattered throughout the second floor of the museum are tables with stone inlay surfaces that push the limit between art and miracle. These aren't classic mosaics (which use tiny chips of stone to create a picture); instead they use chunks of stone to simulate objects lying on the table's surface, such as fruit, paper, and scientific and musical instruments. I've never seen anything like them anywhere else in Europe, and every time I go to Madrid I am dumbfounded at the skill it took to make them.

Top ten museums and galleries

These are the big ones – the ones you can't miss if you're anywhere nearby.

1. **National Gallery, London**. The pride of Britain – a beautiful museum, right on Trafalgar Square, with free admission and dozens of magnificent paintings. These include a Leonardo, brilliant works by Rembrandt, Velazquez, Rubens, Monet, Van Gogh, and many others. If you see one thing in London, see this museum.

2. **Rijksmuseum, Amsterdam**. Three Vermeers, and more Rembrandts than you can shake a brush at. Strong in Dutch paintings, of course, and right around the corner from the Van Gogh Museum. Notice that one of the Vermeers is not nearly as beautiful as the other two: even great artists can't be great all of the time.

3. **Uffizi Gallery, Florence**. Botticelli's two masterpieces (*Birth of Venus* and *Allegory of Spring*), and the one and only easel painting Michelangelo ever completed (*The Holy Family*). These alone are worth the price of admission, but there are dozens of other great works.

4. **Museo del Prado, Madrid**. The greatest museum of painting in the world. More outstanding Goya and Velazquez than the rest of the museums in the world combined, along with critical works by Rubens, Dürer, Bosch, Raphael, and many others. Just the right size, too, to be covered in a day. The perfect museum.

5. **Louvre, Paris**. The Louvre's miles of corridors and staircases have defeated legions of travelers, who have been slowly worn down on the creaking wood floors of this former royal palace. Tons

of Leonardo, rooms full of Rubens, Delacroix, Rembrandt, along with Raphael, a Vermeer or two, and works from every possible French painter. Oh yeah, and the *Mona Lisa*, *Venus de Milo*, *Winged Victory*, Roman sculpture... you get the idea. As previously mentioned, far too much for a single day.

6. **Kunsthistorische Museum**, **Vienna**. Expensive admission, but worth it. Some truly great Rubens (*Little Fur*, *Head of Medusa*, and others), a very sexy Correggio, and some marvelous imperial gewgaws left over from the Hapsburgs.

7. **The Armory, Moscow**. Start with a dozen eggs. Fabergé eggs, that is. Jeweled crowns by the armload. Gilded carriages, illuminated manuscripts, and jeweled icons. All of this, however, pales in comparison with the contents of the diamond vault. The vault contains piles of diamonds. Big diamonds, small diamonds, cut diamonds, uncut diamonds. Piles of gold bars. Giant gold nuggets. Platinum nuggets the size of basketballs. I like this place.

8. **Hermitage Museum, St Petersburg**. The Hermitage is such an overwhelming building that the art it contains is almost of secondary interest. The Hermitage was the Winter Palace of the Russian Royal Family, and it shows. After walking up the Jordan Staircase, even Versailles will look squalid. After an hour or so in the jewelry collections, if it isn't solid gold with diamonds, you won't even bother to look at it (and you'll understand why Russia had a revolution). Oh, yeah, a huge collection of Impressionists, seminal works by Rembrandt, a Leonardo, and all the usual suspects.

9. **British Museum, London**. The best part of my first visit to the British Museum was walking up to this big hunk of rock, reading the info plate to see what the big hunk of rock was, and realizing that I was looking at the Rosetta Stone. Just sitting there. The British Museum houses some of the very best artifacts the British brought home from their various colonies, a couple of copies of the Magna Carta, the Elgin Marbles, and a really cool chess set. Well, well worth a visit.

10. **Vatican Museum, Rome**. The Sistine Chapel, along with three absolute milestones in the history of Western Art – the Apollo Belvedere, the Belvedere Torso, and the Laocoön. The tapestries, frescoes, and bric-a-brac in the corridors are about as fabulous as you would expect from the Vatican. Priceless paintings from major artists of every age? Of course!

The performing arts

The preceding lists in this chapter are related to art and architecture not only because I personally like that sort of thing, but because this is where Europe truly shines. There are, of course, gorgeous national parks and majestic mountains in Europe, but similar sites exist in dozens of spots all over the world. But, no matter where you go or how long you travel, you won't find anything similar to the cathedrals, museums, and old cities of Europe anywhere in the world.

That being said, a reader named Melanie Jacobson sent me a sweet letter recently, which reminded me that "culture" is not just museums and cathedrals, and that the performing arts are also important. She's quite right, and it is in her honor that I include the following thoughts on opera, music, and theater.

Opera

Love opera or hate it, the opera houses of Europe are incredible monuments to the arts, and are worth visiting even if there is no performance scheduled. Nevertheless, the best way to visit an opera house is to actually go to a performance. To their great credit, most opera companies in Europe sell heavily discounted tickets to impoverished students and young people. You may not get the best – or even close to the best – seats in the house, but you'll be able to hear well and you can still wander around the house gaping at the art and architecture.

Having been to opera performances in London, St Petersburg, Budapest, Naples, and Vienna, I strongly recommend them to anyone. The best place to inquire about tickets and performances is the city tourist office. In Vienna and Milan, especially, the opera performances are a major tourist draw, and the tourist office will know exactly how to get tickets.

If you're from North America, be aware when buying a ticket that "balcony" means you will be up in the rafters with the bats. What you might think of as the balcony (an upper tier of seats) is called the mezzanine in Europe. The next tier up is called the "loge" and then, way up in the stratosphere, comes the balcony. The "stalls" or "parterre" refers to the seats on the ground floor. If tickets cost a hundred dollars apiece in the stalls they can be as cheap as seven dollars apiece in the balcony (often with good reason).

If you are in any Eastern European city, especially Prague or Budapest, you can get the best seats in the house for a tenth of what they would cost in Western Europe (or North America or Australia, for that matter). Take advantage of it.

Don't worry about dressing up either. Those who are in the cheap seats with you won't be wearing tuxedos and evening gowns. Put on your best, of course, but if your best is a clean shirt and jeans, you'll fit right in.

Symphonies and the ballet

Ninety percent of what I wrote above about opera applies to symphony and ballet performances as well, except that tickets will be marginally cheaper than those for opera. By the way, don't just look for these sorts of performances in the obvious places. I've seen great ballets in Sweden, outstanding music in Finland, and a piano recital held outdoors in a ruin in the heart of Rome. Even more so than with opera, the symphony orchestras and ballet companies of Eastern Europe offer world-class performances at a fraction of Western European prices.

Theater

Your greatest challange to seeing theater in Europe is, of course, the language barrier. For this reason, you might want to take advantage of the theater arts while you are in Britain or Ireland during your travels. If you are fluent in a second language, say French, Italian, or German, then by all means look into seeing a production while in Paris, Rome, Berlin, or any major European city. As always, check out a local newspaper or look for flyers in the tourist office and you will most likely find discount seats or special deals to a number of productions during your stay.

Music in Prague

For some reason, Prague hosts an incredible number of all sorts of musical performances, from voice recitals by soloists to chamber music to string quartets to full-blown symphony orchestras, often five or six performances in a single night. Many of the smaller performances take place in churches which are hundreds of years old, and are marvelous places to hear music that was being written at about the same time they were being built. If you visit Prague, at least one of these performances is a must.

London is, of course, the epicenter of live theater despite what those in New York might think. There are dozens of ticket outlets in the Leicester Square/Piccadilly/Covent Garden area but, as before, be careful when you buy tickets – the worst seats in British theaters are usually pretty horrible.

Dublin's famous Abbey Theatre is another European standout, founded in 1904 by W.B. Yeats and Lady Gregory, and the theater has played a prominent role in Ireland's rich artistic tradition, by supporting both traditional Irish playwrights and younger up-and-comers. The theater itself is dripping with history and you'll feel that it's a special occasion just being there.

Seven spots that are touristy but still fun

1. **Neuschwanstein Castle**, **Bavaria**. Make sure that after the tour you cross the bridge above the castle and climb up the hill for an incredible view. Lots of Germans visit here, too, so don't go on a weekend if you can avoid it. Long lines even during the week – bring a book and some water and food.

2. **The Hofbräu House**, **Munich**. Lots of tourists, but many of them, at least on weekends, are German. You will also see the occasional older man in full lederhosen get-up. I am convinced that these guys are either hired to add atmosphere to the place, or else are mechanical dummies, like the Pirates of the Caribbean, and are actually drinking motor oil.

3. **The British Crown Jewels (in the Tower of London)**. Absolutely massive lines, and you go past the jewels on a moving sidewalk/conveyor belt. Still, the diamonds are incredibly, unbelievably huge, and the Royal Punch Bowl is both beautiful and utterly tasteless at the same time.

4. **Buckingham Palace**, **London**. Another massive line, probably with the same people you met waiting to see the Crown Jewels. The palace tour may no longer be given when you get there, but if it is, you won't be disappointed. You don't get to look in the Queen's medicine cabinet or lingerie drawer, but the palace is pretty darn impressive.

5. **The Leaning Tower of Pisa**. Pisa is an hour from Florence, and best done as a day-trip from there (about twenty trains a day).

The Tower is actually the bell tower
for a stunning cathedral, with a bap-
tistry, on the same site (known as the Campo dei Miracoli, or
"Field of Miracles"). The tower is really leaning over, but it's completely safe, and you can even walk up it.

6. **Pompeii**. The ruins of a Roman city frozen in time by a volcanic eruption and untouched for centuries. Go early, and bring
plenty of water; Pompeii is a huge site, and will take you much of
the day to see properly.

7. **Trevi Fountain, Rome**. Almost everyone's heard of it ("Three
Coins in the Fountain"), and I've met many who thought such a
"touristy" place was not worth visiting. Don't make this mistake.
The fountain is a marvel – a perfect marriage of art and architecture. Beautiful by day, spectacular at night, it should not be missed
by anyone traveling in Rome. Go early and avoid the mobs.

Five disappointments

1. **Zermatt**. The town, not the surroundings, which are beautiful.
Zermatt is a town in the Alps very close to the Matterhorn, and has
therefore been a tourist mecca for more than a century. For a mere
$700–800, you can hire a guide to take you to the top of the

Matterhorn. Plus the train to the town is private, and charges big bucks even with a Eurail pass. To top it all off, there is a thriving *McDonald's* in town.

2. **Versailles**. Didn't live up to expectations, but then the expectations are pretty high. Still worth going to see, though. The gardens are much better than the interiors. Worst food for the money I've ever eaten at the local snack bar, so bring lunch and spend most of your time outdoors. At this symbol of French majesty and grandeur, you are charged half a buck to use the bathroom.

3. **The Louvre**. Too big, too many tourists. Definitely go, but go very early or during the evening hours on Mondays and Wednesdays, and know what you're looking for before you go. The Louvre is best seen on two or three shorter trips, concentrating on a specific section each time.

4. **Prague**. Still a beautiful city with a wonderful atmosphere, but the cigarette ads, billboards, *Pizza Huts*, and other flotsam of Western society are disgusting. Prague will probably look like New York in five years, so go there now, and try and ignore the pollution that Marlboro and Camel spread all over the city.

5. **The Olympic Museum in Lausanne, Switzerland**. High-tech and glitzy, but a bit superficial and very expensive. Skip this one.

Eight festivals worth building an itinerary around

All these are great – but for accommodation at any you'll need to book way in advance.

1. **The Fiesta of San Fermín**, also known as the Running of the Bulls, in Pamplona, Spain. A massive party, with an incredibly dangerous but exhilarating five minutes every morning. Every July 6 this festival begins at noon with a rocket fired by the mayor over the heads of a delirious crowd in Pamplona's main square. The next day, and for the following six days, at precisely 8am, six bulls and eight steers are run about half a mile through the streets of the town to the bull ring. Anyone who so chooses can run with them, although females are very unwelcome. If you want to see this spectacular event, come a few days early and look very, very hard for a

room. I slept with twelve strangers in a three-bedroom apartment and felt lucky to sleep indoors.

2. **The Edinburgh Festival**. The official Edinburgh Festival, which lasts three weeks at the end of August/beginning of September, is a serious cultural event. At the same time, though, the city hosts a military tattoo, jazz and film festivals, and the Festival Fringe, with thousands of alternative events – comedy, theater, music – and pubbing and clubbing till dawn.

3. **Il Palio, in Siena, Italy**. As wild a party as Pamplona, but somewhat less dangerous. On July 2 and August 16 the ancient neighborhoods of Siena hold a bareback horse race in the main square, a tradition that dates back centuries. Needless to say, there is massive revelry before, during, and after the race. As with Pamplona, get there way early, look hard for a place, and don't be surprised if prices have tripled for the week.

4. **Oktoberfest, in Munich, Germany**. Don't be misled – the Oktoberfest actually begins in mid-September. Everything else is pretty much as advertised: huge tents filled with massive crowds swilling beer and eating chickens and sausages. There are plenty of tourists from all over the world, but that doesn't take away much from the atmosphere of revelry.

5. **Festival of Avignon, France**. Mainly a theater festival, but with the stunning backdrop of the city as a stage, and plenty of off-Festival happenings, the atmosphere is unbeatable. Lasts three weeks from the second week of July.

6. **Holy Week and Feria de Abril, Seville, Spain**. Holy Week or Semana Santa, from Palm Sunday to Good Friday, is celebrated here with a strange mixture of extreme Catholicism and revelry – featuring hooded penitents and vast floats carried bodily by the crowds, along with carousing in the bars. The Feria de Abril, in the second half of April, usually follows soon after: a weeklong party of food, drink, and flamenco.

7. **Roskilde Festival, Denmark**. Roskilde, a small town near Copenhagen, is the unlikely setting for Europe's biggest open-air rock event, held during the last weekend in June. Tens of thousands of tickets are sold in advance, but they claim never to turn anyone away.

8. **Brockworth Cheese Rolling Festival**. Yes, "cheese rolling." In a modern version of what is probably an ancient fertility rite, every year on the last weekend in May thousands of spectators gath-

er in Brockworth, near Gloucester, England, to watch a few hardy souls risk life and limb in the pursuit of cheese. "Pursuit" is actually a pretty good description of what goes on: the contestants start at the top of a 300-yard slope with a one-in-two gradient, then chase a twenty-pound wheel of Gloucester cheese that is rolled down the slope before them. The contest is winner-take-all: first one to grab the cheese keeps it. Three races are run for men and women, then a fourth is run with women only. Injuries abound a few seconds after the race begins as the more clumsy competitors loose their footing, pile into each other, and eat large quantities of dirt as they slide down the slope face-first. Meanwhile, the fleet of foot and deft of balance dash down the slope in search of both cheese and glory. This event is covered by media from all over the world – any non-Briton who takes home a cheese is guaranteed to be a national hero, if only for a few minutes on the evening news.

Seven worthwhile spots you might overlook

1. **El Escorial**, a monastery and palace about an hour outside Madrid. The tombs of Spanish royalty and nobility alone are worth the trip out, and the building itself is quite impressive. It is filled with art treasures, of course.

2. **The Cathedral at Köln (Cologne)**. This is a hot tip. If you are going to take a train through Köln and don't intend on stopping, catch an earlier train, and when you get to Köln jump off and go to the cathedral, which is a two-minute walk from the station. Give yourself an hour or two, then catch the next train to your destination.

3. **London's Imperial War Museum**. Tons of real equipment and some very moving displays. The films of the liberation of Belsen concentration camp are about as horrible as anything ever captured on film, and are definitely not for children. If the British seem a bit proud of their victory over the Germans in World War II, remember that the German occupation plan called for exporting the entire adult male population to the continent as slaves.

4. **Herculaneum**. This Roman town was buried in the same volcanic eruption as Pompeii. As such, it is a similar site, but much less touristy. Excavation is still going on.

5. **The Alhambra, Granada, Spain**. The fortress of the last of the Moorish rulers of southern Spain, and one of the most romantic of all European monuments. Granada is a bit hard to get to by train, but the Alhambra is worth the trip. By all means, visit the gardens of the Generalife while you're there.

6. **Luxembourg**. This small country refers to itself as "Europe in Miniature," with some justification. The countryside, with its river valleys and storybook castles, is beautiful, and there is a small wine-growing region near the capital (actually, the whole country is "near the capital"). If you really want to get to know a small part of Europe, a two-week trip here would be perfect.

7. **Auschwitz/Birkenau**. Not in Germany, as many believe, but rather in southern Poland, about an hour by bus from Cracow. Auschwitz, the original camp of that name, is tiny, and was used to house slave laborers. When most people think of "Auschwitz," they are actually thinking of Birkenau, an enormous complex located about two miles from the original Auschwitz camp. This is the real extermination camp – see it for yourself.

Six great day-trips

1. **San Gimignano via Florence**. San Gimignano is a little town about an hour's bus ride from Florence and is most famous for its thirteen towers, which were built to store grain during times of war during the Middle Ages. Because the city is remarkably well preserved it is a magnet for tourists, most of them on day-trips from Florence. I advise just the opposite: stay in San Gimignano and take the bus into Florence for the day. Your quiet evenings here will make the twenty-first century seem like a memory.

2. **Oxford via London**. The most well-known of all British universities is just an hour by bus from London, and has enough student and budget accommodations to house an army. Oxford University is actually made up of a number of individual "colleges," most of which are centuries old, and housed in truly beautiful old buildings. While the buildings are ancient, the students are not, and you will find a rocking good time if you visit during a festival or as the term ends.

3. **Capri via Naples**. Some visitors skip the island of Capri (about an hour and fifteen minutes by ferry from Naples) because they think it's expensive. That would be a terrible mistake; Capri is breathtakingly beautiful and only a bit more expensive than the rest

of southern Italy. It can get crowded though, so it's not a bad idea to make it a day-trip instead of staying overnight. However you go, don't miss the ski lift to the highest point on the island, and definitely don't miss the Blue Grotto, a sea cave that by a miracle of refraction is filled with a glowing blue light. Strong swimmers can skip the expensive boat trips into the grotto and swim in after 6pm.

4. **Toledo via Madrid**. Toledo (about an hour and a half by train from Madrid) is perhaps the most intensely Spanish town in Spain. Perched on a bluff overlooking the Tajo river, Toledo is filled with winding streets, ancient churches, and a thousand years' worth of architecture, though it's most famous for its religious art, especially that of El Greco, and for its sword making, which made "Spanish steel" a byword for quality during the Middle Ages. (Now, sadly, most of the swords made here are cheap toys for the tourists.)

5. **Monaco via Nice**. Unlike most of the destinations mentioned above, Monaco (thirty minutes by bus from Nice) is not a great place to spend the night for a budget traveler, and should be considered purely as a day-trip. On one hand, it is a pretty place, with steep hills and beautiful homes; on the other, if your yacht doesn't have a helicopter on it, nobody will look twice at you when you pull into Monaco's harbor. That said, the best things in Monaco (the view, the ocean, and the Botanic Gardens or "jardin exotique") are cheap or free, and hey, going to the little place counts as visiting another whole country.

6. **Pont du Gard via Avignon or Nîmes**. Pont du Gard is a jaw-dropping Roman ruin in southern France – a massive, virtually intact triple-arched aqueduct soaring over the Gard River. By some miracle of cultural sensitivity and good taste, the visitor's center/theater/snack bar is about half a mile from the aqueduct, so when you get to the ruin itself, it's as if the modern world doesn't exist. Swimming in the clear water of the Gard River on a hot summer day is pure magic, especially since it's perfectly okay to swim under the 1900-year-old aqueduct itself. Pont du Gard is accessible by bus from Avignon and Nîmes.

Four "fantasy islands"

1. **The Lofotens, Norway**. Way, way, way, up north by the Arctic Circle, off the coast of Norway, are the Lofotens, a magical land of twenty-hour days, wild blueberries, and fresh cod in the summer.

Unfortunately it's a rain-soaked, freezing nightmare of fog and cold in the winter. However, summer visitors should spend at least a week wandering through these islands, which even the Norwegians see as a rugged and somewhat adventurous destination. Bring hiking boots, bug spray, the best raincoat you can afford, and be prepared for friendly people, sweeping vistas, and lots of fish on the menu.

2. **The Isle of Man, Britain**. This island (located between Britain and Ireland in the Irish Sea) technically belongs to England but has its own parliament, dialect, and (most importantly to the British) tax laws. For some reason known only to God, the islanders take great pride in two of the local animals: the Manx cat (which has no tail), and the Manx loghtan sheep (which has four horns). Horny sheep and tail-less cats aside, the island is perfect for hiking and walking and has some of the most impressive scenery in Britain.

3. **Bornholm, Denmark**. This little bit of Denmark stuck way off to the east in the Baltic Sea is a popular summer destination for Scandinavians, and I highly recommend a visit. If you go, take the bus down to the enormous fortress at the northwest end of the island, and by all means take the mail boat (which actually sails most of the way) out to Christianso, a tiny island off the coast of Bornholm where the Danes used to exile the politically inconvenient.

4. **Sifnos, Greece**. Sifnos is in the Cyclades, the most popular of the Greek Islands, but it's far enough off the beaten trail to be semi-livable, even in early July (from mid-July through August, forget it). If you can get there early in the season, you'll understand why these islands are so crowded: the heat, the brilliant white houses with deep-blue roofs, the aquamarine sea, the food, the tiny churches, and the sense of history that seems to hang in the air. Go early, as I said, but go, and you'll understand.

Four beckoning beaches

1. **Sagres, Portugal**. Although once a port of great maritime significance, the Sagres of today is better known for its long stretches of scenic beaches. Within walking distance of the village lie a half dozen pristine beaches, free of crowds and offering up majestic views of the southwesternmost tip of Portugal. If the water is too cold for you (it can get quite chilly), you can stop into the village

market to stock up on picnic provisions and five-liter flagons of the local wine for pennies.

2. **Bol, Croatia**. Stranded on the far side of the Vidova Gora mountains, Bol's beautiful setting and the charm of its old stone houses is unbelievable. However, the main attraction of the village is its beach, Zlatni Rat (Golden Cape). Unusually sandy for this region and stunningly beautiful, the cape juts into the sea in the form of a giant "Y," changing shape slightly from day to day as the wind plays across it.

3. **Amalfi, Italy**. Occupying the southern side of Sorrento's peninsula, the Almalfi coast lays claim to Europe's loveliest stretch of sand, particularly alluring in Amalfi itself. Yes, it can get crowded at times, but the energy level and overwhelming beauty of the beach overshadow any minuses.

4. **Antibes, France**. Although Antibes is a place of residence for some of Europe's very well-off, it's also a place with great, unaffected charm. Plage de la Salis, the longest Antibes beach, runs along the eastern neck of the coastline sans giant Riviera hotels – a rarity – and further along the southern and western shores are a few more public and untrammeled beaches definitely worth exploring. The moneyed are tucked away in the hills and cliffs, leaving the public beaches fairly empty, and perfect for some R&R.

Five preserved pieces of "Ye Olde World"

1. **Bruges, Belgium**. Bruges enjoyed great prosperity from the ninth to the fifteenth centuries, but eventually slipped into decline, finally rediscovered by wealthy nineteenth-century Europeans drawn to the town's quiet, aged charm. Frozen in time, having managed to escape damage in both world wars, Bruges has emerged as the perfect tourist attraction with its intimate, winding steets living up to even the most inflated tourist hype. However, make sure to see it out of season or in the early morning before the hordes have descended, otherwise it can become unbearable.

2. **Vindabona (Hoher Markt), Austria**. Buried below street level in Vienna's oldest square, and accessible through what is now a sushi bar, is the remains of the Roman camp – Vindabona. Today, two large houses still remain, revealing the complex heating systems

which the Romans developed to see them through the harsh Austrian winters. The fact that Vienna bustles stories above the quiet remains of the old Roman ruins adds an eerie edge to the site.

3. **Dubrovnik, Croatia**. Dubrovnik is a beautifully preserved fortified town pressed against the sea within magnificent medieval walls. First settled by Roman refugees in the early seventh century, it has survived centuries of battles between Slavs, Muslims, Christians, Byzantines, Venetians and even an eight-month seige in 1991 by Yugoslav forces. History oozes from the city's medieval gates, Franciscan monestary, fifteenth-century palace, and even from its small city beach. Definitely a sight worth seeing.

4. **Český Krumlov, Czech Republic**. Dramatically squeezed into an S-bend in the River Vltava, Český Krumlov ranks as one of the most superbly preserved medieval towns in Europe. The twisting river divides the town into two segments: the circular old town on the right bank, and the Latrán quarter on the hillier left bank. Start with the castle in the Latrán quarter but be sure not to miss the expansive terrace gardens high above the town, and the (not so medieval) Egon Schiele gallery.

5. **Canterbury, England**. One of England's most venerable cities, Canterbury offers two thousand years of history, with Roman and early Christian ruins, a Norman castle, and a famous cathedral that dominates a medieval warren of time-skewed Tudor dwellings. It does get crowded during high season, but it's still well worth a visit.

Five thrills for outdoor enthusiasts

1. **Hiking down Samarian Gorge, Crete**. At 18km in length, the Samarian Gorge is the largest in Europe, descending dramatically from the Omalos plateau. The walk down the gorge takes between four and seven hours, depending on how fit you feel and how much scenery you stop to take in. You can also walk up the gorge if you're a contrarian at heart; it's six or seven hours at a reasonable pace. The single most rewarding part to a descent of the scenic gorge is the cold sea water which awaits at the bottom – your dive in is likely to live long in your memory.

2. **Surfing in Thurso, Scotland**. Unlikely though it may seem, Scotland is fast gaining a reputation as a surfing destination, with a

good selection of quality breaks. It may not have the sunshine of Hawaii, and the water is generally steely-gray rather than turquoise-blue, but Thurso is a definite surf spot and boasts one of the finest reef breaks in Europe. However, Scotland's northern coastline lies on the same latitude as Alaska and Iceland, so the water temps are very low – you'll need a good wet suit.

3. **Snowboarding in Axamer Lizum, Austria**. This well-equipped resort southwest of Innsbruck is favored by Austrian snowboarders but rarely featured in holiday brochures. If you don't want to stay overnight in Axamer, it's relatively easy to pop out there for the day from Innsbruck. And, if you're not going to be around during the winter months, you can still take to the slopes southwest of Axamer on Stubai Glacier, where skiing is possible year-round. The Innsbruck tourist office runs day-trips for skiers to the glacier in summer for around $45 (includes bus transfer, equipment rental, and lift pass).

4. **Cycling around Inishmore, Ireland**. Inishmore (Inis Mór) is the largest (and most touristed) of the three Aran Islands lying about thirty miles across the mouth of Galway Bay. It is a long strip of an island, a great tilted plateau of limestone, with a scattering of villages along the sheltered northerly coast. Although the most touristed of the three islands, it makes for one of the most idyllic spots in the world to cycle, with a stop here and there for a gaze out to sea or at the maze of stone walls that zigzag throughout the island's grassy fields.

5. **Skiing at Garmisch–Partenkirchen, Germany**. It isn't any accident that this is the most famous resort in the German Alps. It's at the foot of the highest mountain – the Zugspitze – and also hosted the Winter Olympics in 1936. The location is marvelous, and facilities are plentiful for skating and other winter sports as well. In summer, mountaineers and hiking enthusiasts come to explore the craggy heights.

Four "Oh My God" moments in Europe

These are some personal favorites; sights that, when you see them, will leave you with no doubt whatsoever that (1) you are in Europe, and (2) you are seeing something that is totally different from what you normally see in everyday life.

1. **Westminster, London**. (This one is best at night, but pretty darn impressive in the day as well.) When you're in London, before you go anywhere, take the Tube to Westminster Station. Leave the station using Exit Four, and only Exit Four. Look up. You'll understand.

2. **St Peter's, Rome**. Walk in the door at St Peter's. Look all the way to the other end of the room. That big thing in your way, with the pillars, is the tomb of St Peter, the first Pope. That white dove, up there on the window, the one that looks like a fly, is larger than you are. The room you're standing in can hold 95,000 people.

3. **Sainte Chapelle, Paris**. Walk out of the spiral staircase into the upper chapel of Sainte Chapelle, in Paris. Most of what you're looking at, as delicate as it seems, was already centuries old on the day that Columbus was born.

4. **The Trocadero, Paris**. (This is another one that's best at night.) When you get to Paris, take the Metro to Trocadero Station. Leave by the exit marked "Woodrow Wilson" and "Musée". When you get out of the station, you should have a street on your right, a building on your left and, across the street and a little ways in front of you, a statue of a man on a horse. Walk down the street (in the direction of the statue) for about 50m, then turn left around the building. You will have no doubt that you are in Paris.

The worst of Europe

1. **Bullfights**. I love Spain, and some of my fondest travel memories are from that country. However, bullfights are, in my opinion, the unfair, unsporting, and cruel torture of a fine animal. (I would have no problem with bullfighting if the bull had half a chance and more matadors were gored.) If you disagree with me, go see one. If you agree, go see one anyway, so you can talk about how bad it is with authority. Feel free to walk out halfway through.

2. **Secondhand smoke**. We're talking billowing clouds of nicotine death, spewed forth from every man, woman, and child above the age of nine. Well, maybe it's not quite that bad, but it's bad enough. You'll see.

3. **Munich Hauptbahnhof**. This is not so much a railway station as a gigantic ant farm built for human beings. Despite having passed through it at least ten times, I still manage to get lost every time I arrive. Both members of the rock group Milli Vanilli lived in this station for a time. I can understand why they lip-synched their way out of there.

4. **Cynar**. Go into any bar in Italy. Ask for a Cynar (Chee-nar). Drink it. As you feel your insides spasm in disgust, you will understand. That elusive taste, as you may guess, is a distilled extract of the vegetable pictured on the label.

5. **The Vienna train station shuffle**. Vienna has two major train stations, and if you are passing through the city you often have to stop, get out, and take a bus or tram to the other station. This is not only irritating, but for some reason, there are no directions in either station. Every time I've passed through the city it has been a combination fire drill and wrestling match with my map as I frantically try to figure out how to get from one station to the other and then get there in time for my next train.

6. **Avignon TGV station**. Somebody made a fortune building this white elephant: a sterile, grossly over-designed glass-and-chrome nightmare fifteen minutes by (expensive) bus or (more expensive) taxi from the center of Avignon. The place handles roughly five percent of the trains that visit Avignon; it's freezing in the winter, a roasting greenhouse in the summer, and is far too "modern" to bother with luxuries like benches for those who might be waiting for a train. To top it all off, the regular station is perfectly able to handle TGVs.

7. **Graffiti**. Obviously, living in countries with free health care, free education, and governments that throw away money like sailors on a drinking binge isn't enough for some young punks in Europe – they feel the need to express themselves with spray paint, often on buildings that have stood unblemished for hundreds of years. I've noticed that graffiti has exploded all over Europe in the last five years; it's everywhere, but is less common in the poorer countries than in the wealthier welfare states of northern Europe.

8. **La Sagrada Familia**. This may be the ugliest building known to man. It's still under construction, and one can only tremble at the thought of how ugly it will be when completed. They should stop now and spend the money on tearing the place down and

replacing it with something more attractive, like, say, a pig farm, a sewage plant, or a junk yard. There seems to be an "Emperor's New Clothes" dynamic going on in Barcelona; this cathedral is so famous and such a tourist draw that nobody is willing to state the obvious – the damn thing is as ugly as a toilet plunger, and, when compared to other cathedrals, looks like something made by a drunk grade-school student with modeling clay.

9. **Florence luggage storage**. The luggage storage office in the main train station at Florence is nothing more than a legalized den of thieves, Italian-style. Rather than being honest and pulling out a gun and robbing tourists, the local luggage office charges ten dollars a day to store one bag. That's not a misprint. This legal monopoly charges ten dollars a day to throw a bag on a shelf. Last time I was in Florence there had to be five hundred bags in the storage room. At ten dollars a day that's $150,000 a month in revenue generated with minimal cost. Needless to say, somebody is getting rich from this scam.

10. **The *Mona Lisa* Motorway**. The *Mona Lisa* hangs in a little alcove at the end of a very long hallway in the Louvre. As a result, you see hundreds of tourists per hour damn near running down that hallway towards that one picture. After seeing it, most of them leave the Louvre through the convenient exit nearby. Well, by walking down that hallway and not stopping, you have missed roughly ten percent of the total number of Leonardo da Vinci paintings in the world. There's only one Leonardo in the entire Western Hemisphere (in Washington, DC), but thousands of people go to the Louvre, pay to get in, and walk past four of them. Also hanging in that hallway are paintings by Raphael, Bronzino, Caravaggio, Correggio, and Carracci. If I were to take all of those paintings on tour, I could pack millions of people into museums anywhere in the world outside of France.

11. **The Black Hole of Barcelona**. Barcelona sells itself as the Spanish city of the future, and yet it has fewer international trains than your average French farm village. Well, it's not quite that bad, but it sure feels like it. You may think that just because Barcelona is such a huge city, you can take your Eurail pass to the station and hop a train to wherever you want whenever you feel like it. Not A Chance. Getting out of Barcelona, especially in the summer, is a nightmare of roasting heat, full-to-the-roof trains, and a station that resembles a riot. If you choose to go to Barcelona,

Food in Europe – the good, the bad, and the ugly

During your travels you will have many "local delicacies" nudged your way with proud smiles, and you'll find it very hard to turn down your hospitable hosts. A word of advice first – make sure you know exactly what you're digging into before you chow down. There are some scary choices floating around out there, countered, I'm happy to say, by some sensational ones that shouldn't be overlooked. Below, I've listed some of the dishes and places worth scouting out (obviously very abbreviated, as there is great food to be had pretty much everywhere) and those worth avoiding at all costs. If you wind up trying any of the latter, try to put on a happy face and chalk it up to adventure.

The Good

Bulgarian yoghurt. Yoghurt was invented in Bulgaria (or so they claim), and the yoghurt in that country is a totally different substance than the stuff you may have eaten out of a plastic carton at home. For the record, theirs is better and if you are adventurous enough to make it to Bulgaria, you'll eat this stuff two or three times a day and still want more.

Belgian frites. Don't call 'em French fries! Many a backpacker has kept body and soul together while traveling in Belgium thanks to this dish, which, at its most basic form, is half a pound of fried potatoes stuffed in a paper cone. No, it's not exactly health food, but when you're dragging a fifty-pound bag of dirty laundry around Europe, you need those extra calories. When you order, be careful, or you may get a giant blob of mayonnaise plopped on the top of your fries – not for all tastes.

Italian tiramisu. Considering that my whole family is Italian, and that I've eaten a bathtub of this stuff, I'm embarrassed to admit that I only tried tiramisu in Rome a few years ago. Tiramisu is half-cake, half-pudding, consisting of layers of cream, coffee liqueur, and chocolate poured over sponge cake. When it's done well, it's fantastic and if you haven't tried it before, make sure you do in Italy.

St-Nectaire cheese. There are so many different types of cheese in France (more than 400 in total) that many visitors stick to the familiar (ie Brie, Camembert, etc), which are all good. If you want to branch out and try something a bit different, you won't go wrong with the strong, creamy St-Nectaire. Try to get the *fermier* kind, usually meaning that it's made on the farm, rather than at a cooperative or manufacturer.

Basque cuisine. Widely considered Spain's finest cuisine, the gastronomic treats which await you in the Basque provinces will forever change your ideas about food. One taste of a la vasca, chipirones en su tinta (squid cooked in its ink), or txangurro (spider crab), and you'll know why the people here are compulsive eaters (and trust me, they are). The best part is that it's very reasonably priced and easy to find – since it's served up in roadside *caseríos* (*baserri* in Basque) throughout the region. If you're not in the mood or don't have time to sit down for a full-fledged meal, you can always saddle up at virtually any bar in the region, and find finger-friendly snacks known as *pinchos* in the Basque country, or *tapas* throughout Spain, freshly cooked and always excellent.

The Bad

Cynar. Cynar is so vile that it has been promoted from the bad food list to the "Worst of Europe" list, and it richly deserves such status. See p.200 for a proper description.

Blutwurst. My God, if that name (pronounced "bloot-wurst") isn't a warning, what is? I'll make this simple: Blutwurst means "blood sausage." Do you need any further explanation? It's found in Germany, Scotland (where it's known as black pudding), and few other places, thankfully.

Dutch drops. I was introduced to this "candy" by some Dutch girls who took sadistic pleasure in watching my face contort as I foolishly tried the largest "drop" in the bag. Dutch drops are sort of like a licorice-flavored gumdrop, only for some reason they have about five times the normal amount of licorice and what tastes like a pound of salt in each drop. Buy a bag for someone at home you don't like.

Any food served in a café with a view of the Eiffel Tower. To Parisians, the Eiffel Tower is no big deal, and the only people willing to pay extra to eat with a view of the tower are tourists. Owners of cafés with a view delight in charging exorbitant prices for horrible food, and they can get away with it because their customers won't be coming back any time soon.

The Ugly

Haggis. I am convinced that if a hell exists for vegetarians, haggis is served there three times a day. The Scots seem to take a perverse pride in serving their guests this gastronomic horror, which consists of chopped mutton heart, lungs, and liver, mixed with a generous amount of oatmeal and boiled in the sewed-up stomach of a sheep. Better them than me, mate.

El Museo de Jamón. If eating haggis provides a glimpse of the menu in vegetarian's hell, El Museo del Jamón provides a pretty good guess at the decor. This is a small chain of restaurants in Madrid, which, as you might guess, specialize in ham. Every inch of ceiling space, wall area, and countertop is covered with massive hams-with-the-hoofs-still-in-'em. The food is actually quite good, and the sandwiches are cheap and filling, but it's hard to get past the sheer quantity of pig flesh proudly displayed.

Spotted Dick. Formerly, this could be found only in the most traditional English working-class restaurants; however, it has become popular again, for whatever reason. I must admit, I only eat the stuff because I like ordering it. If you can't get the name out without laughing, try ordering "Toad in the Hole." (Any place that has Spotted Dick will probably also have this other traditional English dish). No, I'm not going to say what they are, other than to say that "Toad in the Hole" is a main course, and "Spotted Dick" is a dessert.

check very carefully to see when you can get out of the city - even the pitifully small number of international trains don't run every day. Also, make a reservation for your departure train, and do it the second you know when you want to leave.

13

Going home

S adly, every trip must eventually come to an end. Truth be told, many people are glad to be heading home after two months (or more) on the go, sleeping in a different bed every few days. Returning home should be a piece of cake for the now-experienced traveler, so only a few words of advice are necessary:

- If you are flying home, and stopping on the way, be careful. If you miss one leg of a flight, all other legs are canceled. For example, let's say you are scheduled to fly home from Munich to London to Sydney, with a scheduled stop of one week in London. You are having such a good time in Munich that you no-show for your flight to London, and stay in Munich for six extra days, and take a train to London. Well, your ticket from London to Sydney was canceled when the plane took off from Munich without you. Believe it or not, it is virtually impossible to cancel one segment of a two-part flight even if you call ahead. Hard to believe, but true. If your homeward ticket says that you catch a plane in Munich, and go through London and back on to home, even if the whole trip is on the same airline, you MUST catch that plane in Munich. Yes, I know this is stupid - believe me, I know. I once burned through six phone cards in Paris, trying to get a flight segment canceled so I didn't have to backtrack all the way to Denmark.
- Don't forget to confirm your flight back home, just as when you left. Remember, you must call to confirm within 72 hours of departure.
- Get to the airport at least two hours before takeoff, and be prepared to wait. Security and other procedures at most European airports

always seem to take longer than expected. An extra twenty minutes', leeway can save you a bundle of stress.

- Remember, if you're connecting between two flights on your way home, you can't simply go to the gate for your second flight at your stopover airport, even if you have tickets in hand. Remember to check in at the "further clearance" or "further travel" desk.
- If you are flying Virgin Atlantic out of London Heathrow be aware that (due to strong tensions between British Airways and Virgin) the Virgin Atlantic gates are a LONG way from security checkpoints – I've walked out there a couple of times and was afraid I was going to fall off the edge of the world.
- Those planning to buy statues or bronze cannons as souvenirs, and (seriously) those planning to live in Europe for a while, might not be able to bring everything back with them on the plane. If so, you can contact a shipping company that specializes in overseas moves. The cheapest are in London, and listed in *TNT*, but businesses of this type can be unreliable. Do some serious comparison shopping, and ask if you could talk with some previous customers.
- Duty-free restrictions vary throughout Europe, but are standard for EU countries at one litre of spirits, plus two litres of table wine, plus 200 cigarettes (or 250g tobacco, or fifty cigars) and about 250ml of perfume. Anything more will be taxed. Each country also has a limit on other goods that can be imported without tax. This duty-free limit, in local currency, is $400 in the States, $300 in Canada, £136 in Britain, $400 in Australia, and $700 in New Zealand.
- When you get home, be sure to use all sorts of foreign terms to irritate your friends and let them know that, yes, you went to Europe and they did not. Complain about the coffee. Whine about the lack of art and culture.
- If you intend to learn how to speak a foreign language, do so right away. Resolving to learn a language is very common among people who have just returned from Europe, and the ratio of classes taken to resolutions made is about one to twenty. It's zero to something large with me. . . .
- Start planning your next trip to Europe.

Finally . . . one last request

The trip that gave birth to the original *First-Time Europe* began more than seven years ago. I've been back to Europe eight or ten times since then, including a six-month period when I lived in Italy. Looking back, and after reviewing this book, the advice that rings the truest after all of these years is the simplest. First and foremost, stop worrying about it and make the trip. Do your reading ahead of time, and learn about the regions you want to visit. Travel very, very light. Make your reservations. Take an open mind and lots of film. Learn as much of the language(s) as you can. Go early. If you remember nothing else, remember these things.

Every author hopes that his or her book will somehow benefit the reader. My aim was and is to provide information that makes your trip more enjoyable and successful. If I did that, please let me know. If I didn't, then definitely let me know, and tell me what was wrong and how to fix it. Whether or not I helped you, this book is not perfect, and can certainly be improved when I come to prepare a new edition in a year or two.

Accuracy is a major concern, and I would appreciate hearing of any mistakes or changes. Also, if you had an experience that would help others if they heard about it, please write. This is especially the case if you have some expertise: motorcycle tourists, hard-core campers, travel agents who can talk about airline tickets from a seat on the other side of the counter . . . anybody who has information that could help the budget traveler.

The best people to assist the Europe traveler-to-be are those fresh from their first trip, because they remember the problems they just dealt with. As a fairly experienced traveler I now don't have to struggle as much, which means that I can't anticipate someone else's problems quite as well. So, please help me help the next generation. Contact me at the addresses given below. The best and most helpful letters, postcards, or emails will get the writer a copy of the next edition of this book (or any one of the Rough Guide series); and everyone who writes has my sincere gratitude. Thank you in advance. I will answer all mail that I receive; it may take a while if I am on the road, but I will, without fail, respond to anything you send.

Contact me

Louis CasaBianca

First-Time Europe Update
Rough Guides
80 Strand
London WC2R 0RL

If "mail" means "email" to you, feel free to write to the following address:
LOUISFTE@AOL.com

First-Time Europe

Basics

1 Visas

Visas are pretty much extinct in Western Europe but are still alive and kicking in Eastern Europe. This could change by the time you are reading this, but don't count on it. Regardless, get any visas that you need early. Most visas, though not all, are issued while you wait at any embassy of the country you wish to enter. Be advised that some embassies only issue them at odd hours or on certain days, and some require you to leave your passport overnight or longer. Aussies and Kiwis should get as many visas as they can before they leave home, and avoid wasting travel days in Europe waiting for visas to be issued. Don't buy rail tickets or make tightly scheduled plans without your visas in hand.

Western Europe

Australians traveling in France and Spain no longer require visas for short stays, but will need one for entry into Portugal. For details about stays of longer than 30 days, Aussies should contact the relevant embassy. Also, there is a two-month limit on travel in Portugal for Americans and Canadians without visas. In every other country, Australian, Canadian, New Zealand, UK, or US passports are good for a maximum stay of 90 days.

Eastern Europe

Visa requirements in Eastern Europe have become much more relaxed than they were just a few years ago. While Americans, Canadians, and Brits are practically home free these days, Australians and Kiwis still have to put up with a little red tape.

2 Rail passes

If you plan on getting around a lot, especially to major cities, you've probably made the right decision in choosing a train pass. The next step, picking the right pass, may seem confusing, but with a little time you should be able to pick a pass that suits your trip. The details quoted here were accurate as we went to press, but the exact prices and types of passes available change all the time. To get the most up-to-date information, call one of the agents listed at the end of this section before making your final decision. Most student and discount travel agencies will also have the latest price lists.

Remember that train passes are not good on metros and urban trains, but may be good on some commuter lines. Many superexpress services, such as the French TGV, require payment of a small supplement. When in doubt,

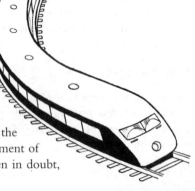

ask before boarding the train. Children aged 4 to 11 get most passes at half price but, as always, call to confirm for your particular pass. Some definitions before we begin the selection process.

Eurail passes

All six of the Eurail passes listed below and on p.216 are good throughout the seventeen Eurail countries: Austria, Belgium, Denmark, Finland, France, Germany, Greece, Holland, Hungary, Ireland, Italy, Luxembourg, Norway, Portugal, Spain (except private railways), Sweden, and Switzerland (except private railways). *Note that Great Britain, Poland, the Czech Republic, and other Eastern European countries are not included.* Fortunately, train or bus travel is very cheap in all countries not included, except Britain.

Also included with the train travel provided by these passes are "free" or discounted ferries between Italy and Greece (see the section on flying within Europe in Chapter 6, "Getting Around," though), France and Ireland, ferries inside of Denmark, from Denmark to Sweden, Sweden to Finland, and several more combinations of the above. Remember the warning about "free" offers, though; anything "free" will cost you a day or force you to validate your pass. You can find Eurail on the Web at ⓦwww.eurail.com.

Eurailpass: All of the passes below are referred to generically as "Eurail passes," but officially the term "Eurailpass" only refers to the most expensive type of pass available. This allows unlimited travel in first class (or second class, if you want to sit there) during their time period – as much as you want, anywhere you want in the seventeen-country Eurail system. Anyone of any age can buy one. They are available in time periods of fifteen days, twenty-one days, one month, two months, and three months. Don't just ask to buy a "Eurailpass" unless you are sure you want one of these, or you may end up paying big bucks in first class.

Eurailpass Youth: Like the above, except only available to those who are under the age of 26 (the day you validate your pass must be before your 26th birthday). Good for unlimited travel anywhere in the Eurail system, in second class only, and available in time periods of fifteen and twenty-one days, one, two, and three months. Because they are only good in second class, they are much cheaper than Eurailpasses.

Flexi Eurailpass: These allow a certain number of days of train travel within a two-month period: passes good for ten or fifteen travel days are currently available. The pass contains a number of boxes, one per day of travel purchased. Before you get on the train, you fill in the day's date in a box. The pass expires when all days are used, or at the end of two months from the day of validation, even if travel days are left over. This version is good for first-class travel, and therefore expensive.

Beat the price increases

The prices of Eurail and other train passes are increased every year on January 1. You then usually have six months after purchasing your pass before you must validate it. (For example, if you buy it on December 17, you have until June 17 to start using it.) What this means is that those who intend on starting their train travel before July 1 can save money by buying their tickets before the prices go up.

Before you do this, be very sure that you are willing to start using the pass before July 1. If you're not sure, it may not be worth the $40–100 you can save, but for those intending on traveling in early June or sooner, this one is a no-brainer. As always, there may be passes that are an exception to the six-month validation rule, so check with your vendor.

Flexi Eurailpass Youth: Exactly the same as a Flexi Eurailpass, except restricted to under-26, and second class only. Same time periods apply, and they're much cheaper.

Eurailpass Saver: This pass gives savings to groups of two to five traveling in first class. Same time periods as Eurailpasses but fifteen percent off. It's good value for couples and groups, but the users must travel together, so be absolutely sure your plans won't change.

Flexi Eurailpass Saver: Like the Eurailpass Saver, except it allows ten or fifteen travel days in a two-month period.

Validating your pass: Before using your pass, you must validate it. Before boarding your first train, go to a ticket window with your passport. The person in the window will enter the date, your passport number, and the last date of eligibility of the pass. You are then good to go for the lifespan of your pass.

Euro Selectpasses plus other country and regional passes

Since the six rail passes mentioned previously are valid all over Europe, they are the most expensive passes available. You're paying for the right to use an enormous system of railroads, from Portugal to Hungary, and from Norway to Greece and Sicily. It's possible that you might not need all that travel power, and don't want to pay for it. If this is the case, you're in luck, because passes for smaller parts of Europe and for individual countries are also available. You can buy these types of passes from most vendors that sell Eurail passes.

Eurail Selectpasses: These passes allow you to create your own smaller version of a Flexi Eurailpass. You can buy a Selectpass for any three, four or five countries out of the seventeen-country Eurail system, as long as they're all connected by a rail or ferry. (For example, you can't buy a pass for Portugal, Finland, Norway, and Hungary, but you could buy a pass for Portugal, Spain, France, and Germany.) Belgium, the Netherlands, and Luxembourg are treated as one country. Selectpasses come with the usual "saver" and "youth" options. Selectpasses are similar to Flexi passes in that they are good for five, six, eight, or ten days of travel in three or four countries, with an additional option of fifteen days of travel if you buy a pass for five countries.

Looking at the prices, these passes only make sense if you are CERTAIN you will only visit a few countries. For example, if you were to buy a fifteen-day Eurail Selectpass Youth for Spain, France, Switzerland, Germany, and Italy, it would cost $556 for fifteen days of travel in those five countries. A seventeen-country Flexi Eurailpass Youth for fifteen days only costs $86 more. Eighty-six bucks for twelve more countries? You've got to be kidding me. The bottom line is that Selectpasses are losers if there is ANY possibility of you traveling further than your original plans.

Not only that, three- and four-country Selectpasses are losers compared to five-country passes. Let's say you planned on visiting France, Switzerland, and Italy. Your Selectpass, for ten days of travel, would cost $379. A four-country pass would only cost you $30 more. For $30 more you could add Germany, Spain, Austria, or Portugal to that pass? That's a no-brainer to me. For $58 you could upgrade that three-country pass to a five-country pass. Also, a no-brainer. I know almost all of us are on tight budgets, but don't save a few dollars in this way unless you are certain of your plans. If you have the slightest doubt, get a seventeen-country pass.

Country and other regional passes: There's a bewildering variety of passes for rail travel within individual countries or specific regions of Europe. Scanrail, Britrail, this rail, that rail: the number, type, and price of train passes can change drastically from year to year, so the only way to decide is to get all the details from a vendor and compare. Some of these passes are good for unlimited travel, some work like Flexi passes, and all reflect the idiosyncrasies of the rail systems of the individual countries involved. When considering a one-country pass within the Euro Selectpass system, compare it with a cheap version of a Euro Selectpass, to see if perhaps you could get a lot more travel for a little more money. Beware: some vendors may only furnish information for the passes they sell. Call more than one company to compare (see list on pp.220–221).

Regional and single-country passes

The following passes were available at the time of publication, but the list does change so check before your travels:

Austria	Czech Republic	Italy
Austria/Czech Republic/ Hungary/Poland/Slovakia	Czech Republic/Germany/ Poland/Slovakia	Netherlands Norway
Belgium	Denmark	Portugal
Belgium/Luxembourg/ Netherlands	Finland France	Scandinavia Scotland
Bulgaria	Germany	Spain
Britain (many types)	Greece	Switzerland
Britain/Ireland	Hungary	

InterRail

InterRail passes are similar to Eurail passes in their intent (to get budget travelers on the rails), but different in operation, coverage, and price. There are also a number of restrictions – you must have been a resident in a particular European country for at least six months, and the pass cannot be used in that country. You can find them on the Web at ⊕www.interrail.net.

InterRail prices are very competitive. The system divides the countries of Europe into a series of zones, and you pay according to the number of zones you wish to travel through. Note that, unlike Eurail passes, InterRail passes are for second-class travel only; you must pay a supplement on "fast" trains such as the TGV and ICE or the AVE, Spain's bullet train. As with Eurail passes, there are discounts ranging from 30 to 50 percent on ferry lines all over Europe.

Europe's InterRail zones

Zone A Ireland/England
Zone B Norway, Sweden, and Finland
Zone C Denmark, Germany, Switzerland, and Austria
Zone D Poland, Czech Republic, Slovakia, Hungary, and Croatia
Zone E France, Belgium, The Netherlands, and Luxembourg
Zone F Spain, Portugal, and Morocco
Zone G Italy, Slovenia, Greece, and Turkey (includes ADN/HML ferry service between Brindisi, Italy, and Patras, Greece)
Zone H Bulgaria, Romania, Macedonia, Bosnia-Hercegovina, and Yugoslavia

Under-26 prices
Any one zone (12 days): €169
Any one zone (22 days): €206
Any two zones (one calendar month): €274
Any three zones (one calendar month): €309
All zones (one calendar month): €375

Over-26 prices
Any one zone (12 days): €248
Any one zone (22 days): €300
Any two zones (one calendar month): €386
Any three zones (one calendar month): €440
All zones (one calendar month): €518

Choosing a rail pass

When deciding which pass is right for you, the two questions you need to answer are (1) where do you want to go, and (2) how definite are your plans? Someone with definite plans has it easy. They can look at where they want to go and how much train travel they need to do, and use a price list obtained by a travel agent to pick a pass that suits their

Some hints for choosing the right rail pass

Think big. I have seldom met travelers who have seen less than they intended. I know several people, myself included, who ended up traveling around a lot more than they expected. If this is your first trip, you will probably end up in places you never expected to go or never heard of until you got to Europe. I doubt you'll regret going for a more powerful pass.

Don't scrimp. Regional passes don't save that much. An example of this is the Eurail Selectpass. In 2003, a fifteen-day Selectpass Youth for Spain, France, Switzerland, Germany, and Italy was only $86 cheaper than a fifteen-day Flexi Eurailpass Youth. That extra $86 spent could save you hundreds if you suddenly decided to go to Norway or Sweden, and you'd be much more likely to go because your trip would be paid for already.

Know your limits. If you are intending to see a lot and cover a lot of ground, then the only decision you have to make is between a two-month Eurailpass and a fifteen-day Flexi Eurailpass, or, if under 26, the youth versions of these passes. In 2002 the price difference was $288 if you were under 26, $410 for over 26. By their very nature, Flexi and unlimited travel passes pull the traveler in opposite directions. Basically, unlimited passes encourage you to travel, because your trip is already paid for. Flexipasses discourage you from traveling because every time you travel you lose one of those precious days. In general, if you plan on traveling on a train for fewer than ten days during the length of your trip, then a fifteen-day Flexipass is better than an unlimited one. (Allow five unplanned trips to be on the safe side, for a total of fifteen days.) If you intend on being on the rails more than ten times in two months, and that's not at all unreasonable, then go unlimited.

Flexibility pays off. If you are spending less than six weeks in Europe, you would probably be better off with a Flexi pass. Overall, fifteen-day and one-month Eurail- and Youthpasses are clear losers in comparison with Flexi passes.

Plan ahead. For shorter trips, where your plans will be more certain, Euro Selectpasses and other regional passes may make sense. As always, think very hard about where you want to go, and whether there is any chance of traveling beyond those plans.

Eligibility counts. While EU citizens and subjects are not eligible for Eurail passes (and with InterRail passes, who cares?), most national and regional rail passes are fair game for anyone not a citizen of the country selling the pass. As always, do some comparison shopping – find a pass that interests you, then make your inquiries to travel agents before buying.

For European residents. If you qualify for an InterRail pass, bear in mind that the differences between the prices of the various zonal tickets is relatively small. Therefore, if you're not sure where you're going to be traveling, it's probably worth investing in an all-zone pass, since it gives much greater flexibility once you're on the road.

needs. If you are sure of where you want to go, get the cheapest pass that takes you there. If you are going to be staying in one or two countries, you don't need a Eurail pass. If you know you are going to be staying in Italy and Germany, for example, a Euro Selectpass will probably be fine for you, or perhaps even individual tickets. In general, though, I recommend regional and country passes only for those who are positive they will be staying in those regions or countries.

Most people headed for Europe aren't certain of their plans. They have some places they know they want to see, but they aren't sure in what order, and they may want to change their plans as they go. If that is the case, and you want the freedom to wander all over Europe if you choose, then skip the regional or country passes. The extra money you pay for the freedom to travel farther will be worth it. My advice in this situation is simple: for your first trip, especially if it's for a whole summer, get the most powerful pass you can afford, either a fifteen-day Flexi Eurailpass or a two- or three-month unlimited Eurailpass, and ride it into the ground.

On a first trip, you are going to want to see a lot. As I said before, I know very few people who have gone to Europe and have traveled less than they expected. If you can afford it, and you have the time, get an unlimited two-month pass and hit the tracks. You won't be worried about saving days or traveling after midnight. If you are in Germany and decide you want to see the midnight sun, two days later you can be above the Arctic Circle. If you get cold while you are there, three days later you can be in sunny Spain. Having an unlimited pass in hand is a powerful incentive to travel to a spot on a whim. To look at a map of Europe and know that you can go absolutely anywhere you like is a great feeling. If you are in doubt, I would go for an unlimited pass.

US rail contacts

BritRail Travel PO Box 416, Hoboken, NJ 07030 ☎1-800/ 4EURAIL, ⓦwww.britrail.com. UK passes. Affiliated with Rail Europe; helpful website, but atrocious phone service.

CIT Tours 342 Madison Ave, Suite 207, New York, NY 10173 ☎1-800/CIT-RAIL or 212/697-2100, ☏212/697-1394,

ⓦwww.cittours.com. Eurail, Euro, and all the other passes, plus point-to-point tickets.

Council Travel 205 E 42nd St, New York, NY 10017 ☎1-800/2COUNCIL, ⓦwww.counciltravel.com. Student travel organization with many local offices, usually near colleges and universities.

Irish Rail and Bus 100 Hanover Ave, Cedar Knolls, NJ 07927 ☎1-800/243-7687, ⓦwww.irisgrail.ie.

Issues vouchers exchangeable in Ireland for Irish rail passes.

Rail Europe 226 Westchester Ave, White Plains, NY 10604 ☎1-800/ 4EURAIL, ✉info@raileurope.com, ⓦwww.raileurope.com. Official Eurail pass agent in North America; sells a wide range of European regional and individual country passes. Horrible phone service, but a good website.

ScanTours 3439 Wade St, Los Angeles, CA 90066 ☎1-800/223-7226, ☏310/390-0493, ⓦwww.scantours.co.uk. Eurail, Scandinavian, and other country passes.

UK rail contacts

European Rail ☎020/7387 0444, ⓦwww.europerail.com. SNCF-owned ticket agents. International rail tickets from anywhere in the UK.

Eurostar EPS House, Waterloo Station, London SE1 8SE Reservations ☎0870/160-6600, ⓦwww.eurostar.co.uk. Moronic website.

Rail Europe ☎0870/584 8848, ⓦwww.raileurope.co.uk. SNCF-owned ticket agents. All European passes and journeys from London.

3 National tourist offices

The old-style tourist office (one that was full of glossy brochures and friendly people who were happy to help prospective travelers) is about as rare today as a flying hippo. Rather than spend money up front in order to help tourists, most European countries are shutting down their overseas offices and relying instead on the Web. That might make short-term economic sense, but it doesn't do you a whole lot of good.

There are a few tourist offices currently operating in the United States, Canada, Britain, Australia, and New Zealand. In North America, many of these offices move around and change phone numbers quite often, so even the most current list may include a bad number or two (though you can always go to ⓦwww.visiteurope.com for an up-to-date directory of the latest information); most of the US offices are in New York, so if you get an invalid number, a call to ☎212/ 555-1212 should get you that office's new number. Some countries also maintain

offices in Los Angeles or Chicago.

Many European countries simply don't want to spend the money to have tourist offices Down Under. There are a few offices in Australia, but almost none in New Zealand. In many cases, the offices are either linked to each country's major national airline or operate as part of an embassy. Even where no tourist office is listed, a call to the national airline (Air France, KLM, etc) or embassy may net you some information. These numbers may be found in any local phone book – look hard for a toll-free number.

When calling these places, if you have a special interest such as biking or walking, mention it when asking for information. Ask for maps, too, especially for countries in Central and Eastern Europe, where up-to-date maps are often scarcer in the country than in their tourist offices abroad.

In a depressing trend, many tourist offices now use computerized answering machines to get information. If you do get hold of a person who does a good job handling your needs, thank him or her for the personal touch.

Austria

US Travel Information Center, PO Box 1142, Times Square, New York, NY 10108-1142 ☎212/944-6880, ⓕ730-4568, ⓔinfo@oewnyc.com, ⓦwww.austria-tourism.at/us.

Canada 2 Bloor St E, Suite 3330, Toronto, ON M4W 1A8 ☎416/967-3381, ⓕ967-4101, ⓔanto-tor@sympatico.ca, ⓦwww.austria-tourism.at.

UK PO Box 2363, London W1A 2QB ☎020/7629 0461, ⓕ7499 6038, ⓔinfo@anto.co.uk, ⓦwww.austria-tourism.at/uk.

Australia 36 Carrington St, Sydney, NSW 2000 ☎02/9299-3621, ⓦwww.austria-tourism.at.

Belgium

US 780 Third Ave, Suite 1501, New York, NY 10017-7076 ☎212/758-8130, ⓕ355-7675, ⓦwww.visitbelgium.com. Poor telephone service,

but you can visit their office from 9.30am to 4.30pm.

Canada 43 rue de Buade, Bureau 525, Quebec City, PQ G1R 4A2 ☎418/692-4939, ⓕ692-4974, ⓔopt.walbru.quebec@videotron.net, ⓦwww.belgique-tourisme.net.

UK 29 Princes St, London W1R 7RG ☎0891/887-799 or ☎020/7629 1988, ⓦwww.visitbelgium.com. The second number has a live human being from 1pm to 5pm.

New Zealand Belgian Embassy, Willis Corroom House, 12th floor, 13 Willeston St, Wellington ☎04/472-9558, ⓕ471-2767, ⓦwww.visitbelgium.com.

Czech Republic

US 1109 Madison Avenue, New York, NY 10028 ☎212/288-0830, ⓕ288-0971, ⓔtravelczech@pop.net or ⓔtourism@czechcenter.com, ⓦwww.czechcenter.com/travel.htm.

Canada 401 Bay St, Suite 1510, Toronto, ON M5H 2Y4 ☎416/363-9928, ⓕ363-0239, ⓔctacanada@iprimus.ca, ⓦwww.visitczechia.cz.

UK Morley House, 320 Regent St, London W1B 3BG ☎020/7631 0427 or ☎09063/640 641 (24-hour enquiry line; calls cost 60p per minute), ⓕ020/7631 0419, ⓔinfo@visitczechia.org.uk, ⓦwww.visitczechia.cz.

Denmark

US 655 Third Ave, New York, NY 10017 ☎212/885-9700, ⓕ885-9726. In the US, Denmark, Norway, Sweden, Finland, and Iceland share facilities as part of the Scandinavian Tourist Board (ⓦwww .goscandi-navia .com). They do not have walk-in facilities, but have a great phone service. To request information on a specific country, call, fax, or write to the Danish, Icelandic, Finnish, etc, Tourist Board at the phone number or address listed above. For general information, the office manager recommends you ask for the "Travel Directory" for the specific country or countries you are interested in visiting.

UK 55 Sloane St, London SW1X 9SY ☎020/7259 5959, ⓕ7259 5955, ⓔdtb.london@dt.dk, ⓦwww.visitdenmark.com.

New Zealand Danish Consulate, PO Box 619, Auckland ☎09/537-3099, ⓕ537-3067, ⓦwww.visitdenmark.com.

Finland

US See entry for Denmark. ☎1-800/FIN-INFO, automated line for brochures.

UK 30 Pall Mall, London SW1Y 5LP ☎020/7839-4048, ⓔfininfo1@mail.idt.net, ⓦwww.mek.fi.

France

US 444 Madison Ave, 16th Floor, New York, NY 10022 ☎212/838-7800 or ☎410/286-8310

(public information service), ⓕ212/838 7855, ⓔinfo@francetourism.com, ⓦwww.francetourism.com.

Canada Suite 490, 1981 Avenue McGill College, Montreal, PQ H3A 2W9 ☎514/876-9871, ⓕ845-4868, ⓔmfrance@attcanada.net, ⓦwww.franceguide.com.

UK 178 Piccadilly, London W1J 9AL ☎09068/244 123 (information line; calls cost 60p per minute), ⓕ020/7493 6594, ⓔinfo@mdlf.co.uk, ⓦwww.franceguide.com.

Australia 25 Bligh St, Level 22, Sydney, NSW 2000 ☎02/9231-5244, ⓦwww.franceguide.com.

Germany

US 52nd Floor, 122 E 42nd St, New York, NY 10168-0072 ☎212/661-7200, ⓕ661-7174, ⓔgntony@aol.com, ⓦwww.visits-to -germany.com.

Canada PO Box 65162, Toronto, ON M4K 322 ☎212/661-7200, ⓕ661-7174, ⓔgntony@aol.com, ⓦwww.visits-to-germany.com.

UK PO Box 2695, London W1A 3TN ☎09001/600 100 (recorded information and brochure request line; calls cost 60p per minute) or ☎020/7317 0908 (general enquiries), ⓕ020/7495 6129, ⓔgntolon@d-z-t.com,

@www.germany-tourism.de.

Australia PO Box A890, Sydney, NSW 2000 ☎02/9267-8148, @www.germany-tourism.de.

New Zealand German Tourist Association of New Zealand, Deutscher Treffpunkt, PO Box 80079, Green Bay, Auckland ☎09/620-0601, @www.germany-tourism.de.

Greece

US Olympic Tower, 645 Fifth Ave, 9th Floor, Suite 903, New York, NY 10022 ☎212/421-5777, ☏826-6940, @gnto@greektourism .com, @www.gnto.gr.

Canada GNTO, 91 Scollard St, 2nd Floor, Toronto, ON M5R 1G4 ☎416/968-2220, ☏968-6533, @grnto.tor@sympatico.ca, @www.gnto.gr;

Office National du Tourisme Grec, 1170 place du Frère André, Suite 300, Montreal, PQ H3B 3C6 ☎514/871-1535, ☏871-1498.

UK 4 Conduit St, London W1S 2DJ ☎020/7734 5997 or 7499 8161, ☏7287 1369, @EOT -greektouristoffice@btinternet.com, @www.gnto.gr.

Australia 51 Pitt St, Sydney, NSW 2000 ☎02/9241-1663, @www.gnto.gr.

Hungary

US 150 E 58th St, New York, NY 10155-3398 ☎212/355-0240, ☏207-4103, @info@gotohungary.com, @www.gotohungary.com.

UK 46 Eaton Pl, London SW1 X8AL ☎020/7823 1032 or 7823 1055 or 09001/171 200 (recorded information; calls cost 60p per minute), ☏020/7823 1459, @htlondon@btinternet.com, @www.hungarytourism.hu.

Iceland

See the entry for Denmark. @www.goiceland.org.

Ireland

US 345 Park Ave, New York, NY 10154 ☎1-800/223-6470 or 212/418-0800, ☏212/371-9052, @info@tourismireland.com, @www.tourismireland.com. Also deals with enquiries from Canada.

Canada 2 Bloor St W, Suite 1501, Toronto, ON M4W 3E2 ☎1-800/223-6470 or 416/925-6368, ☏416/925-6033, @www.tourismireland.com.

UK 150 New Bond St, London W1S 2AQ ☎0800/039 7000 (travel enquiries) or 020/7518 0800, ☏020/7493 9065, @info.uk@tourismireland.com, @www.tourismireland.com.

Australia 36 Carrington St, 5th Floor, Sydney, NSW 2000 ☎02/9299-6177, @www.tourismireland.com.

New Zealand 2nd floor, Dingwall Building, 87 Queen St, Auckland ☎09/379-3708, @www.tourismireland.com.

Italy

US 630 Fifth Ave, Suite 1565, New York, NY 10111 ☎212/245-5618, ☏586-9249, @info@italiantourism.com, @www.italiantourism.com.

Canada, 175 Bloor St East, Suite 907, South Tower, Toronto, ON M4W

3R8 ☎416/925-4882, ℻925-4799,
ⓦwww.italiantourism.com.

UK 1 Princes St, London W1B 2AY
☎020/7408 1254 or 09065/508 925
(brochure line; calls are charged at
£1 per minute), ℻020/7399 3567,
ⓔitaly@italiantouristboard.co.uk,
ⓦwww.enit.it.

Australia 44 Market St, Sydney,
NSW 2000 ☎12/9262-1666,
ⓦwww.enit.it.

Luxembourg

US 17 Beekman Place, New York,
NY 10022 ☎212/935-8888, ℻935-
5896, ⓔluxnto@aol.com,
ⓦwww.visitluxembourg.com.
Open Mon–Fri 9am–5pm.

US 122 Regent St, London W1B
5SA ☎020/7434 2800, ℻7734 1205,
ⓔtourism@luxembourg.co.uk,
ⓦwww.luxembourg.co.uk.

Morocco

US 20 E 46th St, Suite 1201, New
York, NY 10017 ☎212/557-2520,
℻949-8148, ⓦwww.tourism-in-
morocco.com.

UK 205 Regent St, London W1R
7DE ☎020/7437 0073,
ⓦwww.tourism-in-morocco.com.

Canada 1800 McGill College Ave,
Suite 2450, Montreal PQ H3A 3G6
☎514/842-8111, ⓦwww.tourism-in-
morocco.com.

Australia 11 West St N, Sydney,
NSW 2060 ☎12/9922-4999, ℻9923-
1053, ⓦwww.tourism-in
-morocco.com.

Netherlands

US 355 Lexington Ave, 19th Floor,
New York, NY 10017 ☎212/370-
7360, ℻370-9507,
ⓔinfo@goholland.com,
ⓦwww.goholland.com.

Canada 25 Adelaide St East, Suite
710, Toronto, ON M5C 1Y2 ☎1-
888/464-6552 or 416/363-1577,
℻416/363-1470,
ⓔinfo@goholland.com,
ⓦwww.holland.com.

UK PO Box 30783, London WC2B
6DH ☎020/7539 7950 or 09068/
717 777 (recorded information;
calls cost 60p per minute),
℻020/7539 7953,
ⓔinformation@nbt.org.uk,
ⓦwww.holland.com/uk.

Norway

US See entry for Denmark. They
have a separate email, though, at
ⓔusa@ntr.no,
ⓦwww.visitnorway.com.

UK Charles House, 5 Lower Regent
St, London SW1Y 4LR
☎09063/022 033 (brochure request
line; calls costs 60p per minute),
℻020/7839 6014, ⓔinfouk@ntr.no,
ⓦwww.visitnorway.com.

Poland

US 275 Madison Ave, Suite 1711,
New York, NY 10016 ☎212/338-9412,
℻338-9283, ⓦwww.polandtour.org.

UK 310–312 Regent St, London
W1R 5AJ ☎020/7580 8811, ℻7580
8811, ⓦwww.polandtour.org.

Portugal

US 590 Fifth Ave, 4th Floor, New
York, NY 10036–4785 ☎212/719-
3985 or 354-4403, ℻764-6137,
ⓔtourism@portugal.org,
ⓦwww.portugalinsite.com.

Canada 60 Bloor St W, Suite 1005, Toronto, ON M4W 3B8

☎416/921-7376, ℻921-1353, ✉iceptor@idirect.com, ⊛www.portugalinsite.com. Only deals with enquiries within Canada.

UK 2nd Floor, 22–25a Sackville St, London W1S 3LY ☎09063/640 610 (brochure request and information service; calls cost 60p per minute), ℻020/7494 1868, ✉iceplont@aol.com, ⊛www.portugalinsite.com.

Romania

US 14 E 38th St, 12th Floor, New York, NY 10016 ☎212/545-8484, ℻251-0429, ✉ronto@erols.com, ⊛www.romaniatourism.com.

US 22 New Cavendish St, London W1G 8TT ☎020/7224 3692, ℻7935 6435, ✉riarina@hotmail.com, ⊛www.romaniatourism.com.

Slovakia

US 10 E 40th St, Suite 3601, New York, NY 10016 ☎212/213-3865, ℻213-4461, ⊛www.sacr.sk.

UK Slovakian Embassy, 25 Kensington Palace Gardens, London ☎020/7243 0803, ⊛www.sacr.sk. Notice how they changed the name on the building by yanking the letters "Czecho" off the wall.

Slovenia

US 345 E 12th St, New York NY 10003 ☎212/358-9686, ℻358-9025, ⊛www.slovenia-tourism.si.

UK 49 Conduit St, London W1R 9FB ☎020/7287 7133, ℻7287 5476, ⊛www.slovenia-tourism.si.

Spain

US 666 Fifth Ave, 35th Floor, New York, NY 10103 ☎212/265-8822, ℻265-8864, ✉oetny@tourspain.es, ⊛www.okspain.org. Open Mon–Fri 9.30am–5.30pm. Offices also in: Chicago (☎312/642-1992), Los Angeles (☎323/658-7188), and Miami (☎305/358-1992).

Canada 2 Bloor St W, 34th Floor, Suite 3402, Toronto, ON M4W 3E2 ☎416/961-3131, ℻961-1992, ✉toronto@tourspain.es, ⊛www.tourspain.toronto.on.ca.

UK 22–23 Manchester Square, London W1U 3PX ☎020/7486 8077 or 0906/364 0630 (brochure request line; calls cost 60p per minute), ℻020/7486 8034, ✉info.londres@tourspain.es, ⊛www.tourspain.co.uk. Open Mon–Fri 9.15am–4.15pm.

Sweden

US See entry for Denmark. They do have a separate fax number, though, at ℻212/697-0835; ✉info@gosweden.org, ⊛www.gosweden.org.

UK Sweden House, Five Upper Montagu St, London W1H 2AG ☎0800/3080 3080, ℻020/7724 5872, ✉info@swetourism.org.uk, ⊛www.visit-sweden.com. Open Mon–Fri 9am–7pm, Sat 9am–1pm.

Switzerland

International toll free number: ☎011-800/100-200-30.

US 608 Fifth Ave, New York, NY 10020 ☎877/794-8037 (toll free) or 212/757-5944, ℻212/262-6116, ✉stnewyork@switzerlandtourism.com, ⊛www.myswitzerland.com.

Also in: Los Angeles (☎310/640-8900, ⓕ335-5982).

Canada 926 The East Mall, Etobicoke, ON M9B 6K1 ☎1-800/1002-0030 or 416/695-3496, ⓕ1-800/1002-0031 or 416/695-2774, ✉sttoronto@switzerland.com, ⓦwww.myswitzerland.com.

UK 10th Floor, Swiss Centre, Ten Wardour St, London, W1D 6QF ☎00800/1002 0030 (toll free in Europe) or 020/7292 1550, ⓕ00800/1002 0031 (toll free in Europe) or ⓕ020/7292 1599, ✉stc@stlondon.com, ⓦwww.myswitzerland.com.

Turkey

US 821 UN Plaza, 4th Floor, New York, NY 10017 ☎212/687-2194, ⓕ599-7568, ✉ny@tourismturkey.org, ⓦwww.tourismturkey.org.

Canada Suite 801, 360 Albert St, Constitution Square, Ottawa, ON K1R 7X7 ☎613/230-8654, ⓕ230-3683, ✉info@turkishtourism.ca, ⓦwww.turkishtourism.ca.

UK First Floor, 170–173 Piccadilly, London W1J 9EJ ☎020/7629 7771 or 09001/887 755 (brochure request line; calls cost 60p per minute), ⓕ020/7491 0773, ✉tto@turkishtourism.demon.co.uk, ⓦwww.gototurkey.co.uk.

Australia Turkish Information Office, Room 17, 428 George St, Sydney, NSW 2000 ☎02/9223-3055, ⓦwww.turkey.org.

United Kingdom

US 551 Fifth Ave, Suite 701, New York, NY 10176 ☎212/986-2200, ⓕ986-1188 (open Mon–Fri 9am–6pm); 625 N Michigan Ave, Suite 1001, Chicago, IL 60611–1977 ☎1-800/462-2748; ⓦwww.visitbritain.com.

Canada 5915 Airport Rd, Suite 120, Mississauga, ON L4V 1T1 ☎416/961-8124, ⓕ961-2176, ⓦwww.visitbritain.com.

Australia L16 Gateway, 1 Macquarie Pl, Sydney, NSW 2000 ☎02-9377-4400, ⓦwww.visitbritain.com.

New Zealand 17th floor, Fay Richwhite Bldg, 1501 Queen St, Auckland 1 ☎09/303-1446, ⓕ377-6965, ⓦwww.visitbritain.com.

4 Airlines

Aer Lingus in US and Canada ☎1-800/223-6537 or 212/557-1110; in the UK ☎08450/844 444; in the Republic of Ireland ☎0818/365 000; in Australia ☎02/9244-2123; in New Zealand ☎09/308-3351; ⓦwww.aer-lingus.ie. Ireland's national airline.

Air Canada in US and Canada ☎1-888/247-2262; in Australia ☎1300/655-747; in New Zealand ☎09/379-3371; ⓦwww.aircanada.ca. Terrible service.

Air France in US ☎1-800/237-2747; in Canada ☎1-800/667-2747; in UK ☎0845/0845 111; in Australia ☎02/9244-2100; in New Zealand ☎09/308-3352; ⓦwww.airfrance.com.

Air New Zealand in US ☎1-800/262-1234; in Canada ☎1-

800/663-5494; in UK ☎020/8741 2299; in New Zealand ☎0800/737-000; in Australia ☎13-2476; ⓦwww.airnz.com.

Alitalia in US ☎1-800/223-5730; in Canada ☎1-800/361-8336; in UK ☎020/7602 7111; in Australia ☎02/9244-2445; in New Zealand ☎09/308-3357; ⓦwww.alitalia.com. Terrible phone service.

American Airlines in US ☎1-800/433-7300; in UK ☎0845/778 9789; in Australia ☎1-300/650-747; in New Zealand ☎09/309-9159; ⓦwww.aa.com.

Austrian Airlines in US ☎1-800/843-0002; in UK ☎0845/601 0948; ⓦwww.aua.com.

British Airways in US ☎1-800/247-9297; in UK ☎0845/773 3377; in Australia ☎02/8904-8800; in New Zealand ☎09/357-8950; ⓦwww.britishairways.com. The worst website I've ever seen.

Continental Airlines in US and Canada ☎1-800/231-0856; in UK ☎0800/776 464; in Australia ☎1300/361-400; in New Zealand ☎09/308 3350; ⓦwww.continental.com.

Delta Airlines in US ☎1-800/241-4141; in UK ☎0800/414 767; ⓦwww.delta.com.

Finnair in US ☎1-800/950-5000; in UK ☎020/7408 1222; ⓦwww.us.finnair.com.

Icelandair in US and Canada ☎1-800/223-5500; ⓦwww.icelandair.com.

Iberia in US and Canada ☎1-800/772-4642; in UK ☎0845/601 2854; ⓦwww.iberia.com. The Spanish national carrier.

Lufthansa in US ☎1-800/645-3880; in Canada ☎1-800/563-5954; in UK

☎0845/7737 747; in Australia ☎1300/655-727; ⓦwww.lufthansa.com. Germany's national airline.

Malév Hungarian Airlines in US ☎212/757-6446; in Canada ☎416/944-0093; in UK ☎020/7439 0577; ⓦwww.malev.hu.

Martinair Holland in US ☎1-800/627-8462; ⓦwww.martinair.com.

Northwest Airlines/KLM in US and Canada ☎1-800/444-4747; in Australia ☎02/9231-6333; ⓦwww.nwa.com, ⓦwww.klm.com.

Olympic Airways in US and Canada ☎1-800/223-1226 or ☎718/896-7393; in UK ☎0870/606 0460; ⓦwww.olympic-airways.gr. Very friendly; great Greek music while on hold.

Qantas Airways in Australia ☎13/13-13; in New Zealand ☎09/357-8900; in US ☎1-800/227-4500; in UK ☎0845/774 7767; in New Zealand ☎0800/808-767; ⓦwww.Qantas.com. Qantas is the major carrier out of Australia and has great service and the most wonderful flight attendants known to man. (Hi Carolyn!)

SAS (Scandinavian Airlines) in US and Canada ☎1-800/221-2350; in UK ☎0845/607 2772; ⓦwww.scandinavian.net.

Swiss in US and Canada ☎1-877/359-7947; in UK ☎0845/601 0956; in Australia ☎1300/724 666; ⓦwww.swiss.com.

TAP Air Portugal in US and Canada ☎1-800/221-7370 or 201/344-4490; in UK ☎020/7630 0900; ⓦwww.tap-airportugal.pt.

Turkish Airlines in US and Canada ☎1-800/874-8875; in UK

⊕020/7776 9300; ⊛ww.turkishair-
lines.com.

United Airlines in US and Canada
⊕1-800/538-2929; in UK
⊕0845/844 4777; in Australia
⊕13/17-77; in New Zealand ⊕09/
379-3800; ⊛www.ual.com.

Virgin Atlantic Airways in US and
Canada ⊕1-800/862-8621; in UK
⊕01293/747 747; ⊛www.virgin
-atlantic.com. Awful phone service.

No-frills airlines

Buzzaway ⊛www.buzz.co.uk
bmi british midland ⊛www.bmiba-
by.com
Easy Jet ⊛www.easyjet.com
Ryanair ⊛www.ryanair.com
Virgin Express ⊛www.virginexpress
.com

5 Discount flight agents and consolidators

United States and Canada

Air Courier Association ⊕1-
800/282-1202, ⊛www.aircourier.org.
Courier flight resource center.

Airhitch ⊛www.airhitch.org.
Standby-seat broker: For a set
price, they guarantee to get you on
a flight as close to your preferred
destination as possible, within a
week. Western Europe only.

Council Travel ⊕1-800/2COUNCIL,
⊛www.counciltravel.com. Branches
in many US cities. Student travel
organization. A sister company,
Council Charter (⊕1-800/223-7402),
specializes in charter flights to
Europe only.

Educational Travel Center ⊕1-
800/747-5551, ⊛www.edtrav.com.
Student/youth/adult discount agent;
rail passes too.

Interworld Travel ⊕1-800/468-
3796, ⊛www.interworldtravel.com.
Consolidator.

STA Travel ⊕1-800/781-4040,
⊛www.sta.com. Many branches in
the US and Canada. Discount airfares, rail passes and student travel.

TFI Tours International ⊕1-800/
745-8000. Consolidator.

Travac ⊕1-800/872-8800,
⊕212/563-361, ⊛www.travac.com.
Consolidator and discount service.
Great phone service.

Travel CUTS/Voyages Campus
⊕416/979-2406,
⊛www.travelcuts.com. Branches all
over Canada (mostly on or near university campuses). Student travel
specialists, with discounted fares for
non-students, too.

UniTravel ⊕1-800/325-2222,
⊛www.flightsforless.com.
Consolidator.

Britain

North South Travel Moulsham Mill
Centre, Parkway, Chelmsford, Essex
CM2 7PX ⊕01245/608 291.
Friendly, competitive travel agency,
offering discounted fares worldwide
– profits are used to support pro-
jects in the developing world, espe-

cially the promotion of sustainable tourism.

STA Travel 86 Old Brompton Rd, London SW7 3LH; 117 Euston Rd, London NW1 2SX; 38 Store St, London WC1; plus branches around the country. ☎0870/160 0599, ⓦwww.statravel.co.uk. Worldwide specialists in low-cost flights and tours for students and under-26s.

Trailfinders 42–50 Earls Court Rd, London W8 6FT ☎020/7628 7628; ⓦwww.trailfinders.com. Plus branches around the country.

Australia and New Zealand

Anywhere Travel 345 Anzac Parade, Sydney ☎02/9663-0411, ⓔanywhere@ozemail.com.au.

Budget Travel 16 Fort St, Auckland ☎09/366-0061 or 0800/808-480. Call the toll-free number to locate other branches around the city.

Destinations Unlimited 13 Clyde Rd, Browns Bay, Auckland ☎09/373-4033.

Flight Centres 82 Elizabeth St, Sydney ☎02/9235-3522; 19 Bourke St, Melbourne ☎03/650-2899; National Bank Towers, 205–225 Queen St, Auckland ☎09/309-6171. In New Zealand ☎0800/243-544 for information. ⓦwww.flightcentre.com.au.

STA Travel 855 George St, Sydney ☎1300/733-035; Travellers Centre, 10 High St, Auckland ☎0508/782-872; ⓦwww.sta-travel.com. Offices in major cities and university areas across Australia and New Zealand. Student and under-26 discounts.

Student Uni Travel Level 8, 92 Pitt St, Sydney ☎02/9232-8444, ⓦwww.sut.com.au. Other branches in Melbourne ☎03/9662-4666, Perth ☎08/9321-8330, Darwin, Brisbane, and Cairns. A partner of Council Travel.

6 Travel book and map stores

If there is one business listed in this section that I would personally recommend, it's Nation's Travel Mall. They sell books, maps, travel accessories, and luggage (all with an unconditional ninety-day money-back guarantee and free shipping anywhere in the US), along with rail

passes, travel insurance, and airline tickets. Give them a call at ☏1-800/546-8060, seven days a week from 10am to 9pm. They have four stores in the Los Angeles/Santa Barbara area, and can also be found on the Web at ⓦwww.nationstravelmall.com.

The list of bookstores that follows is necessarily very abbreviated – there must be several hundred bookstores specializing in travel products in the United States and Canada. Check your local telephone directory under both "bookstores" and "maps." Many of those that follow have catalogs or newsletters that are worth sending for. If there is a travel bookstore in your area that is not on the list that you feel should be included, please let me know and I'll try to include it in the next edition.

Online bookstores such as Amazon or Barnes and Noble, and their British, Aussie, and Kiwi equivalents, all sell maps, but I don't recommend buying maps online. To really get a feel for how useful a map is going to be you have to actually hold it, see how much it covers, the precise amount of detail it provides, and so forth. Shop for maps in person.

United States and Canada

Book Passage 51 Tamal Vista Blvd, Corte Madera, CA 94925 ☏1-800/999-7909 for orders, ☏415/927-0960 for anything else; ⓦwww.bookpassage.com. Huge selection of travel books and maps.

Distant Lands 56 S Raymond St, Pasadena, CA 91105 ☏1-800/310-3220, ⓔdistantlands@earthlink.net, ⓦwww.distantlands.com.

International Travel Maps and Books 530 W Broadway, Vancouver, BC V5Z 1E9 ☏604/687-3320, ⓕ687-5925, ⓦwww.itmb.com. Books, maps, and globes.

Nations Travel Mall 500–504 Pier Ave, Hermosa Beach, CA 90254 ☏1-800/546-8060 or 310/318-9915, ⓕ318-9115, ⓦwww.nationstravel-mall.com. Books, maps, travel equipment and accessories, plus a travel agency. Ships free anywhere

in the US. Excellent phone service.

Open Air Books and Maps 25 Toronto St, Toronto, ON M5C 2R1 ☏416/363-0719.

Rand McNally 150 E 52nd St, New York, NY 10022 ☏212/758-7488; 595 Market St, San Francisco, CA 94105 ☏415/777-3131; plus more than twenty stores across the US; call ☏1-800/333-0136 (ext 2111) for the nearest one to you; ⓦwww.randmcnally.com. Maps, books, and travel accessories.

Savvy Traveller 310 S Michigan Ave, Chicago, IL 60604 ☏312/913-9800, ⓦwww.savvytraveller.com.

Britain

John Smith and Sons 57–61 St Vincent St, Glasgow G2 5TB ☏0141/221-7472.

National Map Centre 22–24 Caxton St, London SW1H OQU ☏020/7222 2446.

Stanfords 12–14 Long Acre, WC2E 9LP ☎020/7836 1321; 52 Grosvenor Gardens, London SW1W 0AG; 156 Regent St, London W1R 5TA; ⓦwww.stanfords.co.uk.

The Travel Bookshop 13–15 Blenheim Crescent, London W11 2EE ☎020/7229 5260.

Australia

Book & Cranny 168 Belmore Rd, Randwick, NSW 2013 ☎02/9398-6899, ⓕ9398-6899, ⓔbookcranny@att.net.au.

Boyangs 372 Little Bourke St, Melbourne ☎03/9670-4383.

Dymocks Bookstore 424–428 George St, Sydney ☎02/9224-0411, ⓦwww.dymocks.com.au. Nationwide – see website for local shops.

The Map Shop 6–10 Peel St, Adelaide ☎08/8231-2033, ⓦwww.mapshop.net.au.

Perth Map Centre 1/884 Hay St,

Perth, WA 6000 ☎08/9322-5733, ⓔsales@perthmap.com.au, ⓦwww.perthmap.com.au.

Travel Bookshop 175 Liverpool St, Sydney, NSW 2000 ☎02/9261-8200.

New Zealand

Dymocks Bookstore Atrium on Elliot, Elliot St, Auckland ☎09/379-9919, ⓦwww.dymocks.com.au. Plus five more stores nationwide.

London Bookshops Nationwide ☎09/373-5355.

Map Shop Nationwide ☎0800/696-277.

Map World 173 Gloucester St, Christchurch ☎03/374-5399 or ☎0800/627 967, ⓦwww.mapworld.co.nz.

Specialty Maps 58 Albert St, Auckland ☎09/307-2217.

Unity Bookshop 19 High St, Auckland ☎09/307-0731.

7 Travel equipment suppliers

All of the equipment companies listed below sell products which may be of interest to the traveler. I have bought from all the North American ones and have had good experiences. Overseas buyers will probably not be able to use the 1-800 numbers, so try faxing for catalogs. Aussies and Kiwis remember: it is much cheaper to buy this type of travel equipment in the States than in Australia or New Zealand.

United States and Canada

Campmor PO Box 700, Saddle River, NJ 07458-0700 ☎1-888/226-7667 or 201/825-8300, ⓕ1-800/230-2153 or 201/327-2315,

ⓦwww.campmor.com. This place sells outdoor gear, specializing in clothing and, not surprisingly, camping gear.

Mountain Equipment Co-Op With stores in Calgary, Edmonton,

Halifax, Ottawa, Toronto, Vancouver, and Winnipeg. ☎1-888/847-0770 in Canada and the continental United States; ☎604/709-6241 from Vancouver; ⊛www.mec.ca. Satisfied buyers can thank Elizabeth, from Sarniel, Ontario for helping her Canadian compatriots.

Recreational Equipment, Inc Sumner, WA 98352–0001 ☎1-800/426-4840 or 253/891-2500, ⊕253/891-2523, ⊛www.rei.com. A huge mail-order company that also has about sixty retail stores, mainly in the West. Call to see if there is a store in your area or for a catalog. This company is good for outdoor equipment and clothes.

Travelsmith 60 Leveroni Ct, Novato, CA 94949 ☎1-800/950-1600 or 415/884-1350, ⊕415/884-1351, ⊛www.travelsmith.com. Although this operation has some yuppie-looking products, some of their prices are decent, and the catalog is worth a look.

Britain

Cotswold Outdoor Ltd 42–46 Uxbridge Rd, London W12 8ND ☎020/8743 2976, ⊕8740 1490, ⊛www.cotswold-outdoor.com. Plus Harrogate, Manchester, Reading, St Albans, Southampton, and other locations. Sells a huge range of outdoor and adventure gear for pretty much any activity and climate. Mail order is available; to order a catalog, call ☎01285/643 434.

YHA Adventure Shop 152–160 Wardour St, London W1F 8YA ☎020/7025 1900, ⊛www.yhaadventure.co.uk. London

branch of Britain's best outdoor equipment supplier.

Australia

A-Roving 102 Elizabeth St, Melbourne ☎07/654-7264.

Mountain Designs 105 Albert St, Brisbane ☎07/3221-6756; 377 Little Bourke St, Melbourne ☎07/670-3354; ⊛www.mountaindesigns.com. Dozens of stores throughout Australia and New Zealand.

Paddy Palin 507 Kent St, Sydney, NSW 2000 ☎1-800/805-398; 360 Little Bourke St, Melbourne ☎07/670-4845.

Southern Cross 447 Kent St, Sydney, NSW 2000 ☎02/9261-3435.

New Zealand

Outside Adventure Exchange 16 Shortland St, Auckland ☎09/366-1445. Good choice for quality secondhand equipment.

Kathmandu ☎09/309-4615. Upmarket clothing and equipment.

Pack 'n' Pedal 5 Gillies Ave, Auckland ☎09/522-2161, ⊛www.packnpedal.co.nz. Huge selection of climbing, trekkings and travel equipment; additional stores in Auckland and Wellington.

Doyles Clothing and Camping ☎09/377-6998, ⊛www.doyles-outdoors.co.nz. Fourteen stores nationwide. Wide range, great service, and honest prices.

Tisdalls ☎09/379-0254, ⊛www.tisdalls.co.nz. Located in Auckland and Wellington.

8 Insurance providers

Take a good long look at all the restrictions and requirements involved with an insurance policy before buying one. The costs and coverages provided by the companies listed here vary widely, though all are very expensive. For two or three months' coverage, expect to pay $150–300. Be aware that "high risk" activities may not be included or may cost extra. The best procedure if you think you need this kind of insurance is to send away for as much information as possible, and actually read all of the pages of fine print you will receive.

In addition to the companies listed here, most travel agents offer insurance: again, don't just accept what they offer without checking it out first. Remember, if you get an international student, youth, or teacher card, you get insurance that may be as good as that provided by the companies listed; check, too, any health or household insurance you already hold to see if that covers you.

Rough Guides offer their own travel insurance, customized by a leading UK broker and backed by a Lloyds underwriter. It's available for anyone, of any nationality, traveling anywhere in the world. For a policy quote, call on UK freefone ☎0800/015 0906, or, from outside Britain, on ☎44/1243 621 046; you can also get online quotes and buy online at ⓦwww.roughguidesinsurance.com.

United States and Canada

Access America ☎1-800/284-8300.

Carefree Travel Insurance ☎1-800/323-3149.

Council Travel ☎1-800/2-COUNCIL.

Travel Assistance International ☎1-800/821-2828. This company provides medical coverage, as well as trip and luggage insurance.

Travel Guard ☎1-800/826-1300.

Travel Insured International, Inc ☎1-800/243-3174, ☎203/528-8005.

Britain

Columbus Travel Insurance ☎020/7375 0011.

Endsleigh Insurance ☎020/7436 4451.

Marcus Hearn & Co ☎020/7739 3444.

Australia

CIC Insurance ☎09/202-8000.

ⓦwww.travelinsurance.com.au.

New Zealand

AMP ☎0800/806-244.

ⓦwww.brokers.co.nz.

National Insurance ☎0800/808-808.

ⓦwww.uni-care.org.

9 Online travel resources

In addition to consulting books, travel agents, airlines, rail companies and so on, you can find a great deal of useful travel information on the Web. Some sites are more flash than cash, but the ones mentioned in this section are all worth a look. A quick Net search will reveal many more.

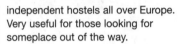

Adventurous Traveler Bookstore
ⓦwww.adventuroustraveler.com. Guidebooks, maps, and videos to help you on your way.

Book Passage
ⓦwww.bookpassage.com. Books of every kind, including a huge travel selection.

CIA World Factbook
ⓦwww.cia.gov/cia/publications/Factbook. An encyclopedic summary of every country's essential statistics: geographical boundaries, international disputes, climate, geography, economic indicators, demographics, government, communications, and defense.

The Cyber Café Search Engine
ⓦwww.cybercaptive.com. A comprehensive search engine of cybercafés throughout Europe as well as the US and Canada. Updated daily.

International Student Travel Confederation ⓦwww.istc.org. Find out where to get an International Student Identity Card and what it's good for.

Internet Guide to Hosteling
ⓦwww.webcom/hostels. Gives details and recommendations for independent hostels all over Europe. Very useful for those looking for someplace out of the way.

Magellans ⓦwww.magellans.com. Primarily an equipment supplier, it has many useful links from its website.

Paris ⓦwww.paris.org. Virtual tour of popular museums, cafés, monuments, stores, rail systems, educational institutions, and other attractions. In English or French.

Rough Guides
ⓦwww.roughguides.com. Rough Guides' home page steers you to a searchable database of 10,000 destinations.

Time Out ⓦwww.timeout.co.uk. *Time Out*, London's weekly listings guide, offers a bonanza of information on how to pass the time in London, Amsterdam, Berlin, Madrid, Paris, and Prague.

Travel Channel Online ⓦwww.travelchannel.com. The cable TV channel on the Web, spotlighting different destinations around the globe, along with discussion forums, photos, and the like.

Travel World
ⓦwww.travel.world.co.uk. Excellent

resource with links to every type of European travel website.

Universal Currency Converter
ⓦ www.xe.net/ucc/.
The online converter allows you to check current conversion rates by selecting the two currencies you're interested in and the amount. Rates are updated every minute.

The Virtual Tourist
ⓦ www.wings.buffalo.edu/world.

Click on the atlas to zoom into the region of your choice.

Visit Europe
ⓦ www.visiteurope.com. Lots of facts and event listings for all of Europe as well as great links to tourist boards.

World Travel Guide ⓦ www.travel -guide.com. Excellent user-friendly site with tons of information on almost all countries in Europe.

10 Final checklist

DOCUMENTS

- ❏ Passport
- ❏ Extra passport-sized photos
- ❏ Passport copy
- ❏ Credit card copies (leave at home)
- ❏ Train pass and copy
- ❏ Youth Hostel membership card
- ❏ ISIC card (or other youth/teacher ID)
- ❏ Driver's license
- ❏ Train timetable
- ❏ Hosteling guide and map
- ❏ Journal
- ❏ Maps

ESSENTIALS

- ❏ Backpack
- ❏ Daypack
- ❏ Backpack lock
- ❏ Clothes/shoes
- ❏ Rain gear/umbrella
- ❏ Money belt
- ❏ Padlock and cable
- ❏ First-aid kit
- ❏ Swiss Army knife
- ❏ Sewing/repair kit
- ❏ Flashlight
- ❏ Sunscreen
- ❏ Sunglasses/lip balm
- ❏ Clock/watch
- ❏ Sleep sack
- ❏ Towel
- ❏ Camera/film/battery
- ❏ Plastic bags

- ❏ Toilet paper
- ❏ Bathroom kit
- ❏ Contact lens stuff
- ❏ Glasses
- ❏ Earplugs
- ❏ Drain plug
- ❏ Guidebook(s)

OPTIONAL

- ❏ Sleeping bag
- ❏ Cooking gear
- ❏ Clothespins/line
- ❏ Tent
- ❏ Sleeping pad
- ❏ Stove
- ❏ Compass
- ❏ Walkman/Discman
- ❏ Whistle
- ❏ Calculator
- ❏ Playing cards
- ❏ Bug repellent
- ❏ Pictures and postcards

First-Time Europe

Index
+ small print

Index

Map entries are in colour.

Twenty years of Rough Guides

In the summer of 1981, Mark Ellingham, Rough Guides' founder, knocked out the first guide on a typewriter, with a group of friends. Mark had been traveling in Greece after university, and couldn't find a guidebook that really answered his needs.There were heavyweight cultural guides on the one hand – good on museums and classical sites but not on beaches and tavernas – and on the other hand student manuals that were so caught up with how to save money that they lost sight of the country's significance beyond its role as a place for a cool vacation. None of the guides began to address Greece as a country, with its natural and human environment, its politics, and its contemporary life.

Having no urgent reason to return home, Mark decided to write his own guide. It was a guide to Greece that tried to combine some erudition and insight with a thoroughly practical approach to travelers' needs. Scrupulously researched listings of places to stay, eat, and drink were matched by careful attention to detail on everything from Homer to Greek music, from classical sites to national parks, and from nude beaches to monasteries. Back in London, Mark and his friends got their Rough Guide accepted by a farsighted commissioning editor at the publisher Routledge and it came out in 1982.

The Rough Guide to Greece was a student scheme that became a publishing phenomenon. The immediate success of the book – shortlisted for the Thomas Cook Award – spawned a series that rapidly covered dozens of countries. The Rough Guides found a ready market among backpackers and budget travelers, but soon acquired a much broader readership that included older and less impecunious visitors. Readers relished the guides' wit and inquisitiveness as much as the enthusiastic, critical approach that acknowledges everyone wants value for money – but not at any price.

Rough Guides soon began supplementing the "rougher" information – the hostel and low-budget listings – with the kind of detail that independent-minded travelers on any budget might expect. These days, the guides – distributed worldwide by the Penguin Group – include recommendations spanning the range from shoestring to luxury, and cover more than 200 destinations around the globe. Our growing team of authors, many of whom come to Rough Guides initially as outstandingly good letter-writers telling us about their travels, are spread all over the world, particularly in Europe, the USA, and Australia. As well as the travel guides, Rough Guides publishes a series of dictionary phrasebooks covering two dozen major languages, an acclaimed series of music guides running the gamut from Classical to World Music, a series of music CDs in association with World Music Network, and a range of reference books on topics as diverse as the Internet, Pregnancy, and Unexplained Phenomena. Visit **www.roughguides.com** to see what's cooking.

Rough Guide credits

Text editor: Claire Saunders
Series editor: Mark Ellingham
Editorial: Martin Dunford, Jonathan Buckley,
Kate Berens, Ann-Marie Shaw, Helena Smith,
Judith Bamber, Orla Duane, Olivia Swift,
Ruth Blackmore, Geoff Howard,
Gavin Thomas, Alexander Mark Rogers,
Polly Thomas, Joe Staines, Richard Lim,
Duncan Clark, Peter Buckley, Lucy Ratcliffe,
Clifton Wilkinson, Alison Murchie,
Matthew Teller, Andrew Dickson,
Fran Sandham, Andrew Rosenberg,
Stephen Timblin, Yuki Takagaki,
Richard Koss, Hunter Slaton, Julie Feiner (US)
Production: Susanne Hillen, Andy Hilliard,
Link Hall, Helen Prior, Julia Bovis,
Michelle Draycott, Katie Pringle, Zoë Nobes,
Rachel Holmes, Andy Turner

Cartography: Melissa Baker, Maxine Repath,
Ed Wright, Katie Lloyd-Jones
Cover art direction: Louise Boulton
Picture research: Sharon Martins,
Mark Thomas
Online: Kelly Cross, Anja Mutic-Blessing,
Jennifer Gold, Audra Epstein,
Suzanne Welles, Cree Lawson (US)
Finance: John Fisher, Gary Singh,
Edward Downey, Mark Hall, Tim Bill
Marketing & Publicity: Richard Trillo, Niki
Smith, David Wearn, Chloë Roberts,
Demelza Dallow, Claire Southern (UK);
Simon Carloss, David Wechsler,
Kathleen Rushforth (US)
Administration: Tania Hummel,
Julie Sanderson

Publishing information

This fifth edition published March 2003 by
Rough Guides Ltd,
80 Strand, London WC2R 0RL
Penguin Putnam, Inc, 375 Hudson Street,
NY 10014, USA
Distributed by the Penguin Group
Penguin Books Ltd,
80 Strand, London WC2R ORL
Penguin Putnam, Inc,
375 Hudson Street, NY 10014, USA
Penguin Books Australia Ltd,
487 Maroondah Highway, PO Box 257,
Ringwood, Victoria 3134, Australia
Penguin Books Canada Ltd,
10 Alcorn Avenue, Toronto, Ontario
M4V 1E4 Canada
Penguin Books (NZ) Ltd,
182–190 Wairau Road, Auckland 10,
New Zealand
Printed in Italy by LegoPrint S.p.A

272pp includes index
A catalogue record for this book is available
from the British Library.

ISBN 1-84353-045-7

The publishers and authors have done their
best to ensure the accuracy and currency of
all the information in **First-Time Europe**;
however, they can accept no responsibility
for any loss, injury, or inconvenience
sustained by any traveler as a result of
information or advice contained in the guide.

Help us update

If you have any comments or update on this book, please write to us. We'll credit all contributions, and send a copy of the next edition (or any other Rough Guide if you prefer) for the best letters. Everyone who writes to us and isn't already a subscriber will receive a copy of our full-color twice-yearly newsletter. Please mark letters: "**Rough Guide First-Time Europe Update**" and send to: Rough Guides, 80 Strand, London WC2 0RL, or Rough Guides, 4th Floor, 345 Hudson St, New York, NY 10014. Or send an email to **mail@roughguides.com**. Have your questions answered and tell others about your trip at **www.roughguides.atinfopop.com**.

Acknowledgements

The editor would like to thank Link Hall for picture layout and typesetting, Louise Boulton for some great pictures, Ed Wright for the maps, Diane Margolis for proofreading, and – especially – Martin Dunford, Kate Berens, and Andrew Rosenberg for all their support and advice.

Readers' letters

From the author: In this fifth edition I would like to thank those who emailed about FTE4, and apologize to anyone whose name may have been omitted. To all those below, and to the many, many more who only left first names, thank you very much and keep those emails coming – they're the best part of my job.

Tara Belcher, Joel Bouwman, Cynthia Brooks, Dennis-Michael Broussard, Rona-Louise Claffey, Allison Douglas, Lee Durdin, Gabrielle Fishman, Pam Harris, Gary Healey, Michael Hiebert, Craig Horne, Chris Iles, Jorge Knizek, Becky Martin, Lalka Morales, Sarah Richardson, Melissa Robinson, Shervin Saleh, Lisie Seilback, Ernesto Silva, Beth Snyder, Mark Sobieraj, Dan Stephenson, Jackie Stein, Alice Williams.

Photo credits

Europe

Algarve
Amsterdam
Andalucia
Austria
Barcelona
Belgium
 & Luxembourg
Berlin
Britain
Brittany
 & Normandy
Bruges & Ghent
Brussels
Budapest
Bulgaria
Copenhagen
Corsica
Costa Brava
Crete
Croatia
Cyprus
Czech & Slovak
 Republics
Devon & Cornwall
Dodecanese
 & East Aegean
Dordogne
 & the Lot
Dublin
Edinburgh
England
Europe
First-Time Europe
Florence
France
French Hotels
 & Restaurants
Germany
Greece
Greek Islands
Holland
Hungary
Ibiza
 & Formentera
Iceland
Ionian Islands
Ireland
Italy
Lake District

Languedoc
 & Roussillon
Lisbon
London
London Mini Guide
London
 Restaurants
Madeira
Madrid
Mallorca
Malta & Gozo
Menorca
Moscow
Norway
Paris
Paris Mini Guide
Poland
Portugal
Prague
Provence & the
 Côte d'Azur
Pyrenees
Romania
Rome
Sardinia
Scandinavia
Scotland
Scottish Highlands
 & Islands
Sicily
Spain
St Petersburg
Sweden
Switzerland
Tenerife & La
 Gomera
Turkey
Tuscany & Umbria
Venice
 & The Veneto
Vienna
Wales

Asia

Bali & Lombok
Bangkok
Beijing
Cambodia
China
First-Time Asia
Goa
Hong Kong
 & Macau
India
Indonesia
Japan
Laos
Malaysia,
 Singapore
 & Brunei
Nepal
Singapore
South India
Southeast Asia
Thailand
Thailand Beaches
 & Islands
Tokyo
Vietnam

Australasia

Australia
Gay & Lesbian
 Australia
Melbourne
New Zealand
Sydney

North America

Alaska
Big Island of
 Hawaii
Boston
California
Canada
Florida
Hawaii
Honolulu
Las Vegas
Los Angeles
Maui
Miami & the
 Florida Keys
Montréal
New England
New Orleans
New York City

New York City
 Mini Guide
New York
 Restaurants
Pacific Northwest
Rocky Mountains
San Francisco
San Francisco
 Restaurants
Seattle
Southwest USA
Toronto
USA
Vancouver
Washington DC
Yosemite

Caribbean & Latin America

Antigua & Barbuda
Argentina
Bahamas
Barbados
Belize
Bolivia
Brazil
Caribbean
Central America
Chile
Costa Rica
Cuba
Dominican
 Republic
Ecuador
Guatemala
Jamaica
Maya World
Mexico
Peru
St Lucia
Trinidad & Tobago

Africa & Middle East

Cape Town
Egypt
Israel & Palestinian
 Territories

Jerusalem
Jordan
Kenya
Morocco
South Africa,
 Lesotho
 & Swaziland
Syria
Tanzania
Tunisia
West Africa
Zanzibar
Zimbabwe

Dictionary Phrase- books

Czech
Dutch
European
 Languages
French
German
Greek
Hungarian
Italian
Polish
Portuguese
Russian
Spanish
Turkish
Hindi & Urdu
Indonesian
Japanese
Mandarin Chinese
Thai
Vietnamese
Mexican Spanish
Egyptian Arabic
Swahili

Maps

Amsterdam
Dublin
London
Paris
San Francisco
Venice

Rough Guides publishes new books every month:

● TRAVEL ● MUSIC ● REFERENCE ● PHRASEBOOKS ●

Rough Guides music, reference & CDs

Music

Acoustic Guitar
Blues: 100 Essential CDs
Cello
Clarinet
Classical Music
Classical Music: 100 Essential CDs
Country Music
Country: 100 Essential CDs
Cuban Music
Drum'n'bass
Drums
Electric Guitar & Bass Guitar
Flute
Hip-Hop
House
Irish Music
Jazz
Jazz: 100 Essential CDs
Keyboards & Digital Piano
Latin: 100 Essential CDs
Music USA: a Coast-To-Coast Tour
Opera
Opera: 100 Essential CDs
Piano
Reading Music
Reggae
Reggae: 100 Essential CDs
Rock
Rock: 100 Essential CDs
Saxophone
Soul: 100 Essential CDs
Techno
Trumpet & Trombone
Violin & Viola
World Music: 100 Essential CDs

World Music Vol1
World Music Vol2

Reference

Children's Books, 0–5
Children's Books, 5–11
China Chronicle
Cult Movies
Cult TV
Elvis
England Chronicle
France Chronicle
India Chronicle
The Internet
Internet Radio
James Bond
Liverpool FC
Man Utd
Money Online
Personal Computers
Pregnancy & Birth
Shopping Online
Travel Health
Travel Online
Unexplained Phenomena
Videogaming
Weather
Website Directory
Women Travel

Music CDs

Africa
Afrocuba
Afro-Peru
Ali Hussan Kuban
The Alps
Americana
The Andes
The Appalachians
Arabesque
Asian Underground
Australian Aboriginal Music
Bellydance
Bhangra
Bluegrass

Bollywood
Boogaloo
Brazil
Cajun
Cajun and Zydeco
Calypso and Soca
Cape Verde
Central America
Classic Jazz
Congolese Soukous
Cuba
Cuban Music Story
Cuban Son
Cumbia
Delta Blues
Eastern Europe
English Roots Music
Flamenco
Franco
Gospel
Global Dance
Greece
The Gypsies
Haiti
Hawaii
The Himalayas
Hip Hop
Hungary
India
India and Pakistan
Indian Ocean
Indonesia
Irish Folk
Irish Music
Italy
Jamaica
Japan
Kenya and Tanzania
Klezmer
Louisiana
Lucky Dube
Mali and Guinea
Marrabenta Mozambique
Merengue & Bachata
Mexico
Native American Music
Nigeria and Ghana
North Africa

Nusrat Fateh Ali Khan
Okinawa
Paris Café Music
Portugal
Rai
Reggae
Salsa
Salsa Dance
Samba
Scandinavia
Scottish Folk
Scottish Music
Senegal & The Gambia
Ska
Soul Brothers
South Africa
South African Gospel
South African Jazz
Spain
Sufi Music
Tango
Thailand
Tex-Mex
Wales
West African Music
World Music Vol 1: Africa, Europe and the Middle East
World Music Vol 2: Latin & North America, Caribbean, India, Asia and Pacific
World Roots
Youssou N'Dour & Etoile de Dakar
Zimbabwe

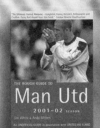

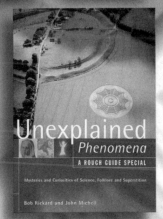

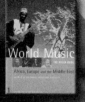

Don't bury your head in the sand!

Take cover!

with Rough Guide Travel Insurance